ALSO BY EVAN OSNOS

Wildland: The Making of America's Fury

Joe Biden: The Life, the Run, and What Matters Now

Age of Ambition: Chasing Fortune, Truth, and Faith in the New China

THE HAVES
AND
HAVE-YACHTS

Dispatches on the Ultrarich

EVAN OSNOS

SCRIBNER

New York Amsterdam/Antwerp London
Toronto Sydney/Melbourne New Delhi

Scribner
An Imprint of Simon & Schuster, LLC
1230 Avenue of the Americas
New York, NY 10020

First Scribner hardcover edition June 2025

SCRIBNER and design are trademarks of Simon & Schuster, LLC

Simon & Schuster strongly believes in freedom of expression and stands against
censorship in all its forms. For more information, visit BooksBelong.com.

For information about special discounts for bulk purchases, please contact
Simon & Schuster Special Sales at 1-866-506-1949 or business@simonandschuster.com.

The Simon & Schuster Speakers Bureau can bring authors to your live event.
For more information, or to book an event, contact the Simon & Schuster Speakers Bureau
at 1-866-248-3049 or visit our website at www.simonspeakers.com.

Interior design by Kyle Kabel

Manufactured in the United States of America

1   3   5   7   9   10   8   6   4   2

Library of Congress Control Number: 2025933402

ISBN 978-1-6682-0448-1
ISBN 978-1-6682-0450-4 (ebook)

For my grandparents,
Jozef and Marta Osnos, and Albert and Carroll Sherer,
whose very different lives
converged around values and love

Contents

THE HAVES
AND
HAVE-YACHTS

Introduction

The makings of history can be hard to discern in the moment, but, occasionally, a scene arrives that is instantly indelible. On January 20, 2025, the world watched American politics embrace plutocracy without shame or pretense. Donald Trump took his oath of office on a stage filled with billionaires. Off his left shoulder stood the world's three richest people: Mark Zuckerberg, Jeff Bezos, and Elon Musk. A few feet to the right were Sergey Brin, the cofounder of Google, who, in the past, had said Trump's rise to power was "deeply offensive," and Tim Cook, the CEO of Apple, who had evidently got over his outrage at the "shameful" riot at the Capitol. There were so many billionaires onstage that the leaders of Congress were relegated to the audience.

The moguls on hand to celebrate Trump's return to the White House had little in common with the old-fashioned corporate conservative elite. They were political players born of the Supreme Court's decision in 2010 to remove limits on political contributions. As a result, candidates no longer needed large pools of rich supporters; they only needed small pools of *ultra*rich supporters, who gave far more and received far more in return. When oil-and-gas executives had visited Trump at Mar-a-Lago, he told them he would remove restrictions on drilling, for which they should raise $1 billion for his campaign. Musk devoted at least $288 million of his fortune to getting Trump and other Republicans elected, and, after Election Day, it proved to be a colossally fruitful investment. In a single week, stock traders, betting that Musk's businesses would prosper from the new era, boosted the value of his shares by an astounding $54 billion.

Trump named thirteen billionaires to the top ranks of his administration. Musk devised the Department of Government Efficiency, a new entity ostensibly charged with finding savings. Within weeks, Musk and a small band of acolytes, some barely out of college, had tipped the federal government into chaos by seizing the powers to fire people, access classified files, and all but close branches of the government. Opponents sued, but Musk was backed by a fortune so large that he could exhaust almost anyone in the courts.

There had, in retrospect, been many signs that this is where we were headed. Days before Trump's inauguration, Joe Biden, in his final speech as president, said belatedly: "Today, an oligarchy is taking shape in America of extreme wealth, power, and influence that literally threatens our entire democracy, our basic rights and freedoms, and a fair shot for everyone to get ahead." In fact, that oligarchy had been taking shape for decades. The tableau at the inauguration was the culmination of ideas and ambitions that run through the pages of this book.

* * *

The effects of great fortunes exist in a conditional state of visibility: they are meant to be unmistakable to a slender stratum of society, but otherwise obscured by jargon and secrecy. Only occasionally, when something collapses—a myth, a confidence, a scrim of propriety—does the true power of the world's biggest fortunes become visible.

I inherited two very different philosophies on money. My mother came from a long line of Midwestern WASPs, and I absorbed some of their threadbare oxford-cloth suspicion of showiness. My grandmother spent years moving from one foreign service post to another, and, when I went abroad as a reporter, she warned me that expats have a weakness for accumulating simulated treasure. "Don't fill your house with junk," she said. (Every midcentury diplomat has at least one cheap ceramic elephant, known as a "Buffy," for "big ugly fucking elephant.") She went on, "All you need are a few fine things."

My father's family had other ideas. He was born in India, to Polish-Jewish refugees who lost everything to the Nazis. His father, one of seven siblings, was the sole survivor of the war. When he and my grandmother eventually made it to the United States, they scratched their way up. Two decades later, they paid $40,000 for an apartment, which they stocked with objects that conjured the world that had been devoured by the war: books, carpets, artworks real and fake. (I still cherish a knockoff sculpture known in the family as the "fake Giacometti.") Money, to them, meant arrival, grace, and cosmic revenge.

My father became a newspaperman, and we moved many times: Moscow, Washington, London. When I was in sixth grade, we moved into my grandmother's house in Greenwich, Connecticut, one of the wealthiest places in America, where the forces of capital and politics jockey amiably, like retirees in line at an omelet station. I learned to recognize the subtle tussles for status, the compromises for proximity to power and wealth.

I developed an appetite for reading about fortunes gained and lost, about the ways that money, like power, might change you, but, first, it will reveal you. *The Gilded Age*, a satire by Mark Twain and Charles Dudley Warner, is a clunky novel but its title gave us the perfect term for a time of superficial splendor. In Twain's early days, there had been fewer than twenty millionaires in the United States; by the century's end, there were four thousand. New technologies were everywhere—the telephone, the typewriter, the gramophone—as was fantastical corruption, inequality, and excess. The new plutocrats indulged on parties, luxuries, and pliant politicians; when the media baron William Randolph Hearst told his wife that he'd bought a Norman castle in Wales, she reputedly replied, "Norman who?"

In the twentieth century, Upton Sinclair, Ida Tarbell, and other muckrakers argued that the country was on an unsustainable course. Louis Brandeis, the future Supreme Court justice, warned of business fortunes "so powerful that the ordinary social and industrial forces existing are insufficient to cope with it." In 1913, he called this the "curse of bigness." A hundred years later, President Barack Obama raised a similar concern, as he called inequality and immobility "the defining challenge of our time." (The hedge fund manager Paul Tudor Jones gave it a more self-interested gloss, worrying that the chasm between the rich and the rest would lead to "revolution, higher taxes or wars.")

I started reporting in earnest about wealth and class in 2016, when Donald Trump confounded our usual instruments for understanding the country. I had written about him as a political figure, but I sensed that if we wanted to grasp the change he represented—to understand why a voter could revile "the elite" and revere the billionaire scion of a New York real estate fortune—we had to look beyond politics. Trump is a creature of the money-world, and, specifically, of a period of American thinking about greed, fairness, liberty, and dominance.

That reporting resulted in *Wildland: The Making of America's Fury*, a book about the ways that extreme inequality had altered life in three places I'd lived: Greenwich, Chicago, and Clarksburg, West Virginia. *Wildland*, published in 2021, was a view from the alarmed middle, animated by the perspective of frustrated residents of Appalachia and the South Side. This new book is a view from the top—a kind of field guide to the ultrarich. It aims to capture the thinking and behavior of some of the world's most powerful people. By assessing their tactics and obsessions, their manners and delusions, it attempts to show how the very rich see themselves and how they see the world that they increasingly control.

*   *   *

In the years between Trump's first and second inaugurations, the scale of wealth held by America's billionaires more than doubled. Our nation's richest citizens now control an even greater percentage of its money than they did during the reign of the Vanderbilts and Rockefellers—the run-up to what F. Scott Fitzgerald called "the greatest, gaudiest spree in history." The pieces in this book, originally published in *The New Yorker*, were written over those same eight years, against a backdrop of immense contrast, of rising homelessness and environmental peril, and a dawning sense of how technology could affect our sources of work, income, and meaning. Some of these essays reach back to the Middle Ages, to explore debates around inheritance and philanthropy; others inquire into present-day practices and standards. They hover around a set of persistent concerns—ambition and fakery, status and shame, duty and disregard.

Reporting in the enclaves of the very rich—Monte Carlo, Palm Beach, Palo Alto, and Hollywood—is complicated. It's not a world that relishes scrutiny. Often, the subjects have been reluctant; in some cases, their lawyers tried to run me off. At times, though, I found myself in real-world scenarios that evoked the morality plays of Oscar Wilde: an heiress, in thrall to Bernie Sanders but also to her millions; a white-collar ex-con who returned to the dating scene and found that prison talk was a turn-off, except when it wasn't.

These pieces are unified by a desire for lucid facts, not abstractions. It's easy to become numb to headlines reporting that billionaires pay a lower effective tax rate than the working class, but it's startling to see the precise mechanics laid out by a disgruntled private wealth manager. Frivolous things often prove revealing. Thorstein Veblen, the economist who coined the idea of "conspicuous consumption," studied spending (on "food, drink, narcotics, shelter") to make sense of a culture of excess. In the current era, I wanted to grasp how "gigayachts" (leisure vessels as long as naval ships) became the most expensive objects our species has ever owned—and, as a Silicon Valley CEO put it to me, the best way to "absorb the most excess capital." Understanding why Mark Zuckerberg, the precocious and polarizing tycoon, is so preoccupied with Roman emperors that he named his children after them, helps clarify his thinking about the "trade-offs" between profit and harm. To see what this age means for culture, I joined the rapper Flo Rida for a big-money bar mitzvah before an audience of thirteen-year-olds—the oligarchs of tomorrow.

In assembling a consolidated portrait of the ultrarich, including some scenes that appear in *Wildland*, my hope is that patterns emerge: how money monumentalizes itself in steel and stone; how self-interest and civic duty shape philanthropy; how the technologies of influence determine what we see, hear, and believe. As I worked on this book, it was sometimes tempting to wonder if America was approaching the point of untenable imbalance, a pattern that has repeated across the centuries. Near the end of the Roman Empire, in the fourth century AD, inequality had become so severe that a Roman senator could earn 120,000 pieces of gold a year, while a farmer earned five. The fall of Rome took five hundred years, but, as the distinguished historian Ramsay MacMullen once wrote, it could be compressed into three words: "fewer have more."

On the ground, reporting these stories, I often contemplated what future historians might make of a generation that splurges not only on its share of Norman castles but also on high-tech fortresses, fifteen stories underground, with artificial windows that play videos of Central Park, in case the world aboveground becomes inhospitable.

The present debates around wealth in society have moved far beyond the old dichotomy of my childhood, between restraint and exhibition—far beyond even the inequalities of the Obama era, which look almost quaint by today's standards. Private empires, of the scale of Elon Musk's, have achieved such power that they bring to mind Brandeis's warning about a "curse of bigness" that imperils democracy. Musk, who condemns an "unelected" bureaucracy, is, himself, unelected, having acquired his sway over the government by paying more than anyone else to ensure a president's election.

However far it goes, the alliance between the world's most powerful officeholder and the world's richest man has already achieved one clear effect: Musk has pulled the ultrarich into public attention more squarely than at any moment since the New Deal, nearly a century ago. At that time, Franklin Roosevelt pointed back to the lessons of the Gilded Age and the Roaring Twenties, a time when, as he put it, "privileged princes of these new economic dynasties, thirsting for power, reached out for control over Government itself."

THE REWARDS

How to Spend It

The Floating World

*Outrageously luxurious superyachts are attracting
political scrutiny—and buyers in record numbers*

— 2022 —

I n the Victorian era, it was said that the length of a man's boat, in feet,
should match his age, in years. The Victorians would have had some
questions at the fortieth annual Palm Beach International Boat Show,
which convened in March 2022 on Florida's Gold Coast. A typical
offering: a 203-foot superyacht named *Sea Owl*, selling secondhand for
$90 million. The owner, Robert Mercer, the hedge fund tycoon and
Republican donor, was throwing in furniture and accessories, including several auxiliary boats, a Steinway piano, a variety of frescoes, and
a security system that requires fingerprint recognition. Nevertheless,
Mercer's package was a modest one; the largest superyachts are more
than five hundred feet, on a scale with naval destroyers, and cost six or
seven times what he was asking.

For the small, tight-lipped community around the world's biggest
yachts, the Palm Beach show has the promising air of Spring Training.
On the cusp of the summer season, it affords brokers and builders and
owners (or attendants from their family offices) a chance to huddle
over the latest merchandise and to gather intelligence: Who's getting
in? Who's getting out? And, most pressingly, who's ogling a bigger
boat?

On the docks, brokers parse the crowd according to a taxonomy of potential. Guests asking for tours face a gantlet of greeters, trained to distinguish "superrich clients" from "ineligible visitors," in the words of Emma Spence, a former greeter at the Palm Beach show. Spence looked for promising clues (the right shoes, jewelry, pets) as well as for red flags (cameras, ornate business cards, clothes with pop culture references). For greeters from elsewhere, Palm Beach is a challenging assignment. Unlike in Europe, where money can still produce some visible tells—Hunter Wellies, a Barbour jacket—the habits of wealth in Florida offer little that's reliable. One colleague resorted to binoc-ulars to spot a passerby with a $100,000 watch. According to Spence, people judged to have insufficient buying power are quietly marked for "dissuasion."

For the uninitiated, a pleasure boat the length of a football field can be bewildering. Andy Cohen, the talk show host, recalled his first visit to a superyacht owned by the media mogul Barry Diller: "I was like the Beverly Hillbillies." The boats have grown so vast that some owners place unique works of art outside the elevator on each deck, so that lost guests don't barge into the wrong stateroom.

At the Palm Beach show, I lingered in front of a gracious vessel called *Namasté*, until I was dissuaded by a wooden placard: "Private yacht, no boarding, no paparazzi." In a nearby berth was a 280-foot superyacht called *Bold*, which was styled like a warship, with its own helicopter hangar, three Sea-Doos, two sailboats, and a color scheme of gunmetal gray. The rugged look is a trend; "explorer" vessels, equipped to handle remote journeys, are the sport-utility vehicles of yachting.

If you hail from the realm of ineligible visitors, you may not be aware that we are living through the "greatest boom in the yacht business that's ever existed," as Bob Denison—whose firm, Denison Yachting, is one of the world's largest brokers—told me. "Every broker, every builder, up and down the docks, is having some of the best years they've ever expe-rienced." In 2021, the industry sold a record 887 superyachts worldwide, nearly twice the previous year's total. With more than a thousand new superyachts on order, shipyards are so backed up that clients unaccustomed to being told no have been shunted to waiting lists.

One reason for the increased demand for yachts is the pandemic. Some buyers invoke social distancing; others, an existential awakening. John Staluppi, of Palm Beach Gardens, who made a fortune from car dealerships, is looking to upgrade from his current, $60 million yacht. "When you're forty or fifty years old, you say, 'I've got plenty of time,'" he told me. But, at seventy-five, he is ready to throw in an extra fifteen million if it will spare him three years of waiting. "Is your life worth five million dollars a year? I think so," he said. A deeper reason for the demand is the widening imbalance of wealth. Since 1990, the United States' supply of billionaires has increased from sixty-six to more than eight hundred, even as the median hourly wage has risen only 20 percent. In that time, the number of truly giant yachts—those longer than 250 feet—has climbed from less than ten to more than 170. Raphael Sauleau, the CEO of Fraser Yachts, told me bluntly, "COVID and wealth—a perfect storm for us."

And yet the marina in Palm Beach was thrumming with anxiety. Ever since Russian president Vladimir Putin launched his assault on Ukraine, the superyacht world has come under scrutiny. At a port in Spain, a Ukrainian engineer named Taras Ostapchuk, working aboard a ship that he said was owned by a Russian arms dealer, threw open the sea valves and tried to sink it to the bottom of the harbor. Under arrest, he told a judge, "I would do it again." Then he returned to Ukraine and joined the military. Western allies, in the hope of pressuring Putin to withdraw, have sought to cut off Russian oligarchs from businesses and luxuries abroad. "We are coming for your ill-begotten gains," President Joe Biden declared in his State of the Union address.

*   *   *

Nobody can say precisely how many of Putin's associates own superyachts—known to professionals as "white boats"—because the white-boat world is notoriously opaque. Owners tend to hide behind shell companies, registered in obscure tax havens, attended by private bankers and lawyers. But, with unusual alacrity, authorities have used subpoenas and police powers to freeze boats suspected of having links to the Russian elite. In Spain, the government detained a $150 million yacht associated with Sergei Chemezov, the head of the conglomerate Rostec, whose bond with Putin reaches back to their time as KGB officers in East Germany. (As in many cases, the boat is not registered to Chemezov; the official owner is a shell company connected to his stepdaughter, a teacher whose salary is likely about $2,200 a month.) In Germany, authorities impounded the world's most voluminous yacht, *Dilbar*, for its ties to the mining-and-telecom tycoon Alisher Usmanov. And in Italy police have grabbed a veritable armada, including a boat owned by one of Russia's richest men, Alexei Mordashov, and a colossus suspected of belonging to Putin himself, the 459-foot *Scheherazade*.

In Palm Beach, the yachting community worried that the same scrutiny might be applied to them. "Say your superyacht is in Asia, and there's some big conflict where China invades Taiwan," Denison told me. "China could spin it as 'Look at these American oligarchs!'" He wondered if the seizures of superyachts marked a growing political animus toward the very rich. "Whenever things are economically or politically disruptive," he said, "it's hard to justify taking an insane amount of money and just putting it into something that costs a lot to maintain, depreciates, and is only used for having a good time."

Nobody pretends that a superyacht is a productive place to stash your wealth. The *Financial Times*, in a column headlined "A Superyacht Is a Terrible Asset," observed, "Owning a superyacht is like owning a stack of 10 Van Goghs, only you are holding them over your head as you tread water, trying to keep them dry."

Not so long ago, status transactions among the elite were denominated in Old Masters and in the sculptures of the Italian Renaissance. Joseph Duveen, the dominant art dealer of the early twentieth century, kept the oligarchs of his day—Andrew Mellon, Jules Bache, J. P.

Morgan—jockeying over Donatellos and Van Dycks. "When you pay high for the priceless," he liked to say, "you're getting it cheap."

In the 1950s, the height of aspirational style was fine French furniture—FFF, as it became known in certain precincts of Fifth Avenue and Palm Beach. Before long, more and more money was going airborne. Hugh Hefner, a pioneer in the private-jet era, decked out a plane he called Big Bunny, where he entertained Elvis Presley, Raquel Welch, and James Caan. The oil baron Armand Hammer circled the globe on his Boeing 727, paying bribes and recording evidence on microphones hidden in his cuff links. But once it seemed that every plutocrat had a plane, the thrill was gone.

In any case, an airplane is just transportation. A big ship is a floating manse, with a hierarchy written right into the nomenclature. If it has a crew working aboard, it's a yacht. If it's more than ninety-eight feet, it's a superyacht. After that, definitions are debated, but people generally agree that anything more than 230 feet is a megayacht, and more than 295 is a gigayacht. The world contains about 5,400 superyachts, and about a hundred gigayachts.

For the moment, a gigayacht is the most expensive item that our species has figured out how to own. In 2019, the hedge fund billionaire Ken Griffin bought a quadruplex on Central Park South for $240 million, the highest price ever paid for a home in America. In May, an unknown buyer spent about $195 million on an Andy Warhol silk screen portrait of Marilyn Monroe. In luxury-yacht terms, those are ordinary numbers. "There are a lot of boats in build well over two hundred and fifty million dollars," Jamie Edmiston, a broker in Monaco and London, told me. His buyers are getting younger and more inclined to spend long stretches at sea. "High-speed internet, telephony, modern communications have made working easier," he said. "Plus, people made a lot more money earlier in life."

A Silicon Valley CEO told me that one appeal of boats is that they can "absorb the most excess capital." He explained, "Rationally, it would seem to make sense for people to spend half a billion dollars on their house and then fifty million on the boat that they're on for two weeks a year, right? But it's gone the other way. People don't want to live in a hundred-thousand-square-foot house. Optically, it's weird. But a half-billion-dollar boat, actually, is quite nice." Staluppi, of Palm Beach Gardens, is content to spend three or four times as much on his yachts as on his homes. Part of the appeal is flexibility. "If you're on your boat and you don't like your neighbor, you tell the captain, 'Let's go to a different place,'" he said. On land, escaping a bad neighbor requires more work: "You got to try and buy him out or make it uncomfortable or something." The preference for sea-based investment has altered the proportions of taste. Until recently, the Silicon Valley CEO said, "a fifty-meter boat was considered a good-sized boat. Now that would be a little bit embarrassing." In the past twenty years, the length of the average luxury yacht has grown by a third, to 160 feet.

Thorstein Veblen, who published *The Theory of the Leisure Class* in 1899, argued that the power of conspicuous consumption sprang not from artful finery but from sheer needlessness. "In order to be reputable," he wrote, "it must be wasteful." In the yachting world, stories circulate about exotic deliveries by helicopter or seaplane: Dom Pérignon, bagels from Zabar's, sex workers, a rare melon from the island of Hokkaido. The industry excels at selling you things that you didn't know you needed. When you flip through the yachting press, it's easy to wonder how you've gone this long without a personal submarine, or a cryosauna that "blasts you with cold" down to minus 110 degrees Celsius, or the full menagerie of "exclusive leathers," such as eel and stingray.

But these shrines to excess capital operate, as vast fortunes do, on a principle of controlled visibility—radiant to the right audience, but veiled from the wider world. Even before Russia's invasion of Ukraine, the yachting community was straining to manage its reputation as a gusher of carbon emissions (one well-stocked diesel yacht is estimated to produce as much greenhouse gas as fifteen hundred passenger cars), not to mention the fact that the world of white boats is overwhelmingly white. In a candid aside to a French documentarian, the American yachtsman Bill Duker said, "If the rest of the world learns what it's like to live on a yacht like this, they're gonna bring back the guillotine." In 2022, the Dutch press reported that Jeff Bezos, the founder of Amazon, was building a sailing yacht so tall that the city of Rotterdam might temporarily dismantle a bridge that had survived the Nazis in order to let the boat pass to the open sea. Rotterdammers were not pleased. On Facebook, a local man urged people to "take a box of rotten eggs with you and let's throw them en masse at Jeff's superyacht when it sails through." At least thirteen thousand people expressed interest. Amid the uproar, a deputy mayor announced that the dismantling plan had been abandoned "for the time being." (Bezos modeled his yacht partly on the vessel owned by Diller, who has hosted him many times. The appreciation eventually extended to personnel, and Bezos hired one of Diller's captains.)

As social media has heightened the scrutiny of extraordinary wealth, some of the very people who created those platforms have sought less observable places to spend it. But they occasionally indulge in some coded provocation. In 2006, when the venture capitalist Tom Perkins unveiled his boat in Istanbul, most passersby saw it adorned in colorful flags, but people who could read naval signals were able to decode a message: "Rarely does one have the privilege to witness vulgar ostentation displayed on such a scale." As a longtime owner told me, "If you don't have some guilt about it, you're a rat."

Alex Finley, a former CIA officer who has seen yachts proliferate near her home in Barcelona, has weighed the superyacht era and its discontents in writings and on Twitter, using the hashtag #YachtWatch. "To me, the yachts are not just yachts," she told me. "In Russia's case, these are the embodiment of oligarchs helping a dictator destabilize our democracy while utilizing our democracy to their benefit." But, Finley added, it's a mistake to think the toxic symbolism applies only to Russia. "The yachts tell a whole story about a Faustian capitalism—this idea that we're ready to sell democracy for short-term profit," she said.

"They're registered offshore. They use every loophole that we've put in place for illicit money and tax havens. So they play a role in this battle, writ large, between autocracy and democracy."

*   *   *

After a morning on the docks at the Palm Beach show, I headed to a more secluded marina nearby, which had been set aside for what an attendant called "the really big hardware." It felt less like a trade show than like a boutique resort, with a swimming pool and a terrace restaurant. Kevin Merrigan, a relaxed Californian with horn-rimmed glasses and a high forehead pinked by the sun, was waiting for me at the stern of *Unbridled*, a superyacht with a brilliant blue hull that gave it the feel of a personal cruise ship. He invited me to the bridge deck, where a giant screen showed silent video of dolphins at play.

Merrigan is the chairman of the brokerage Northrop & Johnson, which has ridden the tide of growing boats and wealth since 1949. Lounging on a sofa mounded with throw pillows, he projected a nearly postcoital level of contentment. He had recently sold the boat we were on, accepted an offer for a behemoth beside us, and begun negotiating the sale of yet another. "This client owns three big yachts," he said. "It's a hobby for him. We're at 191 feet now, and last night he said, 'You know, what do you think about getting 250?'" Merrigan laughed. "And I was, like, 'Can't you just have dinner?'"

Among yacht owners, there are some unwritten rules of stratification: a Dutch-built boat will hold its value better than an Italian; a custom design will likely get more respect than a "series yacht"; and, if you want to disparage another man's boat, say that it looks like a wedding cake. But, in the end, nothing says as much about a yacht, or its owner, as the delicate matter of LOA—length over all.

The imperative is not usually length for length's sake (though the longtime owner told me that at times there is an aspect of "phallic sizing"). LOA is a byword for grandeur. In most cases, pleasure yachts are permitted to sleep no more than twelve passengers, a rule set by the International Convention for the Safety of Life at Sea, which was conceived after the sinking of the *Titanic*. But those limits do not apply to crew. "So, you might have anything between twelve and fifty crew looking after those twelve guests," Jamie Edmiston, the broker, said. "It's a level of service you cannot really contemplate until you've been fortunate enough to experience it."

As yachts have grown more capacious, and the limits on passengers have not, more and more space on board has been devoted to staff and to novelties. The latest fashions include IMAX theaters, hospital equipment that tests for dozens of pathogens, and ski rooms where guests can suit up for a helicopter trip to a mountaintop. The longtime owner, who had returned the previous day from his yacht, told me, "No one today—except for assholes and ridiculous people—lives on land in what you would call a deep and broad luxe life. Yes, people have nice houses and all of that, but it's unlikely that the ratio of staff to them is what it is on a boat." After a moment, he added, "Boats are the last place that I think you can get away with it."

Even among the truly rich, there is a gap between the haves and the have-yachts. One boating guest told me about a conversation with a famous friend who keeps one of the world's largest yachts. "He said, 'The boat is the last vestige of what real wealth can do.' What he meant is, You have a chef, and I have a chef. You have a driver, and I have a driver. You can fly privately, and I fly privately. So, the one place where I can make clear to the world that I am in a different fucking category than you is the boat."

After Merrigan and I took a tour of *Unbridled*, he led me out to a waiting tender, staffed by a crew member with an earpiece on a coil. The tender, Merrigan said, would ferry me back to the busy main dock of the Palm Beach show. We bounced across the waves under a pristine sky, and pulled into the marina, where my fellow-gawkers were still trying to talk their way past the greeters. As I walked back into the scrum, *Namasté* was still there, but it looked smaller than I remembered.

*   *   *

For owners and their guests, a white boat provides a discreet marketplace for the exchange of trust, patronage, and validation. To diagram the precise workings of that trade—the customs and anxieties, strategies and slights—I talked to Brendan O'Shannassy, a veteran captain who is a curator of white-boat lore. Raised in Western Australia, O'Shannassy joined the navy as a young man, and eventually found his way to skippering some of the world's biggest yachts. He has worked for Paul Allen, the late cofounder of Microsoft, along with a few other billionaires he declines to name. Now in his early fifties, with patient green eyes and tufts of curly brown hair, O'Shannassy has had a vantage from which to monitor the social traffic. "It's all gracious, and everyone's kiss-kiss," he said. "But there's a lot going on in the background."

O'Shannassy once worked for an owner who limited the number of newspapers on board, so that he could watch his guests wait and squirm. "It was a mind game amongst the billionaires. There were six couples, and three newspapers," he said, adding, "They were ranking themselves constantly." On some boats, O'Shannassy has found himself playing host in the awkward minutes after guests arrive. "A lot of them are savants, but some are very un-socially aware," he said. "They need someone to be social and charming for them." Once everyone settles in, O'Shannassy has learned, there is often a subtle shift, when a mogul or a politician or a pop star starts to loosen up in ways that are rarely possible on land. "Your security is relaxed—they're not on your hip," he said. "You're not worried about paparazzi. So you've got all this extra space, both mental and physical."

O'Shannassy has come to see big boats as a space where powerful "solar systems" converge and combine. "It is implicit in every interaction that their sharing of information will benefit both parties; it is an obsession with billionaires to do favors for each other. A referral, an introduction, an insight—it all matters," he wrote in *Superyacht Captain*, a memoir. A guest told O'Shannassy that, after a lavish display of hospitality, he finally understood the business case for buying a boat. "One deal secured on board will pay it all back many times over," the guest said, "and it is pretty hard to say no after your kids have been hosted so well for a week."

Take the case of David Geffen, the former music and film executive. He is long retired, but he hosts friends (and potential friends) on the 454-foot *Rising Sun*, which has a double-height cinema, a spa and salon, and a staff of fifty-seven. In 2017, shortly after Barack and Michelle Obama departed the White House, they were photographed on Geffen's boat in French Polynesia, accompanied by Bruce Springsteen, Oprah Winfrey, Tom Hanks, and Rita Wilson. For Geffen, the boat keeps him connected to the upper echelons of power. There are wealthier Americans, but not many of them have a boat so delectable that it can induce both a Democratic president and the workingman's crooner to risk the aroma of hypocrisy.

The binding effect pays dividends for guests, too. Once people reach a certain level of fame, they tend to conclude that its greatest advantage is access. Spend a week at sea together, lingering over meals, observing one another floundering on a paddleboard, and you have something of value for years to come. Call to ask for an investment, an introduction, an internship for a wayward nephew, and you'll at least get the call returned. It's a mutually reinforcing circle of validation: she's here, I'm here, we're here.

But if you want to get invited back, you are wise to remember your part of the bargain. If you work with movie stars, bring fresh gossip. If you're on Wall Street, bring an insight or two. Don't make the transaction obvious, but don't forget why you're there. "When I see the guest list," O'Shannassy wrote, "I am aware, even if not all names are familiar, that all have been chosen for a purpose."

For O'Shannassy, there is something comforting about the status anxieties of people who have everything. He recalled a visit to the Italian island of Sardinia, where his employer asked him for a tour of the boats nearby. Riding together on a tender, they passed one colossus after another, some twice the size of the owner's superyacht. Eventually, the man cut the excursion short. "Take me back to my yacht, please," he said. They motored in silence for a while. "There was a time when my yacht was the most beautiful in the bay," he said at last. "How do I keep up with this new money?"

*   *   *

The summer season in the Mediterranean cranks up in May, when the really big hardware heads east from Florida and the Caribbean to escape the coming hurricanes, and reconvenes along the coasts of France, Italy, and Spain. At the center is the Principality of Monaco, the sun-washed tax haven that calls itself the "world's capital of advanced yachting." In Monaco, which is among the richest countries on earth, superyachts bob in the marina like bath toys.

The nearest hotel room at a price that would not get me fired was an Airbnb over the border with France. But an acquaintance put me on the phone with the Yacht Club de Monaco, a members-only establishment created by the late monarch His Serene Highness Prince Rainier III, whom the website describes as "a true visionary in every respect." The club occasionally rents rooms—"cabins," as they're called—to visitors in town on yacht-related matters. Claudia Batthyany, the elegant director of special projects, showed me to my cabin and later explained that the club does not aspire to be a hotel. "We are an association," she said. "Otherwise, it becomes"—she gave a gentle wince—"not that exclusive."

Inside my cabin, I quickly came to understand that I would never be fully satisfied anywhere else again. The space was silent and aromatically upscale, bathed in soft sunlight that swept through a wall of glass overlooking the water. If I was getting a sudden rush of the onboard experience, that was no accident. The clubhouse was designed by the British architect Lord Norman Foster to evoke the opulent indulgence of ocean liners of the interwar years, like the *Queen Mary*. I found a handwritten welcome note, on embossed club stationery, set alongside an orchid and an assemblage of chocolate truffles: "The whole team remains at your entire disposal to make your stay a wonderful experience. Yours sincerely, Service Members." I saluted the nameless Service Members, toiling for the comfort of their guests. Looking out at the water, I thought, intrusively, of a line from Santiago, Hemingway's old man of the sea. "Do not think about sin," he told himself. "It is much too late for that and there are people who are paid to do it."

I had been assured that the Service Members would cheerfully bring dinner, as they might on board, but I was eager to see more of my surroundings. I consulted the club's summer dress code. It called for white trousers and a blue blazer, and it discouraged improvisation: "No pocket handkerchief is to be worn above the top breast-pocket bearing the Club's coat of arms." The handkerchief rule seemed navigable, but I did not possess white trousers, so I skirted the lobby and took refuge in the bar. At a table behind me, a man with flushed cheeks and a British accent had a head start. "You're a shitty negotiator," he told another man, with a laugh. "Maybe sales is not your game." A few seats away, an American woman was explaining to a foreign friend how to talk with conservatives: "If they say, 'The earth is flat,' you say, 'Well, I've sailed around it, so I'm not so sure about that.'"

In the morning, I had an appointment for coffee with Gaëlle Tallarida, the managing director of the Monaco Yacht Show, which the *Daily Mail* has called the "most shamelessly ostentatious display of yachts in the world." Tallarida was not born to that milieu; she grew up on the French side of the border, swimming at public beaches with a view of boats sailing from the marina. But she had a knack for highly organized spectacle. While getting a business degree, she worked on a student theater festival and found it thrilling. Afterward, she got a job in corporate events, and in 1998 she was hired at the yacht show as a trainee.

With this year's show five months off, Tallarida was already getting calls about what she described as "the most complex part of my work": deciding which owners get the most desirable spots in the marina. "As you can imagine, they've got very big egos," she said. "On top of that,

I'm a woman. They are sometimes arriving and saying"—she pointed into the distance, pantomiming a decree—"'OK, I want that!'"

Just about everyone wants his superyacht to be viewed from the side, so that its full splendor is visible. Most harbors, however, have a limited number of berths with a side view; in Monaco, there are only twelve, with prime spots arrayed along a concrete dike across from the club. "We reserve the dike for the biggest yachts," Tallarida said. But try telling that to a man who blew his fortune on a small superyacht.

Whenever possible, Tallarida presents her verdicts as a matter of safety: the layout must insure that "in case of an emergency, any boat can go out." If owners insist on preferential placement, she encourages a yachting version of the Golden Rule: "What if, next year, I do that to you? Against you?"

Does that work? I asked. She shrugged. "They say, 'Eh.'" Some would gladly risk being a victim next year in order to be a victor now. In the most awful moment of her career, she said, a man who was unhappy with his berth berated her face-to-face. "I was in the office, feeling like a little girl, with my daddy shouting at me. I said, 'OK, OK, I'm going to give you the spot.'"

Securing just the right place, it must be said, carries value. Back at the yacht club, I was on my terrace, enjoying the latest delivery by the Service Members—an airy French omelet and a glass of preternaturally fresh orange juice. I thought guiltily of my wife, at home with our kids, who had sent a text overnight alerting me to a maintenance issue that she described as "a toilet debacle."

Then I was distracted by the sight of a man on a yacht in the marina below. He was staring up at me. I went back to my brunch, but, when I looked again, there he was—a middle-aged man, on a mid-tier yacht, juiceless, on a greige banquette, staring up at my perfect terrace. A surprising sensation started in my chest and moved outward like a warm glow: the unmistakable pang of superiority.

*   *   *

That afternoon, I made my way to the bar, to meet the yacht club's general secretary, Bernard d'Alessandri, for a history lesson. The general secretary was up to code: white trousers, blue blazer, club crest over the heart. He has silver hair, black eyebrows, and a tan that evokes high-end leather. "I was a sailing teacher before this," he said, and gestured toward the marina. "It was not like this. It was a village."

Before there were yacht clubs, there were *jachten*, from the Dutch word for "hunt." In the seventeenth century, wealthy residents of Amsterdam created fast-moving boats to meet incoming cargo ships before they hit port, in order to check out the merchandise. Soon, the Dutch owners were racing one another, and yachting spread across Europe. After a visit to Holland in 1697, Peter the Great returned to Russia with a zeal for pleasure craft, and he later opened Nevsky Flot, one of the world's first yacht clubs, in St. Petersburg.

For a while, many of the biggest yachts were symbols of state power. In 1863, the viceroy of Egypt, Isma'il Pasha, ordered up a steel leviathan called *El Mahrousa*, which was the world's longest yacht for a remarkable 119 years, until the title was claimed by King Fahd of Saudi Arabia. In the United States, Franklin Delano Roosevelt received guests aboard the USS *Potomac*, which had a false smokestack containing a hidden elevator so that the president could move by wheelchair between decks.

But yachts were finding new patrons outside politics. In 1954, the Greek shipping baron Aristotle Onassis bought a Canadian navy frigate and spent $4 million turning it into *Christina O*, which served as his home for months on end—and, at various times, as a home to his companions Maria Callas, Greta Garbo, and Jacqueline Kennedy. *Christina O* had its flourishes—a Renoir in the master suite, a swimming pool with a mosaic bottom that rose to become a dance floor—but none were more distinctive than the appointments in the bar, which included whales' teeth carved into pornographic scenes from the *Odyssey* and stools upholstered in whale foreskins.

For Onassis, the extraordinary investments in *Christina O* were part of an epic tit for tat with his archrival, Stavros Niarchos, a fellow shipping tycoon, which was so entrenched that it continued even after Onassis's death, in 1975. Six years later, Niarchos launched a yacht fifty-five feet longer than *Christina O*: *Atlantis II*, which featured a swimming pool on a gyroscope so that the water would not slosh in heavy seas. *Atlantis II*, now moored in Monaco, sat before the general secretary and me as we talked.

Over the years, d'Alessandri had watched waves of new buyers arrive from one industry after another. "First, it was the oil. After, it was the telecommunications. Now, they are making money with crypto," he said. "And, each time, it's another size of the boat, another design." What began as symbols of state power had come to represent more diffuse aristocracies—the fortunes built on carbon, capital, and data that migrated across borders. As early as 1908, the English writer G. K. Chesterton wondered what the big boats foretold of a nation's fabric. "The poor man really has a stake in the country," he wrote. "The rich man hasn't; he can go away to New Guinea in a yacht."

Each iteration of fortune left its imprint on the industry. Sheikhs, who tend to cruise in the world's hottest places, wanted baroque indoor spaces and were uninterested in sundecks. Silicon Valley favored acres of beige, more Sonoma than Saudi. And buyers from Eastern Europe became so abundant that shipyards perfected the onboard banya, a traditional Russian sauna stocked with birch and eucalyptus. The collapse of the Soviet Union in 1991 had minted a generation of new billionaires, whose approach to money inspired a popular Russian joke: One oligarch brags to another, "Look at this new tie. It cost me two hundred bucks!" To which the other replies, "You moron. You could've bought the same one for a thousand!"

In 1998, around the time that the Russian economy imploded, the young tycoon Roman Abramovich reportedly bought a secondhand yacht called *Sussurro*—Italian for "whisper"—which had been so carefully engineered for speed that each individual screw was weighed before installation. Soon, Russians were competing to own the costliest ships. "If the most expensive yacht in the world was small, they would still want it," Maria Pevchikh, a Russian investigator who helps lead the Anti-Corruption Foundation, told me.

In 2008, a thirty-six-year-old industrialist named Andrey Melnichenko spent some $300 million on *Motor Yacht A*, a radical experiment conceived by the French designer Philippe Starck, with a dagger-shaped hull and a bulbous tower topped by a master bedroom set on a turntable that pivots to capture the best view. The shape was ridiculed as "a giant finger pointing at you" and "one of the most hideous vessels ever to sail," but it marked a new prominence for Russian money at sea. Today, post-Soviet elites are thought to own a fifth of the world's gigayachts.

Even Putin has signaled his appreciation, being photographed on yachts in the Black Sea resort of Sochi. In an explosive report in 2012, Boris Nemtsov, a former deputy prime minister, accused Putin of amassing a storehouse of outrageous luxuries, including four yachts, twenty homes, and dozens of private aircraft. Less than three years later, Nemtsov was fatally shot while crossing a bridge near the Kremlin. The Russian government, which officially reports that Putin collects a salary of about $140,000 and possesses a modest apartment in Moscow, denied any involvement.

* * *

Many of the largest, most flamboyant gigayachts are designed in Monaco, at a sleek waterfront studio occupied by the naval architect Espen Øino. At sixty, Øino has a boyish mop and the mild countenance of a country parson. He grew up in a small town in Norway, the heir to a humble maritime tradition. "My forefathers built wooden rowing boats for four generations," he told me. In the late 1980s, he was designing sailboats when his firm won a commission to design a megayacht for Emilio Azcárraga, the autocratic Mexican who built Televisa into the world's largest Spanish-language broadcaster. Azcárraga was nicknamed El Tigre, for his streak of white hair and his comfort with confrontation;

he kept a chair in his office that was unusually high off the ground, so that visitors' feet dangled like children's.

In early meetings, Øino recalled, Azcárraga grew frustrated that the ideas were not dazzling enough. "You must understand," he said. "I don't go to port very often with my boats, but, when I do, I want my presence to be felt."

The final design was suitably arresting; after the boat was completed, Øino had no shortage of commissions. In 1998, he was approached by Paul Allen of Microsoft to build a yacht that opened the way for the Goliaths that followed. The result, called *Octopus*, was so large that it contained a submarine marina in its belly, as well as a helicopter hangar that could be converted into an outdoor performance space. Mick Jagger and Bono played on occasion. I asked Øino why owners obsessed with secrecy seem determined to build the world's most conspicuous machines. He compared it to a luxury car with tinted windows. "People can't see you, but you're still in that expensive, impressive thing," he said. "We all need to feel that we're important in one way or another."

In recent months, Øino has seen some of his creations detained by governments in the sanctions campaign. When we spoke, he condemned the news coverage. "Yacht equals Russian equals evil equals money," he said disdainfully. "It's a bit tragic, because the yachts have become synonymous with the bad guys in a James Bond movie."

What about *Scheherazade*, the giant yacht that U.S. officials have alleged is held by a Russian businessman for Putin's use? Øino, who designed the ship, rejected the idea. "We have designed two yachts for heads of state, and I can tell you that they're completely different, in terms of the layout and everything, from *Scheherazade*." He meant that the details said plutocrat, not autocrat.

For the time being, *Scheherazade* and other Øino creations under detention across Europe have entered a strange legal purgatory. As lawyers for the owners battle to keep the ships from being permanently confiscated, local governments are duty-bound to maintain them until a resolution is reached. In a comment recorded by a hot mike in 2022,

Jake Sullivan, the U.S. national security advisor, marveled that "people are basically being paid to maintain Russian superyachts on behalf of the United States government." (It usually costs about 10 percent of a yacht's construction price to keep it afloat each year. In May, officials in Fiji complained that a detained yacht named *Amadea* was costing them more than $171,000 a day.)

Stranger still are the Russian yachts on the lam. Among them is Melnichenko's much-maligned *Motor Yacht A*. On March 9, Melnichenko was sanctioned by the European Union, and although he denied having close ties to Russia's leadership, Italy seized one of his yachts—a $600 million sailboat. But *Motor Yacht A* slipped away before anyone could grab it. Then the boat turned off the transponder required by international maritime rules so that its location could no longer be tracked. The last ping was somewhere near the Maldives, before it went dark on the high seas.

*   *   *

The very largest yachts come from Dutch and German shipyards, which have experience in naval vessels, known as "gray boats." But the majority of superyachts are built in Italy, partly because owners prefer to visit the Mediterranean during construction. (A British designer advises those who are weighing their choices to take the geography seriously, "unless you like schnitzel.")

In the past twenty-two years, nobody has built more superyachts than the Vitellis, an Italian family whose patriarch, Paolo Vitelli, got his start in the 1970s, manufacturing smaller boats near a lake in the mountains. By 1985, their company, Azimut, had grown large enough to buy the Benetti shipyards, which had been building enormous yachts since the nineteenth century. Today, the combined company builds its largest boats near the sea, but the family still works in the hill town of Avigliana, where a medieval monastery towers above a valley. When I visited in April, Giovanna Vitelli, the vice president and the founder's daughter, led me through the experience of customizing a yacht.

"We're using more and more virtual reality," she said, and a staffer fitted me with a headset. When the screen blinked on, I was inside a 3-D mockup of a yacht that is not yet on the market. I wandered around my suite for a while, checking out swivel chairs, a modish sideboard, blond wood paneling on the walls. It was convincing enough that I collided with a real-life desk.

After we finished with the headset, it was time to pick the décor. The industry encourages an introspective evaluation: What do you want your yacht to say about you? I was handed a vibrant selection of wood, marble, leather, and carpet. The choices felt suddenly grave. Was I cut out for the chiseled look of Cream Vesuvio, or should I accept that I'm a gray Cardoso Stone? For carpets, I liked the idea of Chablis Corn White—Paris and the prairie, together at last. But, for extra seating, was it worth splurging for the VIP Vanity Pouf?

Some designs revolve around a single piece of art. The most expensive painting ever sold, Leonardo da Vinci's *Salvator Mundi*, reportedly was hung on the Saudi crown prince Mohammed bin Salman's 439-foot yacht *Serene*, after the Louvre rejected a Saudi demand that it hang next to the *Mona Lisa*. Art conservators blanched at the risks that excess humidity and fluctuating temperatures could pose to a five-hundred-year-old painting. Often, collectors who want to display masterpieces at sea commission replicas.

If you've just put half a billion dollars into a boat, you may have qualms about the truism that material things bring less happiness than experiences do. But this, too, can be finessed. Andrew Grant Super, a cofounder of the "experiential yachting" firm Berkeley Rand, told me that he served a uniquely overstimulated clientele: "We call them the bored billionaires." He outlined a few of his experience products. "We can plot half of the Pacific Ocean with coordinates, to map out the Battle of Midway," he said. "We re-create the full-blown battles of the giant ships from America and Japan. The kids have haptic guns and haptic vests. We put the smell of cordite and cannon fire on board, pumping around them." For those who aren't soothed by the scent of cordite, Super offered an alternative. "We fly 3-D-printed, architectural freestanding restaurants into the middle of the Maldives, on a sand shelf that can only last another eight hours before it disappears."

For some, the thrill lies in the engineering. John Staluppi, born in Brooklyn, was an auto mechanic who had no experience with the sea until his boss asked him to soup up a boat. "I took the six-cylinder engines out and put V-8 engines in," he recalled. Once he started commissioning boats of his own, he built scale models to conduct tests in water tanks. "I knew I could never have the biggest boat in the world, so I says, 'You know what? I want to build the *fastest* yacht in the world.' The Aga Khan had the fastest yacht, and we just blew right by him."

In Italy, after decking out my notional yacht, I headed south along the coast, to Tuscan shipyards that have evolved with each turn in the country's history. Close to the Carrara quarries, which yielded the marble that Michelangelo turned into *David*, ships were constructed in the nineteenth century to transport giant blocks of stone. Down the coast, the yards in Livorno made warships under the Fascists, until they were bombed by the Allies. Later, they began making and refitting luxury yachts. Inside the front gate of a Benetti shipyard in Livorno, a set of models depicted the firm's famous modern creations. Most notable was the megayacht *Nabila*, built in 1980 for the high-living arms dealer Adnan Khashoggi, with a hundred rooms and a disco that was the site of legendary decadence. (Khashoggi's budget for prostitution was so extravagant that a French prosecutor later estimated he paid at least half a million dollars to a single madam in a single year.)

In 1987, shortly before Khashoggi was indicted for mail fraud and obstruction of justice (he was eventually acquitted), the yacht was sold to the real estate developer Donald Trump, who renamed it *Trump Princess*. Trump was never comfortable on boats—"Couldn't get off fast enough," he once said—but he liked to impress people with his yacht's splendor. In 1991, while $3 billion in debt, Trump ceded the vessel to creditors. Later in life, though, he discovered enthusiastic support among what he called "our beautiful boaters," and he came to see quality watercraft as a mark of virtue—a way of beating the so-called elite. "We got better houses, apartments, we got nicer boats, we're smarter than they are," he told a crowd in Fargo, North Dakota. "Let's call ourselves, from now on, the super-elite."

*   *   *

In the age of oversharing, yachts are a final sanctum of secrecy, even for some of the world's most inveterate talkers. Oprah, after returning from her sojourn with the Obamas, rebuffed questions from reporters. "What happens on the boat stays on the boat," she said. "We talked, and everybody else did a lot of paddleboarding."

I interviewed six American superyacht owners at length, and almost all insisted on anonymity or held forth with stupefying blandness. "Great family time," one said. Another confessed, "It's really hard to talk about it without being ridiculed." None needed to be reminded of David Geffen's misadventure during the early weeks of the pandemic, when he Instagrammed a photo of his yacht in the Grenadines and posted that he was "avoiding the virus" and "hoping everybody is stay-ing safe." It drew thousands of responses, many marked #EatTheRich, others summoning a range of nautical menaces: "At least the pirates have his location now."

The yachts extend a tradition of seclusion as the ultimate luxury. The Medici, in sixteenth-century Florence, built elevated passageways, or *corridoi,* high over the city to escape what a scholar called the "clash of classes, the randomness, the smells and confusions" of pedestrian life below. More recently, owners of prized townhouses in London have headed in the other direction, building three-story basements so vast that their construction can require mining engineers—a trend that researchers in the United Kingdom named "luxified troglodytism."

Water conveys a particular autonomy, whether it's ringing the foot of a castle or separating a private island from the mainland. Peter Thiel, the billionaire venture capitalist, gave start-up funding to the Seasteading

Institute, a nonprofit group cofounded by Milton Friedman's grandson, which seeks to create floating mini-states—an endeavor that Thiel considered part of his libertarian project to "escape from politics in all its forms." Until that fantasy is realized, a white boat can provide a start. A recent feature in *Boat International*, a glossy trade magazine, noted that the new $125 million megayacht *Victorious* has four generators and "six months' autonomy" at sea. The builder, Vural Ak, explained, "In case of emergency, god forbid, you can live in open water without going to shore and keep your food stored, make your water from the sea."

Much of the time, superyachts dwell beyond the reach of ordinary law enforcement. They cruise in international waters, and, when they dock, local cops tend to give them a wide berth; the boats often have private security, and their owners may well be friends with the prime minister. According to leaked documents known as the Paradise Papers, handlers proposed that the Saudi crown prince take delivery of a $420 million yacht in "international waters in the western Mediterranean," where the sale could avoid taxes.

Builders and designers rarely advertise beyond the trade press, and they scrupulously avoid leaks. At Lürssen, a German shipbuilding firm, projects are described internally strictly by reference number and code name. "We are not in the business for the glory," Peter Lürssen, the CEO, told a reporter. The closest thing to an encyclopedia of yacht ownership is a site called SuperYachtFan, run by a longtime researcher who identifies himself only as Peter, with a disclaimer that he relies partly on "rumors" but makes efforts to confirm them. In an email, he told me that he studies shell companies, navigation routes, paparazzi photos, and local media in various languages to maintain a database with more than thirteen hundred supposed owners. Some ask him to remove their names, but he thinks that members of that economic echelon should regard the attention as a "fact of life."

To work in the industry, staff must adhere to the culture of secrecy, often enforced by NDAs. On one yacht, O'Shannassy, the captain, learned to communicate in code with the helicopter pilot who regularly flew the owner from Switzerland to the Mediterranean. Before takeoff, the pilot would call with a cryptic report on whether the party included the presence of a Pomeranian. If any guest happened to overhear, their cover story was that a customs declaration required details about pets. In fact, the lapdog was a constant companion of the owner's wife; if the Pomeranian was in the helicopter, so was she. "If no dog was in the helicopter," O'Shannassy recalled, the owner was bringing "somebody else." It was the captain's duty to rebroadcast the news across the yacht's internal radio: "Helicopter launched, no dog, I repeat no dog today"— the signal for the crew to ready the main cabin for the mistress, instead of the wife. They swapped out dresses, family photos, bathroom supplies, favored drinks in the fridge. On one occasion, the code got garbled, and the helicopter landed with an unanticipated Pomeranian. Afterward, the owner summoned O'Shannassy and said, "Brendan, I hope you never have such a situation, but if you do I recommend making sure the correct dresses are hanging when your wife comes into your room."

*   *   *

In the hierarchy on board a yacht, the most delicate duties tend to trickle down to the least powerful. Yacht crew—yachties, as they're known—trade manual labor and obedience for cash and adventure. On a well-staffed boat, the "interior team" operates at a forensic level of detail: they'll use Q-tips to polish the rim of your toilet, tweezers to lift your fried-chicken crumbs from the teak, a toothbrush to clean the treads of your staircase.

Many are English-speaking twentysomethings, who find work by doing the "dock walk," passing out résumés at marinas. The deals can be alluring: $3,500 a month for deckhands; $50,000 in tips for a decent summer in the Med. For captains, the size of the boat matters—they tend to earn about a thousand dollars per foot per year.

Yachties are an attractive lot, a community of the toned and chipper, which does not happen by chance; their résumés circulate with head shots. Before Andy Cohen was a talk show host, he was the head of production and development at Bravo, where he green-lighted a reality show about a yacht crew: "It's a total pressure cooker, and they're actually living together while they're working. Oh, and by the way, half of them are having sex with each other. What's not going to be a hit about that?" The result, the gleefully seamy *Below Deck* has been among the network's top-rated shows for nearly a decade.

To stay in the business, captains and crew must absorb varying degrees of petty tyranny. An owner once gave O'Shannassy "a verbal beating" for failing to negotiate a lower price on champagne flutes etched with the yacht's logo. In such moments, the captain responds with a deferential mantra: "There is no excuse. Your instruction was clear. I can only endeavor to make it better for next time."

The job comes with perilously little protection. A big yacht is effectively a corporation with a rigid hierarchy and no HR department. In recent years, the industry has fielded increasingly outspoken complaints about sexual abuse, toxic impunity, and a disregard for mental health. A 2018 survey by the International Seafarers' Welfare and Assistance Network found that more than half of the women who work as yacht crew had experienced harassment, discrimination, or bullying on board. More than four-fifths of the men and women surveyed reported low morale.

Karine Rayson worked on yachts for four years, rising to the position of "chief stew," or stewardess. Eventually, she found herself "thinking of business ideas while vacuuming," and tiring of the culture of entitlement. She recalled an episode in the Maldives when "a guest took a Jet Ski and smashed into a marine reserve. That damaged the coral, and broke his Jet Ski, so he had to clamber over the rocks and find his way to the shore. It was a private hotel, and the security got him and said, 'Look, there's a large fine, you have to pay.' He said, 'Don't worry, the boat will pay for it.'" Rayson went back to school and became a psychotherapist. After a period of counseling inmates in maximum-security prisons, she now works with yacht crew, who meet with her online from around the world.

Rayson's clients report a range of scenarios beyond the boundaries of ordinary employment: guests who did so much cocaine that they had no appetite for a chef's meals; armed men who raided a boat offshore and threatened to take crew members to another country; owners who vowed that if a young stew told anyone about abuse she suffered on board they'd call in the Mafia and "skin me alive." Bound by NDAs, crew at sea have little recourse. "We were paranoid that our emails were being reviewed, or we were getting bugged," Rayson said.

She runs an "exit strategy" course to help crew find jobs when they're back on land. The adjustment isn't easy, she said: "You're getting paid good money to clean a toilet. So, when you take your CV to land-based employers, they might question your skill set." Despite the stresses of yachting work, Rayson said, "a lot of them struggle with integration into land-based life, because they have all their bills paid for them, so they don't pay for food. They don't pay for rent. It's a huge shock."

*   *   *

It doesn't take long at sea to learn that nothing is too rich to rust. The ocean air tarnishes metal ten times as fast as on land; saltwater infiltrates from below. Left untouched, a single corroding ulcer will puncture tanks, seize a motor, even collapse a hull. There are tricks, of course—shield sensitive parts with resin, have your staff buff away blemishes—but you can insulate a machine from its surroundings for only so long.

Hang around the superyacht world for a while and you see the metaphor everywhere. In the months after Putin's invasion of Ukraine, the war ate a hole in his myths of competence. The Western campaign to isolate him and his oligarchs was far from perfect, but it had revealed and quantified a realm of commerce that was otherwise hard to measure. Even if the seizures of yachts were mired in legal disputes, Finley, the former CIA officer, saw them as a vital "pressure point." She said, "The oligarchs supported Putin because he provided stable authoritarianism, and he can no longer guarantee that stability. And that's when you start to have cracks."

For all its profits from Russian clients, the yachting industry was unsentimental. Brokers stripped photos of Russian yachts from their websites; Peter Lürssen, the German builder, sent questionnaires to clients asking who, exactly, they were. Business was roaring, and, if some Russians were cast out of the have-yachts, other buyers would replace them.

On a cloudless morning in Viareggio, a Tuscan town that builds almost a fifth of the world's superyachts, a family of first-time owners from Tel Aviv made the final, fraught preparations. Down by the docks, their new boat was suspended above the water on slings, ready to be lowered for its official launch. The scene was set for a ceremony: white flags in the wind, a plexiglass lectern. It felt like the obverse of the dockside scrum at the Palm Beach show; by this point in the buying process, nobody was getting vetted through binoculars. Waitresses handed out glasses of wine. The yacht vendors were in suits, but the new owners were in upscale Euro casual: untucked linen, tight jeans, twelve-hundred-dollar Prada sneakers. The family declined to speak to me (and the company declined to identify them). They had come asking for a smaller boat, but the sales staff had talked them up to a hundred and eleven feet. The Victorians would have been impressed.

The CEO of Azimut Benetti, Marco Valle, was in a buoyant mood. "Sun. Breeze. Perfect day to launch a boat, right?" he told the owners. He applauded them for taking the "first step up the big staircase." The selling of the next vessel had already begun.

Hanging aloft, their yacht looked like an artifact in the making; it was easy to imagine a future civilization sifting the sediment and discovering that an earlier society had engaged in a building spree of sumptuous arks, with accommodations for dozens of servants but only a few lucky passengers, plus the occasional Pomeranian.

We approached the hull, where a bottle of spumante hung from a ribbon in Italian colors. Two members of the family pulled back the

bottle and slung it against the yacht. It bounced off and failed to shat-
ter. "Oh, that's bad luck," a woman murmured beside me. Tales of that
unhappy omen abound. In one memorable case, the bottle failed to
break on *Zaca*, a schooner that belonged to Errol Flynn. In the years that
followed, the crew mutinied and the boat sank; after being refloated,
it became the setting for Flynn's descent into cocaine, alcohol, orgies,
and drug smuggling. When Flynn died, new owners brought in a cleric
for an onboard exorcism.

In the present case, the bottle broke on the second hit, and confetti
rained down. As the family crowded around their yacht for photos, I
asked Valle, the CEO, about the shortage of new boats. "Twenty-six
years I've been in the nautical business—never been like this," he said.
He couldn't hire enough welders and carpenters. "I don't know for how
long it will last, but we'll try to get the profits right now."

Whatever comes, the white-boat world is preparing to insure future
profits, too. In recent years, big builders and brokers have sponsored
a rebranding campaign dedicated to "improving the perception of
superyachting." (Among its recommendations: fewer ads with girls
in bikinis and high heels.) The goal is partly to defuse #EatTheRich,
but mostly it is to soothe skittish buyers. Even the dramatic increase in
yacht ownership has not kept up with forecasts of the global growth in
billionaires—a disparity that represents the "one dark cloud we can see
on the horizon," as Øino, the naval architect, said during an industry
talk in Norway. He warned his colleagues that they needed to reach
those "potential yacht owners who, for some reason, have decided not
to step up to the plate."

But, to a certain kind of yacht buyer, even aggressive scrutiny can
feel like an advertisement—a reminder that, with enough access and
cash, you can ride out almost any storm. Weeks after the fugitive *Motor
Yacht A* went silent, it was rediscovered, buffed to a shine and moored
along a creek in the United Arab Emirates. The owner, Melnichenko,
had been sanctioned by the E.U., Switzerland, Australia, and the U.K.
Yet the Emirates had rejected requests to join those sanctions and had

become a favored wartime haven for Russian money. *Motor Yacht A* was once again arrayed in almost plain sight, like signal flags in the wind.

Amadea, the yacht seized in Fiji, was transported to San Diego, where it stayed in detention while the case moved through the courts; the U.S. government maintained the vessel at a cost of at least $600,000 dollars a month. In 2024, the yachting press reported that Mark Zuckerberg had paid a bargain price of $300 million for the largest gigayacht ever built in the Netherlands. (The boat was relatively cheap because it had been commissioned by Russian billionaire Vladimir Potanin, who proved unable to take possession after Europe banned the export of yachts to Russia.) That summer, Russian authorities added Maria Pevchikh, the anti-corruption investigator, to an official list of "extremists and terrorists." In December 2024, Dutch prosecutors levied a fine of $157,000 on the company that built Bezos's superyacht for importing teak harvested from Myanmar, in violation of European law. In 2025, the Palm Beach International Boat Show announced the addition of a "preview day," to give "serious buyers the opportunity to explore the show before larger crowds arrive."

Survival of the Richest

Some of the wealthiest people in America—in Silicon Valley, New York, and beyond—are getting ready for the crackup of civilization

— 2017 —

Steve Huffman, the thirty-three-year-old cofounder and CEO of Reddit, which is valued at $600 million, was nearsighted until November 2015, when he arranged to have laser eye surgery. He underwent the procedure not for the sake of convenience or appearance but, rather, for a reason he doesn't usually talk much about: he hopes that it will improve his odds of surviving a disaster, whether natural or man-made. "If the world ends—and not even if the world ends, but if we have trouble—getting contacts or glasses is going to be a huge pain in the ass," he told me. "Without them, I'm fucked."

Huffman, who lives in San Francisco, has large blue eyes, thick, sandy hair, and an air of restless curiosity; at the University of Virginia, he was a competitive ballroom dancer, who hacked his roommate's website as a prank. He is less focused on a specific threat—a quake on the San Andreas, a pandemic, a dirty bomb—than he is on the aftermath, "the temporary collapse of our government and structures," as he puts it. "I own a couple of motorcycles. I have a bunch of guns and ammo. Food. I figure that, with that, I can hole up in my house for some amount of time."

Survivalism, the practice of preparing for a crackup of civilization, tends to evoke a certain picture: the woodsman in the tinfoil hat, the

33

hysteric with the hoard of beans, the religious doomsayer. But in recent years survivalism has expanded to more affluent quarters, taking root in Silicon Valley and New York City, among technology executives, hedge fund managers, and others in their economic cohort.

In 2016, when the presidential campaign exposed increasingly toxic divisions in America, Antonio García Martínez, a forty-year-old former Facebook product manager living in San Francisco, bought five wooded acres on an island in the Pacific Northwest and brought in generators, solar panels, and thousands of rounds of ammunition. "When society loses a healthy founding myth, it descends into chaos," he told me. The author of *Chaos Monkeys*, an acerbic Silicon Valley memoir, García Martínez wanted a refuge that would be far from cities but not entirely isolated. "All these dudes think that one guy alone could somehow withstand the roving mob," he said. "No, you're going to need to form a local militia. You just need so many things to actually ride out the apocalypse." Once he started telling peers in the Bay Area about his "little island project," they came "out of the woodwork" to describe their own preparations, he said. "I think people who are particularly attuned to the levers by which society actually works understand that we are skating on really thin cultural ice right now."

In private Facebook groups, wealthy survivalists swap tips on gas masks, bunkers, and locations safe from the effects of climate change. One member, the head of an investment firm, told me, "I keep a helicopter gassed up all the time, and I have an underground bunker with an air-filtration system." He said that his preparations probably put him at the "extreme" end among his peers. But he added, "A lot of my friends do the guns and the motorcycles and the gold coins. That's not too rare anymore."

Tim Chang, a forty-four-year-old managing director at Mayfield Fund, a venture capital firm, told me, "There's a bunch of us in the Valley. We meet up and have these financial-hacking dinners and talk about backup plans people are doing. It runs the gamut from a lot of people stocking up on Bitcoin and cryptocurrency, to figuring out how to get second passports if they need it, to having vacation homes in other countries that could be escape havens." He said, "I'll be candid: I'm stockpiling now on real estate to generate passive income but also to have havens to go to." He and his wife, who is in technology, keep a set of bags packed for themselves and their four-year-old daughter. He told me, "I kind of have this terror scenario: 'Oh, my God, if there is a civil war or a giant earthquake that cleaves off part of California, we want to be ready.'"

When Marvin Liao, a former Yahoo executive who is now a partner at 500 Startups, a venture capital firm, considered his preparations, he decided that his caches of water and food were not enough. "What if someone comes and takes this?" he asked me. To protect his wife and daughter, he said, "I don't have guns, but I have a lot of other weaponry. I took classes in archery."

For some, it's just "brogrammer" entertainment, a kind of real-world sci-fi, with gear; for others, like Huffman, it's been a concern for years. "Ever since I saw the movie *Deep Impact*," he said. The film, released in 1998, depicts a comet striking the Atlantic, and a race to escape the tsunami. "Everybody's trying to get out, and they're stuck in traffic. That scene happened to be filmed near my high school. Every time I drove through that stretch of road, I would think, I need to own a motorcycle because everybody else is screwed."

Huffman has been a frequent attendee at Burning Man, the annual, clothing-optional festival in the Nevada desert, where artists mingle with moguls. He fell in love with one of its core principles, "radical self-reliance," which he takes to mean "happy to help others, but not wanting to require others." (Among survivalists, or "preppers," as some call themselves, FEMA, the Federal Emergency Management Agency, stands for "Foolishly Expecting Meaningful Aid.") Huffman calculated that in the event of a disaster he would seek out some form of community: "Being around other people is a good thing. I also have this somewhat egotistical view that I'm a pretty good leader. I will probably be in charge, or at least not a slave, when push comes to shove."

Over the years, Huffman became increasingly concerned about basic American political stability and the risk of large-scale unrest. He said, "Some sort of institutional collapse, then you just lose shipping—that sort of stuff." (Prepper blogs call such a scenario WROL, "without rule of law.") Huffman has come to believe that contemporary life rests on a fragile consensus. "I think, to some degree, we all collectively take it on faith that our country works, that our currency is valuable, the peaceful transfer of power—that all of these things that we hold dear work because we believe they work. While I do believe they're quite resilient, and we've been through a lot, certainly we're going to go through a lot more."

In building Reddit, a community of thousands of discussion threads, into one of the most frequently visited sites in the world, Huffman has grown aware of the way that technology alters our relations with one another, for better and for worse. He has witnessed how social media can magnify public fear. "It's easier for people to panic when they're together," he said, pointing out that "the internet has made it easier for people to be together," yet it also alerts people to emerging risks. Long before the financial crisis became front-page news, early signs appeared in user comments on Reddit. "People were starting to whisper about mortgages. They were worried about student debt. They were worried about debt in general. There was a lot of, 'This is too good to be true. This doesn't smell right.'" He added, "There's probably some false positives in there as well, but, in general, I think we're a pretty good gauge of public sentiment. When we're talking about a faith-based collapse, you're going to start to see the chips in the foundation on social media first."

*   *   *

How did a preoccupation with the apocalypse come to flourish in Silicon Valley, a place known, to the point of cliché, for unstinting confidence in its ability to change the world for the better?

Those impulses are not as contradictory as they seem. Technology rewards the ability to imagine wildly different futures, Roy Bahat, the head of Bloomberg Beta, a San Francisco–based venture capital firm, told me. "When you do that, it's pretty common that you take things ad infinitum, and that leads you to utopias and dystopias," he said. It can inspire radical optimism—such as the cryonics movement, which calls for freezing bodies at death in the hope that science will one day revive them—or bleak scenarios. Tim Chang, the venture capitalist who keeps his bags packed, told me, "My current state of mind is oscillating between optimism and sheer terror."

In recent decades, survivalism has been edging deeper into mainstream culture. In 2012, National Geographic Channel launched *Doomsday Preppers*, a reality show featuring a series of Americans bracing for what they called SHTF (when the "shit hits the fan"). The premiere drew more than four million viewers, and by the end of the first season it was the most popular show in the channel's history. A survey commissioned by National Geographic found that 40 percent of Americans believed that stocking up on supplies or building a bomb shelter was a wiser investment than a 401(k). Online, the prepper discussions run from folksy ("A Mom's Guide to Preparing for Civil Unrest") to grim ("How to Eat a Pine Tree to Survive").

Around the time that *Doomsday Preppers* was becoming a hit, the reelection of Barack Obama was a boon for the prepping industry. Conservatives who accused Obama of stoking racial tensions, restricting gun rights, and expanding the national debt loaded up on the types of freeze-dried cottage cheese and beef stroganoff promoted by commentators like Glenn Beck and Sean Hannity. A network of "readiness" trade shows attracted conventioneers with classes on suturing (practiced on a pig trotter) and photo opportunities with survivalist stars from the TV show *Naked and Afraid*.

The fears were different in Silicon Valley. Around the same time that Huffman, on Reddit, was watching the advance of the financial crisis, Justin Kan heard the first inklings of survivalism among his peers. Kan cofounded Twitch, a gaming network that was later sold to Amazon for nearly a billion dollars. "Some of my friends were, like, 'The breakdown of society is imminent. We should stockpile food,'" he said. "I tried to. But then we got a couple of bags of rice and five cans of tomatoes. We would have been dead if there was actually a real problem." I asked Kan what his prepping friends had in common. "Lots of money and resources," he said. "What are the other things I can worry about and prepare for? It's like insurance."

Yishan Wong, an early Facebook employee, was the CEO of Reddit from 2012 to 2014. He, too, had eye surgery for survival purposes, eliminating his dependence, as he put it, "on a nonsustainable external aid for perfect vision." In an email, Wong told me, "Most people just assume improbable events don't happen, but technical people tend to view risk very mathematically." He continued, "The tech preppers do not necessarily think a collapse is likely. They consider it a remote event, but one with a very severe downside, so, given how much money they have, spending a fraction of their net worth to hedge against this . . . is a logical thing to do."

How many wealthy Americans are really making preparations for a catastrophe? It's hard to know exactly; a lot of people don't like to talk about it. ("Anonymity is priceless," one hedge fund manager told me, declining an interview.) Sometimes the topic emerges in unexpected ways. Reid Hoffman, the cofounder of LinkedIn and a prominent investor, recalls telling a friend that he was thinking of visiting New Zealand. "Oh, are you going to get apocalypse insurance?" the friend asked. "I'm, like, Huh?" Hoffman told me. New Zealand, he discovered, is a favored refuge in the event of a cataclysm. Hoffman said, "Saying you're 'buying a house in New Zealand' is kind of a wink, wink, say no more. Once you've done the Masonic handshake, they'll be, like, 'Oh, you know, I have a broker who sells old ICBM silos, and they're nuclear-hardened, and they kind of look like they would be interesting to live in.'"

I asked Hoffman to estimate what share of fellow Silicon Valley billionaires have acquired some level of "apocalypse insurance," in the form of a hideaway in the U.S. or abroad. "I would guess fifty-plus percent," he said, "but that's parallel with the decision to buy a vacation home. Human motivation is complex, and I think people can say, 'I now have a safety blanket for this thing that scares me.'" The fears vary, but many worry that, as artificial intelligence takes away a growing share of jobs, there will be a backlash against Silicon Valley, America's second-highest concentration of wealth. (The Gold Coast of Connecticut is first.) "I've heard this theme from a bunch of people," Hoffman said. "Is the country going to turn against the wealthy? Is it going to turn against technological innovation? Is it going to turn into civil disorder?"

The CEO of another large tech company told me, "It's still not at the point where industry insiders would turn to each other with a straight face and ask what their plans are for some apocalyptic event." He went on, "But, having said that, I actually think it's logically rational and appropriately conservative." He noted the vulnerabilities exposed by the Russian cyberattack on the Democratic National Committee in 2016, and also by a large-scale but little-noticed hack that fall, which disrupted the internet in North America and Western Europe. "Our food supply is dependent on GPS, logistics, and weather forecasting," he said, "and those systems are generally dependent on the internet, and the internet is dependent on DNS"—the system that manages domain names. "Go risk factor by risk factor by risk factor, acknowledging that there are many you don't even know about, and you ask, 'What's the chance of this breaking in the next decade?' Or invert it: 'What's the chance that nothing breaks in fifty years?'"

One measure of survivalism's spread is that some people are starting to speak out against it. Max Levchin, a founder of PayPal and of Affirm, a lending start-up, told me, "It's one of the few things about Silicon Valley that I actively dislike—the sense that we are superior giants who move the needle and, even if it's our own failure, must be spared."

To Levchin, prepping for survival is a moral miscalculation; he prefers to "shut down party conversations" on the topic. "I typically ask people, 'So you're worried about the pitchforks. How much money have you donated to your local homeless shelter?' This connects the most, in my mind, to the realities of the income gap. All the other forms of fear that people bring up are artificial." In his view, this is the time to invest in solutions, not escape. "At the moment, we're actually at a relatively benign point of the economy. When the economy heads south, you will have a bunch of people that are in really bad shape. What do we expect then?"

*   *   *

On the opposite side of the country, similar awkward conversations have been unfolding in some financial circles. Robert H. Dugger worked as a lobbyist for the financial industry before he became a partner at the global hedge fund Tudor Investment Corporation in 1993. After seventeen years, he retired to focus on philanthropy and his investments. "Anyone who's in this community knows people who are worried that America is heading toward something like the Russian Revolution," he told me.

To manage that fear, Dugger said, he has seen two very different responses. "People know the only real answer is, Fix the problem," he said. "It's a reason most of them give a lot of money to good causes." At the same time, though, they invest in the mechanics of escape. He recalled a dinner in New York City after 9/11 and the bursting of the dot-com bubble: "A group of centimillionaires and a couple of billionaires were working through end-of-America scenarios and talking about what they'd do. Most said they'll fire up their planes and take their families to Western ranches or homes in other countries." One of the guests was skeptical, Dugger said. "He leaned forward and asked, 'Are you taking your pilot's family, too? And what about the maintenance guys? If revolutionaries are kicking in doors, how many of the people in your life will you have to take with you?' The questioning continued. In the end, most agreed they couldn't run."

Elite anxiety cuts across political lines. Even financiers who supported Trump for president, hoping that he would cut taxes and regulations, have been unnerved at the ways his insurgent campaign seems to have hastened a collapse of respect for established institutions. Dugger said, "The media is under attack now. They wonder, Is the court system next? Do we go from 'fake news' to 'fake evidence'? For people whose existence depends on enforceable contracts, this is life or death."

Robert A. Johnson sees his peers' talk of fleeing as the symptom of a deeper crisis. At fifty-nine, Johnson has tousled silver hair and a soft-spoken, avuncular composure. He earned degrees in electrical engineering and economics at MIT, got a PhD in economics at Princeton, and worked on Capitol Hill before entering finance. He became a managing director at the hedge fund Soros Fund Management. In 2009, after the onset of the financial crisis, he was named head of a think tank, the Institute for New Economic Thinking.

When I visited Johnson at his office on Park Avenue South, he described himself as an accidental student of civic anxiety. He grew up outside Detroit, in Grosse Pointe Park, the son of a doctor, and he watched his father's generation experience the fracturing of Detroit. "What I'm seeing now in New York City is sort of like old music coming back," he said. "These are friends of mine. I used to live in Belle Haven, in Greenwich, Connecticut. Louis Bacon, Paul Tudor Jones, and Ray Dalio"—hedge fund managers—"were all within fifty yards of me. From my own career, I would just talk to people. More and more were saying, 'You've got to have a private plane. You have to assure that the pilot's family will be taken care of, too. They have to be on the plane.'"

Johnson started sounding the alarm: the tensions produced by acute income inequality were becoming so pronounced that some of the world's wealthiest people were taking steps to protect themselves. In 2015, at the World Economic Forum in Davos, Switzerland, Johnson told the audience, "I know hedge fund managers all over the world who are buying airstrips and farms in places like New Zealand because they think they need a getaway."

Johnson wishes that the wealthy would adopt a greater "spirit of stewardship," an openness to policy change that could include, for instance, a more aggressive tax on inheritance. "Twenty-five hedge fund managers make more money than all of the kindergarten teachers in America combined," he said. "Being one of those twenty-five doesn't feel good. I think they've developed a heightened sensitivity." The gap is widening further. In 2016, the National Bureau of Economic Research published an analysis by the economists Thomas Piketty, Emmanuel Saez, and Gabriel Zucman, which found that half of American adults have been "completely shut off from economic growth since the 1970s." Approximately 117 million people earned, on average, the same income that they did in 1980, while the typical income for the top one percent had nearly tripled. That gap was comparable to the gap between average incomes in the U.S. and the Democratic Republic of the Congo, the authors wrote.

Johnson said, "If we had a more equal distribution of income, and much more money and energy going into public school systems, parks and recreation, the arts, and health care, it could take an awful lot of sting out of society. We've largely dismantled those things."

As public institutions deteriorate, elite anxiety has emerged as a gauge of our national predicament. "Why do people who are envied for being so powerful appear to be so afraid?" Johnson asked. "What does that really tell us about our system?" He added, "It's a very odd thing. You're basically seeing that the people who've been the best at reading the tea leaves—the ones with the most resources, because that's how they made their money—are now the ones most preparing to pull the rip cord and jump out of the plane."

*   *   *

On a cool evening just before Thanksgiving, I rented a car in Wichita, Kansas, and drove north from the city through slanting sunlight, across the suburbs and out beyond the last shopping center, where the horizon settles into farmland. After a couple of hours, just before the town of Concordia, I headed west, down a dirt track flanked by corn and soybean fields, winding through darkness until my lights settled on a large steel gate. A guard, dressed in camouflage, held a semiautomatic rifle.

He ushered me through, and, in the darkness, I could see the outline of a vast concrete dome, with a metal blast door partly ajar. I was greeted by Larry Hall, the CEO of the Survival Condo Project, a fifteen-story luxury apartment complex built in an underground Atlas missile silo. The facility housed a nuclear warhead from 1961 to 1965, when it was decommissioned. At a site conceived for the Soviet nuclear threat, Hall has erected a defense against the fears of a new era. "It's true relaxation for the ultrawealthy," he said. "They can come out here, they know there are armed guards outside. The kids can run around."

Hall got the idea for the project about a decade ago, when he read that the federal government was reinvesting in catastrophe planning, which had languished after the Cold War. During the September 11 attacks, the Bush administration activated a "continuity of government" plan, transporting selected federal workers by helicopter and bus to fortified locations, but, after years of disuse, computers and other equipment in the bunkers were out of date. Bush ordered a renewed focus on continuity plans, and FEMA launched annual government-wide exercises. (They simulated hurricanes, improvised nuclear devices, earthquakes, and cyberattacks.)

"I started saying, 'Well, wait a minute, what does the government know that we don't know?'" Hall said. In 2008, he paid $300,000 for the silo and finished construction in 2012, at a cost of nearly $20 million. He created twelve private apartments: full-floor units were advertised at $3 million; a half-floor was half the price. He sold every unit, except one for himself, he said.

Most preppers don't actually have bunkers; hardened shelters are expensive and complicated to build. The original silo of Hall's complex was built by the Army Corps of Engineers to withstand a nuclear strike. The interior can support a total of seventy-five people. It has enough food and fuel for five years off the grid; by raising tilapia in fish tanks, and hydroponic vegetables under grow lamps, with renewable power, it could function indefinitely, Hall said. In a crisis, his SWAT-team-style trucks ("the Pit-Bull VX, armored up to fifty-caliber") will pick up any owner within four hundred miles. Residents with private planes can land in Salina, about thirty miles away. In his view, the Army Corps did the hardest work by choosing the location. "They looked at height above sea level, the seismology of an area, how close it is to large population centers," he said.

Hall, in his late fifties, is barrel-chested and talkative. He studied business and computers at the Florida Institute of Technology and went on to specialize in networks and data centers for Northrop Grumman, Harris Corporation, and other defense contractors. He now goes back and forth between the Kansas silo and a home in the Denver suburbs, where his wife, a paralegal, lives with their twelve-year-old son.

Hall led me through the garage, down a ramp, and into a lounge, with a stone fireplace, a dining area, and a kitchen to one side. It had the feel of a ski condo without windows: pool table, stainless steel appliances, leather couches. To maximize space, Hall took ideas from cruise ship design. We were accompanied by Mark Menosky, an engineer who manages day-to-day operations. While they fixed dinner—steak, baked potatoes, and salad—Hall said that the hardest part of the project was planning for the social dynamics underground. He studied how to avoid depression (add more lights), prevent cliques (rotate chores), and simulate life aboveground. The condo walls are fitted with LED "windows" that show a live video of the prairie above the silo. Owners can opt instead for pine forests or other vistas. One prospective resident from New York City wanted video of Central Park. "All four seasons, day and night," Menosky said. "She wanted the sounds, the taxis and the honking horns."

Some survivalists disparage Hall for creating an exclusive refuge for the wealthy and have threatened to seize his bunker in a crisis. Hall waved away this possibility when I raised it with him over dinner. "You can send all the bullets you want into this place." If necessary, his guards would return fire, he said. "We've got a sniper post."

Later that fall, I spoke on the phone with Tyler Allen, a real estate developer in Lake Mary, Florida, who told me that he paid $3 million for one of Hall's condos. Allen said he worried that America faces a future of "social conflict" and government efforts to deceive the public. He suspects that the Ebola virus was allowed to enter the country in order to weaken the population. When I asked how friends usually responded to his ideas, he said, "The natural reaction that you get most of the time is for them to laugh, because it scares them." But, he added, "my credibility has gone through the roof. Ten years ago, this just seemed crazy that all this was going to happen: the social unrest and the cultural divide in the country, the race-baiting and the hate-mongering." I asked how he planned to get to Kansas from Florida in a crisis. "If a dirty bomb goes off in Miami, everybody's going to go in their house and congregate in bars, just glued to the TV. Well, you've got forty-eight hours to get the hell out of there."

Allen told me that, in his view, taking precautions is unfairly stigmatized. "They don't put tinfoil on your head if you're the president and you go to Camp David," he said. "But they do put tinfoil on your head if you have the means and you take steps to protect your family should a problem occur."

*   *   *

Why do our dystopian urges emerge at certain moments and not others? Doomsday—as a prophecy, a literary genre, and a business opportunity—is never static; it evolves with our anxieties. The earliest Puritan settlers saw in the awe-inspiring bounty of the American wilderness the prospect of both apocalypse and paradise. When in May of 1780 sudden darkness settled on New England, farmers perceived it as a cataclysm heralding the return of Christ. (In fact, the darkness was caused by enormous wildfires in Ontario.) D. H. Lawrence diagnosed a specific strain of American dread. "Doom! Doom! Doom!" he wrote in 1923. "Something seems to whisper it in the very dark trees of America."

Historically, our fascination with the End has flourished at moments of political insecurity and rapid technological change. "In the late nineteenth century, there were all sorts of utopian novels, and each was coupled with a dystopian novel," Richard White, a historian at Stanford University, told me. Edward Bellamy's *Looking Backward*, published in 1888, depicted a socialist paradise in the year 2000, and became a sensation, inspiring "Bellamy Clubs" around the country. Conversely, Jack London, in 1908, published *The Iron Heel*, imagining an America under a fascist oligarchy in which "nine-tenths of one per cent" hold "seventy per cent of the total wealth."

At the time, Americans were marveling at engineering advances—attendees at the 1893 World's Fair in Chicago beheld new uses for electric light—but were also protesting low wages, poor working conditions, and corporate greed. "It was very much like today," White said. "It was a sense that the political system had spun out of control, and was no longer able to deal with society. There was a huge inequity in wealth, a stirring of working classes. Lifespans were getting shorter. There was a feeling that America's advance had stopped, and the whole thing was going to break."

Business titans grew uncomfortable. In 1889, Andrew Carnegie, who was on his way to being the richest man in the world, worth more than $4 billion in today's dollars, wrote, with concern, about class tensions; he criticized the emergence of "rigid castes" living in "mutual ignorance" and "mutual distrust." John D. Rockefeller, of Standard Oil, America's first actual billionaire, felt a Christian duty to give back. "The novelty of being able to purchase anything one wants soon passes," he wrote in 1909, "because what people most seek cannot be bought with money." Carnegie went on to fight illiteracy by creating nearly three thousand public libraries. Rockefeller founded the University of Chicago. According to Joel Fleishman, the author of *The Foundation*, a study of American philanthropy, both men dedicated themselves to "changing the systems that produced those ills in the first place."

During the Cold War, Armageddon became a matter for government policymakers. The Federal Civil Defense Administration, created by

Harry Truman, issued crisp instructions for surviving a nuclear strike, including "Jump in any handy ditch or gutter" and "Never lose your head." In 1958, Dwight Eisenhower broke ground on Project Greek Island, a secret shelter, in the mountains of West Virginia, large enough for every member of Congress. Hidden beneath the Greenbrier Resort in White Sulphur Springs for more than thirty years, it maintained separate chambers-in-waiting for the House and the Senate. (Congress now plans to shelter at undisclosed locations.) There was also a secret plan to whisk away the Gettysburg Address from the Library of Congress, and the Declaration of Independence from the National Archives.

In 1961, prepping acquired the aroma of patriotism, when John F. Kennedy encouraged "every citizen" to help build fallout shelters, saying, in a televised address, "I know you would not want to do less." In 1976, tapping into fear of inflation and the Arab oil embargo, a far-right publisher named Kurt Saxon launched *The Survivor*, an influential newsletter that celebrated forgotten pioneer skills. (Saxon claimed to have coined the term "survivalist.") The growing literature on decline and self-protection included *How to Prosper During the Coming Bad Years*, a 1979 bestseller, which advised collecting gold in the form of South African Krugerrands. The "doom boom," as it became known, expanded under Ronald Reagan. The sociologist Richard G. Mitchell Jr., a professor emeritus at Oregon State University who spent twelve years studying survivalism, said, "During the Reagan era, we heard, for the first time in my life, and I'm seventy-four years old, from the highest authorities in the land that government has failed you, the collective institutional ways of solving problems and understanding society are no good. People said, 'OK, it's flawed. What do I do now?'"

The movement received another boost from the George W. Bush administration's mishandling of Hurricane Katrina. Neil Strauss, a former *New York Times* reporter who chronicled his turn to prepping in his book *Emergency*, told me, "We see New Orleans, where our government knows a disaster is happening, and is powerless to save its own citizens." Strauss got interested in survivalism a year after Katrina, when a tech entrepreneur who was taking flying lessons and hatching escape plans introduced him to a group of like-minded "billionaire and centimillionaire preppers." Strauss acquired citizenship in St. Kitts, put assets in foreign currencies, and trained to survive with "nothing but a knife and the clothes on my back."

These days, when North Korea tests a bomb, Larry Hall can expect an uptick of phone inquiries about space in the Survival Condo Project. But he points to a deeper source of demand. "Seventy percent of the country doesn't like the direction that things are going," he said. After dinner, Hall and Menosky gave me a tour. The complex is a tall cylinder that resembles a corncob. Some levels are dedicated to private apartments and others offer shared amenities: a seventy-five-foot-long pool, a rock-climbing wall, an AstroTurf "pet park," a classroom with a line of Mac desktops, a gym, a movie theater, and a library. It felt compact but not claustrophobic. We visited an armory packed with guns and ammo in case of an attack by nonmembers, and then a bare-walled room with a toilet. "We can lock people up and give them an adult time-out," he said. In general, the rules are set by a condo association, which can vote to amend them. During a crisis, a "life-or-death situation," Hall said, each adult would be required to work for four hours a day, and would not be allowed to leave without permission. "There's controlled access in and out, and it's governed by the board," he said.

The "medical wing" contains a hospital bed, a procedure table, and a dentist's chair. Among the residents, Hall said, "we've got two doctors and a dentist." One floor up, we visited the food-storage area, still unfinished. He hopes that once it's fully stocked it will feel like a "miniature Whole Foods," but for now it holds mostly cans of food.

We stopped in a condo. Nine-foot ceilings, Wolf range, gas fireplace. "This guy wanted to have a fireplace from his home state"—Connecticut—"so he shipped me the granite," Hall said. Another owner, with a home in Bermuda, ordered the walls of his bunker-condo painted in island pastels—orange, green, yellow—but, in close quarters, he found it oppressive. His decorator had to come fix it.

That night, I slept in a guest room appointed with a wet bar and handsome wood cabinets, but no video windows. It was eerily silent, and felt like sleeping in a well-furnished submarine.

I emerged around eight the next morning to find Hall and Menosky in the common area, drinking coffee and watching a campaign-news brief on *Fox & Friends*. It was five days before the election, and Hall, who is a Republican, described himself as a cautious Trump supporter. "Of the two running, I'm hoping that his business acumen will override some of his knee-jerk stuff." Watching Trump's rallies on television, he was struck by how large and enthusiastic the crowds appeared. Polls suggested he was trailing, but Hall said, "I just don't believe the polls."

He thought that mainstream news organizations were biased, and he subscribes to theories that he knew some found implausible. He surmised that "there is a deliberate move by the people in Congress to dumb America down." Why would Congress do that? I asked. "They don't want people to be smart to see what's going on in politics," he said. He told me he had read a prediction that 40 percent of Congress will be arrested, because of a scheme involving the Panama Papers, the Catholic Church, and the Clinton Foundation. "They've been working on this investigation for twenty years," he said. I asked him if he really believed that. "At first, you hear this stuff and go, Yeah, right," he said. But he wasn't ruling it out.

Before I headed back to Wichita, we stopped at Hall's latest project— a second underground complex, in a silo twenty-five miles away. As we pulled up, a crane loomed overhead, hoisting debris from deep below the surface. The complex will contain three times the living space of the original, in part because the garage will be moved to a separate structure. Among other additions, it will have a bowling alley and LED windows as large as French doors to create a feeling of openness.

Hall said that he was working on private bunkers for clients in Idaho and Texas, and that two technology companies had asked him to design "a secure facility for their data center and a safe haven for their key personnel if something were to happen." To accommodate demand, he had paid for the possibility to buy four more silos.

*   *   *

If a silo in Kansas is not remote or private enough, there is another option. In the first seven days after Donald Trump's election, 13,401 Americans registered with New Zealand's immigration authorities, the first official step toward seeking residency—more than seventeen times the usual rate. *The New Zealand Herald* reported the surge beneath the headline "Trump Apocalypse."

In fact, the influx had begun well before Trump's victory. In the first ten months of 2016, foreigners bought nearly fourteen hundred square miles of land in New Zealand, more than quadruple what they bought in the same period the previous year, according to the government. American buyers were second only to Australians. The U.S. government does not keep a tally of Americans who own second or third homes overseas. Much as Switzerland once drew Americans with the promise of secrecy, and Uruguay tempted them with private banks, New Zealand offers security and distance. In the past six years, nearly a thousand foreigners have acquired residency there under programs that mandate certain types of investment of at least a million dollars.

Jack Matthews, an American who is the chairman of MediaWorks, a large New Zealand broadcaster, told me, "I think, in the back of people's minds, frankly, is that, if the world really goes to shit, New Zealand is a First World country, completely self-sufficient, if necessary—energy, water, food. Life would deteriorate, but it would not collapse." As someone who views American politics from a distance, he said, "The difference between New Zealand and the U.S., to a large extent, is that people who disagree with each other can still talk to each other about it here. It's a tiny little place, and there's no anonymity. People have to actually have a degree of civility."

Auckland is a thirteen-hour flight from San Francisco. I arrived in early December, the beginning of New Zealand's summer: blue skies, mid-seventies, no humidity. Top to bottom, the island chain runs roughly the distance between Maine and Florida, with half the population of New York City. Sheep outnumber people seven to one. In global rankings, New Zealand is in the top ten for democracy, clean government, and security. In World Bank reports, New Zealand has supplanted Singapore as the best country in the world to do business.

The morning after I arrived, I was picked up at my hotel by Graham Wall, a cheerful real estate agent who specializes in what his profession describes as HNWI (high-net-worth individuals). Wall, whose clients include Peter Thiel, the billionaire venture capitalist, was surprised when Americans told him they were coming precisely because of the country's remoteness. "Kiwis used to talk about the 'tyranny of distance,'" Wall said as we crossed town in his Mercedes convertible. "Now the tyranny of distance is our greatest asset."

Before my trip, I had wondered if I was going to be spending more time in luxury bunkers. But Peter Campbell, the managing director of Triple Star Management, a New Zealand construction firm, told me that, by and large, once his American clients arrive, they decide that underground shelters are gratuitous. "It's not like you need to build a bunker under your front lawn, because you're several thousand miles away from the White House," he said. Americans have other requests. "Definitely, helipads are a big one," he said. "You can fly a private jet into Queenstown or a private jet into Wanaka, and then you can grab a helicopter and it can take you and land you at your property." American clients have also sought strategic advice. "They're asking, 'Where in New Zealand is not going to be long-term affected by rising sea levels?'"

The growing foreign appetite for New Zealand property has generated a backlash. The Campaign Against Foreign Control of Aotearoa—the Maori name for New Zealand—opposes sales to foreigners. In particular, the attention of American survivalists has generated resentment. In a discussion about New Zealand on the *Modern Survivalist*, a prepper website, a commentator wrote, "Yanks, get this in your heads. Aotearoa NZ is not your little last resort safe haven."

I met for coffee with an American hedge fund manager in his forties—tall, tanned, athletic—who had bought two houses in New

Zealand and acquired local residency. He agreed to tell me about his thinking, if I would not publish his name. Brought up on the East Coast, he said that he expects America to face at least a decade of political turmoil, including racial tension, polarization, and a rapidly aging population. "The country has turned into the New York area, the California area, and then everyone else is wildly different in the middle," he said. He worries that the economy will suffer if Washington scrambles to fund Social Security and Medicare for people who need it. "Do you default on that obligation? Or do you print more money to give to them? What does that do to the value of the dollar? It's not a next-year problem, but it's not fifty years away, either."

New Zealand's reputation for attracting doomsayers is so well known in the hedge fund manager's circle that he prefers to differentiate himself from earlier arrivals. He said, "This is no longer about a handful of freaks worried about the world ending." He laughed, and added, "Unless I'm one of those freaks."

*   *   *

Every year since 1947, the *Bulletin of the Atomic Scientists*, a magazine founded by members of the Manhattan Project, has gathered a group of Nobel laureates and other luminaries to update the Doomsday Clock, a symbolic gauge of our risk of wrecking civilization. In 1991, as the Cold War was ending, the scientists set the clock to its safest point ever—seventeen minutes to "midnight."

Since then, the direction has been inauspicious. In January 2016, after increasing military tensions between Russia and NATO, and the earth's warmest year on record, the *Bulletin* set the clock at three minutes to midnight, the same level it held at the height of the Cold War. (In 2018, they dropped it to two minutes, a level unseen since America's first test of the hydrogen bomb in 1953.)

Fear of disaster is healthy if it spurs action to prevent it. But elite survivalism is not a step toward prevention; it is an act of withdrawal.

Philanthropy in America is still three times as large, as a share of GDP, as philanthropy in the next closest country, the United Kingdom. But it is now accompanied by a gesture of surrender, a quiet disinvestment by some of America's most successful and powerful people. Faced with evidence of frailty in the American project, in the institutions and norms from which they have benefited, some are permitting themselves to imagine failure. It is a gilded despair.

As Steve Huffman of Reddit observed, our technologies have made us more alert to risk, but have also made us more panicky; they facilitate the tribal temptation to cocoon, to seclude ourselves from opponents, and to fortify ourselves against our fears, instead of attacking the sources of them. Justin Kan, the technology investor who had made a half-hearted effort to stock up on food, recalled a recent phone call from a friend at a hedge fund. "He was telling me we should buy land in New Zealand as a backup. He's, like, 'What's the percentage chance that Trump is actually a fascist dictator? Maybe it's low, but the expected value of having an escape hatch is pretty high.'"

There are other ways to absorb the anxieties of our time. "If I had a billion dollars, I wouldn't buy a bunker," Elli Kaplan, the CEO of the digital health start-up Neurotrack, told me. "I would reinvest in civil society and civil innovation. My view is you figure out even smarter ways to make sure that something terrible doesn't happen." Kaplan, who worked in the White House under Bill Clinton, was appalled by Trump's victory, but said that it galvanized her in a different way: "Even in my deepest fear, I say, 'Our union is stronger than this.'"

That view is, in the end, an article of faith—a conviction that even degraded political institutions are the best instruments of common will, the tools for fashioning and sustaining our fragile consensus. Believing that is a choice.

I called a Silicon Valley sage, Stewart Brand, the author and entrepreneur whom Steve Jobs credited as an inspiration. In the 1960s and '70s, Brand's *Whole Earth Catalog* attracted a cult following with its mixture of hippie and techie advice. (The motto: "We are as gods and might as well get good at it.") Brand told me that he explored survivalism in the 1970s, but not for long. "Generally, I find the idea that 'Oh, my God, the world's all going to fall apart' strange," he said.

At seventy-seven, living on a tugboat in Sausalito, Brand is less impressed by signs of fragility than by examples of resilience. In the past decade, the world survived, without violence, the worst financial crisis since the Great Depression; Ebola, without cataclysm; and, in Japan, a tsunami and nuclear meltdown, after which the country has persevered. He sees risks in escapism. As Americans withdraw into smaller circles of experience, we jeopardize the "larger circle of empathy," he said, the search for solutions to shared problems. "The easy question is, How do I protect me and mine? The more interesting question is, What if civilization actually manages continuity as well as it has managed it for the past few centuries? What do we do if it just keeps on chugging?"

After a few days in New Zealand, I could see why one might choose to avoid either question. Under a cerulean blue sky one morning in Auckland, I boarded a helicopter beside a thirty-eight-year-old American named Jim Rohrstaff. After college in Michigan, Rohrstaff worked as a golf pro, and then in the marketing of luxury golf clubs and property. Upbeat and confident, with shining blue eyes, he moved to New Zealand two and a half years ago, with his wife and two children, to sell property to HNWI who want to get "far away from all the issues of the world," he said.

Rohrstaff, who co-owns Legacy Partners, a boutique brokerage, wanted me to see Tara Iti, a new luxury housing development and golf club that appeals mostly to Americans. The helicopter nosed north across the harbor and banked up the coast, across lush forests and fields beyond the city. From above, the sea was a sparkling expanse, scalloped by the wind.

The helicopter eased down onto a lawn beside a putting green. The new luxury community will have three thousand acres of dunes and forestland, and seven miles of coastline, for just 125 homes. As we toured the site in a Land Rover, he emphasized the seclusion: "From the outside, you won't see anything. That's better for the public and better for us, for privacy."

As we neared the sea, Rohrstaff parked the Land Rover and climbed out. In his loafers, he marched over the dunes and led me down into the sand, until we reached a stretch of beach that extended to the horizon without a soul in sight.

Waves roared ashore. He spread his arms, turned, and laughed. "We think it's the place to be in the future," he said. For the first time in weeks—months, even—I wasn't thinking about Trump. Or much of anything.

———————

The Tara Iti resort is open to members and their guests. Outsiders, with a letter of recommendation, can pay to visit, but only once in the course of a lifetime.

In 2017, Peter Thiel's citizenship in New Zealand became the subject of controversy when officials revealed that he had acquired it after spending only twelve days in the country—less than one percent of the usual time required to become a citizen. (Officials had concluded that providing him citizenship would benefit New Zealand business.) Spurred partly by the Thiel case, the government moved the following year to ban the sale of existing homes to nonresident foreigners. In 2021, the controversy reemerged after the government confirmed that Larry Page, the cofounder of Google and the world's sixth-richest person, had gained residency and entered New Zealand on a medevac with his son, when the nation's borders were still closed because of Covid-19.

In 2023, after the downfall of Sam Bankman-Fried, the CEO of FTX, the firm alleged, in a lawsuit, that he had discussed plans to buy the island nation of Nauru as a doomsday refuge, where fellow adherents to the philosophy of effective altruism could build a lab and explore, as an internal memo put it, "human genetic enhancement." Later that year, Steve Huffman, the Reddit CEO who underwent eye surgery to protect himself in the event of a social collapse, received a pay package worth $193 million in salary and stock, drawing a wave of criticism from Reddit moderators, because they are unpaid. Defending himself, he said, "If the company does well, I will do well."

In recent years, the experts who maintain the Doomsday Clock have heightened their warnings, because of the pandemic, political fragility, and Putin's lowering of the threshold for launching nuclear weapons. In January 2025, they moved the symbolic clock to 89 seconds to midnight, the direst warning of catastrophe in its eight-decade history.

One for the Money

How to hire a pop star for your private party

— 2023 —

At ten o'clock on a recent Saturday night, the rapper Flo Rida was in his dressing room with a towel over his head, in a mode of quiet preparation. Along one wall, a handsome buffet—lobster, sushi, Dom Pérignon—sat untouched. Flo Rida, whose stage name honors his home state but is pronounced like "flow ridah," is fastidious about his physique. He is six feet three, 220 pounds, and often travels with a trainer, though on this occasion the trip was brief enough that he would do without. That afternoon, a private jet had carried him, along with eight of his backup performers and assistants, from South Florida to Chicago. By the following night, he would be back at his mansion in Miami.

Flo Rida, who is forty-three, attained celebrity in 2008 with his song "Low," an admiring ode to a Rubenesque beauty on the dance floor. "Low" went platinum ten times over and was No. 1 on the Billboard charts for ten weeks—a longer run than any other song that year, including Beyoncé's "Single Ladies." In 2009, Flo landed another No. 1 hit, "Right Round," which broke a world record, jointly held by Eminem, 50 Cent, and Dr. Dre, for the most downloads in an opening week. Flo never matched the stardom of those peers, but he has recorded another nine Top Ten hits, sold at least a hundred million records, and secured for himself a lucrative glide from ubiquity. His endorsement deals are of sufficient scale that, in a recent breach-of-contract dispute with one of his brand partners, Celsius energy drinks, a jury awarded him $83 million.

A man with this kind of nest egg might never need to leave home again. But on this evening, Flo had journeyed north on business: he was playing a bar mitzvah, for a thirteen-year-old boy and three dozen of his friends, in the well-to-do Chicago suburb of Lincolnshire. The bar mitzvah boy, in keeping with the customs of his forebears, had chanted his way into adulthood; then, following a more recent tradition, the celebrants had relocated to a warehouse-size event venue that is highly regarded on Chicago's mitzvah circuit. A production company had installed the décor, including roller coasters stenciled across the dance floor and a banquet table made to resemble a red Ferrari. The whole affair was invisible to the outside world, except for the word "Andrew" projected by brilliant red floodlights onto an exterior wall.

The entertainment had been arranged by Andrew's father, an executive at a financial services company. At first, he had doubted that Flo Rida, his son's favorite artist, would agree to come, but an agent informed him that most big-name musicians are available these days under the right conditions. Flo Rida's fee for private gigs in the United States runs between $150,000 and $300,000, depending on location, scale, and other particulars. Reginald Mathis, his lawyer, told me, "Internationally, it could run you up to a million." For the Lincolnshire bar mitzvah, the contract stipulated private-jet travel, suitable accommodations, and a fee "in the six figures," Mathis said; Flo Rida would perform for thirty minutes. When I saw Andrew's father at the event, he was thrilled with the outcome but declined to have his name in this story. "I work on Wall Street," he told me. "I don't want to end up on Page Six."

As showtime approached, Flo changed from his travel T-shirt and jeans into performance attire: a much nicer T-shirt (vintage Kiss concert merch), a sleeveless black biker jacket, and cat-eye shades speckled with rhinestones. While the opening act finished up, I stepped out of the dressing room to assess the crowd. From a balcony overlooking the dance floor, surrounded by a hefty array of professional-grade lights and speakers, I watched a desultory turn of the hora, backed by a recorded "Hava Nagila." The children seemed preoccupied. Then a platoon of production staff started handing out flashing LED sticks, and the kids rushed toward the stage in anticipation.

I was joined on the balcony by one of Flo's bandmates, a younger rapper known as Int'l Nephew, who wore a red sweatband and a black puffy vest over a tank top. We peered across the railing toward the back of the room, where a few dozen parents were sipping cocktails. In the realm of private gigs, those secondary guests are a high-priority demographic—future clients who don't yet know it. Int'l Nephew saw the makings of a worthwhile trip. "They're all big-money people," he said. "And they're, like, 'Oh, we want you, Flo.'"

By the time Flo Rida bounded onstage, his hands to the heavens, the kids were bouncing to the opening strains of "Good Feeling," one of his club hits, featuring the sampled voice of Etta James. The edge of the stage was lined by teenage boys in untucked shirts and jeans, alongside girls in spaghetti-strap dresses and chunky sneakers. Flo was flanked by dancers in black leather bikini tops and mesh leggings. Out of the audience's view, he kept a set list inscribed with the names of his hosts, as an aide-mémoire. "We love you, Andrew!" he shouted, and barreled into "Right Round," a rowdy track about visiting a strip club and showering a pole dancer with hundred-dollar bills. When he pulled Andrew onstage, the bar mitzvah boy didn't miss a beat, dancing along to Flo's verse: "From the top of the pole I watch her go down / She got me throwing my money around."

*   *   *

A private, as it's known in the music business, is any performance off limits to the public; the term applies to a vast spectrum of gigs, from suburban Sweet Sixteens and Upper East Side charity galas to command performances in the Persian Gulf. For years, the world of privates was dominated by aging crooners, a category known delicately as "nostalgia performers." Jacqueline Sabec, an entertainment lawyer in San Francisco, who has negotiated many private-gig contracts, told me, "Artists used to say no to these all the time, because they just weren't cool."

But misgivings have receded dramatically. In January 2023, Beyoncé did her first show in more than four years—not in a stadium of screaming fans but at a new hotel in Dubai, earning a reported $24 million for an hour-long set. More than a few Beyoncé fans winced; after dedicating a recent album to pioneers of queer culture, she was plumping for a hotel owned by the government of Dubai, which criminalizes homosexuality. (As a popular tweet put it, "I get it, everyone wants their coin, but when you're THAT rich, is it THAT worth it?") Artists, by and large, did not join the critics. Charles Ruggiero, a drummer in Los Angeles who is active in jazz and rock, told me, "The way musicians look at it, generally speaking, is: It's a fucking gig. And a gig is a gig is a gig."

If you have a few million dollars to spare, you can hire Drake for your bar mitzvah or the Rolling Stones for your birthday party. Robert Norman, who heads the private-events department at the talent agency CAA, recalls that when he joined the firm, a quarter century ago, "we were booking one or two hundred private dates a year, for middle-of-the-road artists that you'd typically suspect would play these kinds of events—conventions and things like that." Since then, privates have ballooned in frequency, price, and genre. "Last year, we booked almost six hundred dates, and we've got a team of people here who are dedicated just to private events," Norman said. An agent at another big firm told me, "A lot of people will say, 'Hey, can you send me your private/corporate roster?' And I'm, like, 'Just look at our whole roster, because everybody's pretty much willing to consider an offer.'"

The willingness extends to icons who might seem beyond mortal reach, including three Englishmen honored by Her Late Majesty: Sir Paul McCartney, Sir Elton John, and Sir Rod Stewart. "We just did Rod Stewart for $1.25 million here in Las Vegas," Glenn Richardson, an event producer, told me. It was a corporate gig for Kia, the car company. "He'll do those now, because Rod's not doing as many things as in his heyday," Richardson added. A random selection of other acts who do privates (Sting, Andrea Bocelli, Jon Bon Jovi, John Mayer, Diana Ross, Maroon 5, Black Eyed Peas, OneRepublic, Katy Perry, Eric Clapton) far exceeds the list of those who are known for saying no (Bruce Springsteen, Taylor Swift, and, for reasons that nobody can quite clarify, AC/DC).

Occasionally, the music press notes a new extreme of the private market, like hits on the charts. *Billboard* reported that the Eagles received $6 million from an unnamed client in New York for a single performance of "Hotel California," and *Rolling Stone* reported that Springsteen declined a quarter of a million to ride motorcycles with a fan. But privates typically are enveloped in secrecy, with both artists and clients demanding nondisclosure agreements and prohibitions on photos and social media posts. Sabec told me, "They don't want anybody to know how much they paid the artist, for example, or the details of the party. And the musician might not necessarily want it to be discussed, either." (After the news of Beyoncé's fee leaked, Adam Harrison, a veteran manager, told me, "That is my nightmare." Then he reconsidered the effect on Beyoncé's operation: "It probably raises their rates.")

Until recently, the stigma extended beyond style. A prominent music executive said, "There was a phase where artists would take a private show—a cancer benefit—and somebody would find out that they're getting paid to perform, and then they look like complete cocks in the media, because they took money and some child was dying of cancer. There was risk in the money."

The risk could be especially high overseas. Before the Libyan dictator Muammar Qaddafi was toppled in 2011, members of his family organized events enlivened by 50 Cent, Mariah Carey, Usher, and Nelly Furtado. During the Arab Spring, when Qaddafi unleashed his forces on protesters, Carey expressed regret, and the rest of the performers announced plans to donate their windfall to charity. That kerfuffle did not deter others, however. In 2013, Jennifer Lopez was hired by the

China National Petroleum Corporation to do an event for executives in Turkmenistan, which culminated in her singing "Happy Birthday, Mr. President" to Gurbanguly Berdimuhamedow—one of the world's most repressive despots. After a video of the serenade emerged, Lopez's spokesman assured fans, "Had there been knowledge of human-rights issues of any kind, Jennifer would not have attended." But the Human Rights Foundation, an advocacy group based in New York, subsequently estimated that Lopez had garnered at least $10 million in fees performing for "crooks and dictators from Eastern Europe and Russia." The foundation's president, Thor Halvorssen, asked, "What is the next stop on her tour, Syria?"

The opprobrium dissipated before long. In 2015, when critics urged Nicki Minaj to forsake a reported fee of $2 million for a concert sponsored by a company linked to Angola's dictator, she dismissed them with a tweet: "every tongue that rises up against me in judgement shall be condemned." The music executive told me that there is even a sense of commercial competition among stars, who now measure themselves as entrepreneurs. "If you're Kevin Durant, and you don't have five businesses, you're a schmuck," he said. "'I made twenty-five million dollars playing ten birthday parties.' That used to be seen as 'You fucking piece-of-shit sellout.' Now it's 'How do I get me some of those?'"

At bottom, the boom in private gigs reflects two contrasting trends. One has to do with the music industry. For more than a century after sound was first captured on wax cylinders in the 1880s, the money came mostly from selling recordings. But sales of recordings peaked in 1999, and, as CDs vanished, revenue sank by more than 50 percent. The industry has recovered slightly since then on digital subscriptions, but the new digital giants—Spotify, Apple, YouTube—pay artists only a fraction of what physical sales once delivered.

The other trend is the birth of a new aristocracy, which since 2000 has tripled the number of American billionaires and produced legions of the merely very rich. As musicians have faced an increasingly uncertain market, another slice of humanity has prospered: the limited partners and angel investors and ciphers of senior management who used to splurge on front-row seats at an arena show. Charles Ruggiero, the drummer, told me, "People didn't use to do this, because they couldn't afford to have, like, the Foo Fighters come to their backyard. But now they can. They're, like, 'I can blow a hundred and fifty grand on a Thursday.'"

* * *

Ask a dozen event producers if they'd rather work with a hip young phenom or a pro in the second act of a career, and you'll hear a consistent reply. "The one you have to watch out for is the up-and-comer," Colin Cowie, an event planner in New York and Miami, told me. He aped a litany of demands: "I need this car! I need my DJ rig to be in the middle of the room! And I need this type of room!" Willie Nelson, by contrast, is still booking privates at the age of ninety, playing a guitar so ancient that he has strummed a hole in its face.

Flo, whose real name is Tramar Dillard, is the workmanlike kind of star. The youngest of eight children, he was raised in Miami's Carol City housing projects—a shy kid who became a performer only in the seventh grade, after a teacher punished an infraction by forcing him to join the speech-and-debate team. Two years later, he became a member of the Groundhoggz, a rap group that opened for local artists, and soon he was a hype man for 2 Live Crew, the X-rated pioneers of the Miami sound known as booty bass. Flo did brief stints in college in Nevada and Florida, but he spent most of his time cold-calling studios, seeking someone who would record him. At one point, he rode a Greyhound bus to Los Angeles but was rejected by the major rap labels, and ended up sleeping in motels and, occasionally, on the street. In 2006, he signed with Poe Boy Entertainment, a hip-hop label in Miami. Within two years, he was on the charts, building a reputation as a purveyor of technically adept, if unchallenging, ladies'-man tracks about partying, spending, and vamping. An article in *Vice* once summed up his success with the headline "Flo Rida Is Boring. Flo Rida Is Perfect."

Reginald Mathis, his attorney, is a former prosecutor and corporate lawyer who joined Flo's operation in 2011, agreeing to help oversee its growing presence on the private-gig circuit. In that milieu, blandness can be a superpower. Flo can get along with "any- and everybody, from the emirs in Dubai to the thugs in Carol City," Mathis said. First, though, there were some adjustments to make. During one foray into corporate work, Flo arrived late for a Samsung event, and the CEO had already left for a flight to South Korea. "It's been ten years to repair that situation," Mathis said. "For Asians, in particular, punctuality is important."

Mathis took it upon himself to help the performers make sense of the worlds they were suddenly encountering. In 2012, Flo was hired to play at a benefit for veterans alongside the Democratic National Convention. Mathis, a savvy political observer, briefed the team: "I'm, like, 'Yo, Bill Clinton is speaking tonight, and you're the entertainment for when he finishes.'" Members of Flo's entourage appeared unmoved, so Mathis laid out the stakes: "He's the guy coming to make the case for Barack Obama's reelection, because he has a problem with working-class white men over fifty. So this is a real important night."

Over time, Flo honed a routine for private and corporate gigs. "He'll bring the CEO on and have all the workers and employees and sponsors cheering," Mathis said. He'll put his sunglasses on one of the bosses. He'll shake up champagne and spray the crowd, or hand out roses, pre-positioned in the DJ booth, for when he does "Where Them Girls At." It's all part of what Mathis calls "the formula." He told me, "The formula is definitely tried-and-true. It works." In all, Mathis said, Flo does at least thirty private gigs a year.

At the bar mitzvah, Flo cycled through his oeuvre—"Low," "Club Can't Handle Me," "Wild Ones." He did a reliable bit where he took off his sneakers, autographed them, and handed them to Andrew, who tossed one into the crowd. For the finale, Flo, who has perhaps mellowed since the days when he and DJ Khaled dazzled clubgoers with "Bitch I'm from Dade County," shouted, "Chicago, baby!," and a shower of red confetti rained down, sticking to the kids' sweaty foreheads.

Back in his dressing room, Flo slumped into a Philippe Starck–style translucent chair, toweled off his pate, and slipped into gray rubber slides, to replace the sneakers he gave away. One-on-one, he is soft-spoken, and I wondered how he generates the gusto that the formula requires. "I've been doing this for fifteen years," he said. "I just take it like an invitation to a party. If you come out there and you don't reciprocate, then it's just a waste of everyone's time."

He takes some pleasure in managing the eccentricities of the cohort that can afford him. He recalled arriving for a gig on a megayacht in Sardinia, and finding children at play on deck. "I'm thinking I'm going to perform for all these kids," he said. Instead, he was summoned to a quiet section of the yacht and thrust in front of three adults, who were seated patiently at a round table. It was a notable departure from his experience in 2016 of playing for eighty thousand festival-goers at Wembley Stadium. It was also, he knew, the only way he was getting off that boat with his fee. "I come for a purpose," he said. "Once I learned that, that's where the longevity comes in."

An assistant approached with flutes of champagne. Flo waved him off and asked for a Red Bull. A moment later, the door of the dressing room swung open, and a dozen kids crowded in for the "meet and greet," as stipulated in the contract. The guests posed for photos—the boys making tough-guy faces, the girls giggling madly—while Flo projected a look of serene forbearance.

It was the look of a man who has done so many privates in Europe, the Middle East, and Asia that he says he feels like "I lived in China and Japan"—a man who has made multiple trips to Necker Island, the private getaway owned by Richard Branson. ("He gets wild onstage," Flo said.) In the dressing room, Flo asked one of his bandmates, a rapper called Oya Baby, to jog his memory about where they had stayed for the last gig there. "Guana Island," she said. "It's known for lizards everywhere. Not far from the Richard Branson island."

Both of them lingered on one incident in particular: a wedding in Beirut that started under unpleasant circumstances. "The plane had us late, and this guy was so upset," Flo said. The bride was in tears, and the groom was livid, pestering the performers while they tried to set up. "I was, like, 'Are you done? Because I'm going to the stage,'" Flo recalled. "And then, after I performed, he was so happy!" Flo was not quite so forgiving: "I was, like, 'No, don't try to hang out with me now.'"

*   *   *

Smokey Robinson still books privates, but at the age of eighty-three he finds ways of conserving energy on the job. Glenn Richardson, the event producer, hired him not long ago, and watched Smokey engage in such protracted patter with the audience that he wondered if patter was all they were going to get. "I went over to the road manager and said, 'Is he going to sing anything?' And he goes, 'Glenn, you don't tell the vice president of Motown Records when they need to start singing.'"

The tension between the talent and the money has a long history. In ancient Rome, wealthy music lovers had enslaved performers put on private concerts, known as *symphoniae*—even as Seneca, the Stoic philosopher, scolded those who preferred the "sweetness of the songs" to "serious matters." The emperor Caligula liked to be serenaded aboard his yachts, and to pantomime with the performers in a kind of premodern air guitar.

Even geniuses have had to navigate the servitude to their sponsors. Mozart fumed about the Archbishop of Salzburg, who "treats me like a street urchin and tells me to my face to clear out, adding that he can get hundreds to serve him better than I." But some artists learned to cultivate their sources of capital. In 1876, Tchaikovsky was an unhappy professor at the Moscow Conservatory when he received a letter from Nadezhda Filaretovna von Meck, the lonesome widow of a railway tycoon. Madame von Meck asked him to expand one of his pieces, which, she wrote, "drives me mad." He obliged, and before long she had put him on a salary and installed him at a villa in Florence. Tchaikovsky wrote to his brother, "N.F. asked me when to send the June remittance.

Instead of replying 'Darling, for goodness' sake at once!' I played the gentleman." But the relationship soured, and the composer had to find new sources of income; he wrote glumly, "It has all turned out to be a vulgar, silly farce of which I am ashamed and sick."

In the early decades of rock 'n' roll, its stars advertised their allergy to materialism. During a press conference in 1965, Bob Dylan was asked, "If you were going to sell out to a commercial interest, which one would you choose?" Dylan's response—"Ladies' garments"—suggested that the question was absurd. In a similar spirit, The Who released an album called *The Who Sell Out*, bearing a parody ad on the cover of Roger Daltrey selling Heinz baked beans and Pete Townsend selling deodorant. Bands could be shunned for any perceived transgression. In 1985, the Del Fuegos, a New England rock group favored by critics, appeared in a TV ad for Miller beer. Longtime fans revolted, and another band wrote lyrics mocking their commercial appearance ("I'd even drink Pepsi if you paid me enough"). Warren Zanes, a guitarist in the Del Fuegos, told me, "The general position was: That's the earmark of a true sellout." Looking back, though, it seems like the first rumble of a quake along the fault line between art and commerce. "We didn't want to be fathers of that movement, but in some very small way we were," Zanes said. "Once it's the age of streaming, suddenly people weren't as pure as they thought."

The advent of Napster in 1999 not only reduced musicians' revenues but also scrambled the pieties surrounding art; fans who gleefully downloaded stolen music had to cede some moral high ground. In the coming years, Dylan fulfilled his prophecy and starred in a Victoria's Secret commercial, The Who licensed a song to Pepsi, and Pearl Jam, which had been so averse to consumerism that it largely avoided music videos, took to promoting an album in partnerships with Target and Verizon. In 2011, after the duo Sleigh Bells had its music in a Honda commercial, one member told an interviewer, "It's almost pretentious to avoid the opportunity, especially in this climate." Rock, after all, was playing catch-up to the cultural triumph of hip-hop, which had celebrated capitalism ever since the Sugar Hill Gang rhapsodized about a Lincoln Continental, a color TV, and "more money than a sucker could ever spend."

The forthright attitude toward commerce also became visible in the private-gig market. Doug Sandler, known as DJ Doug on the mitzvah circuit around Washington, D.C., remembers the first time he was told to make room for more famous talent: "They had, as the main act, the Village People." In 2002, David Bonderman, a Texas venture capitalist, booked the Stones for his birthday, at a reported fee of $7 million, and word spread. Jennifer Gilbert, the founder of Save the Date, an event-planning company in New York, noticed that clients were becoming overtly competitive: "They started hearing it more and more—'Oh, they had this person perform.' So now someone says, 'We want something totally unique and over the top.'" Over time, the preferences showed a pattern: whoever was popular with young men about twenty-five years earlier was in renewed demand, as a rising cohort achieved private-gig-level wealth. (Current favorites include the Counting Crows and Sir Mix-a-Lot.)

In 2007, on the eve of the financial crisis, the financier Stephen Schwarzman treated himself to performances by Rod Stewart and Patti LaBelle at a sixtieth-birthday party so lavish that it prompted what *The New York Times* called an "existential crisis on Wall Street about the evils of conspicuous consumption." A decade later, when Schwarzman threw a party for his seventieth—featuring not only Gwen Stefani but also trapeze artists, camels, and fireworks over Palm Beach—it barely protruded above the tide line of the Trump era.

As the market grew, there was an inherent friction between the instinct to show off and the instinct to keep quiet. In 2012, shortly before the Silicon Valley entrepreneur David Sacks sold his company Yammer for $1.2 billion, he threw a costume party for his fortieth birthday, where guests were under orders not to leak details. The embargo was broken by the hired entertainer, Snoop Dogg, who posted a photo of himself posing with the birthday boy. Sacks was wearing an eighteenth-century waistcoat, a wig, and a lacy cravat, in the mode of Marie Antoinette. The party slogan was "Let Him Eat Cake."

*   *   *

Musicians, on the whole, don't get into the business because they dream of playing for tiny audiences, under the shroud of an NDA. Hamilton Leithauser, who helped found the indie band the Walkmen before launching a solo career, recalls peering out one night into a dark club filled with "older, heavyset Philly finance guys." He had been hired as the dinner entertainer at a business conference. "They must have spent a million dollars on the party, and they had pulled in all these huge leather couches and spread them out throughout the room." The remoteness was not only physical, he said: "The closest person is probably thirty feet away, and it's a banker eating a lobster tail."

David (Boche) Viecelli, a well-known booking agent in Chicago, has tried to help musicians navigate unfamiliar territory. Viecelli, who founded the independent agency the Billions Corporation, has represented Arcade Fire, Bon Iver, and other big acts. I asked him how musicians react when they get a private offer. "Every artist always thinks, Well, this is either going to be a total shit show or at least a drag," he said. "That goes all the way up to when you have Beyoncé going to play for some emir."

Despite all the luxuries, "corporate events can be sort of soul-destroying," Viecelli said. "It's not really an audience. It's a convention or a party, and you just happen to be making noise at one end of it." When musicians are uncertain, he has some reliable tools to help them decide: "If you can say, 'Hey, I'm going to go have a bad time for an afternoon, but it's going to pay for my kid's entire college education,' then that's a trade-off I think most responsible adults will make." But these days he has less persuading to do. "If you talk to a twenty-year-old in the music business now, and you bring up this idea of the weirdness of doing corporate events, they'll just stare at you, like, 'What are you talking about?' You might as well say, 'Don't you feel guilty for eating pizza?'"

The realities of making a living in music have changed radically in the past decade or two. Viecelli used to counsel emerging artists to plan for a long-term career: "It might not necessarily make you incomprehensibly rich, but it would give you a way to continue to make music the way you want, while doing it as a full-time job and being secure." In the streaming economy, audience attention is shallow and promiscuous. "A kid could know a track inside out, listen to it a thousand times that summer, and not know the artist's name. They're just surfing along the wave of whatever's getting spit out," he said. "The truth is, now young artists know they're going to have—even if they're successful—two to four years. Maybe. And so that means that they want to monetize everything as fast and hard as they can."

Given the pace of that churn, artists tend to obsess less about impressing A&R executives than about elbowing their way onto top-ranked playlists, with names like RapCaviar and Songs to Sing in the Car. "They know there's this giant unthinking audience that just keeps streaming these playlists and racking up those counts," Viecelli said. "Everything is geared towards treating artists essentially as disposable."

Even as streaming has diminished the returns on recording, social media has created an expectation of accessibility. Fans no longer assume that their favorite artists are remote figures. Viecelli told me, "I'll get emails from people saying, 'I live in Philadelphia, and I see that they're coming to town, and my daughter is a big, big fan. Could you stop off at our house to play a few songs?'" He laughed. "It's, like, 'Are you nuts?' But if that person says, 'And I'd be happy to pay five hundred thousand dollars for the privilege,' well, then, actually it begins to change."

*   *   *

In the spring of 2015, Steely Dan was hired to play a fiftieth-birthday party for Robert Downey Jr. in a converted airplane hangar in Santa Monica. Steely Dan didn't do many privates, but Downey had endeared himself to the singer Donald Fagen. Downey, who had built a thriving late career playing Iron Man in Marvel movies, was celebrating with friends from Hollywood. "Phones were taken away. Downey came up and sang 'Reelin' in the Years' with us," Michael Leonhart, who was playing trumpet that night, recalled. When the evening's other band, Duran Duran, took the stage, Leonhart quickly realized what it meant to generate stadium campiness on a small scale: "Simon Le Bon has his back to the audience. Then he turns around, the drum machine starts, and he goes, 'Is anybody hungry—like the wolf? Two, three, four!' And I'm, like, 'Oh, my God, this guy gives good privates.'"

Leonhart, who has also played private gigs with Lenny Kravitz, learned to expect odd moments when the disparate tribes of cultural capital and financial capital meet: "Either they're in awe of your group or you're the paid servant. You're never sure which meal you're going to get, or which entrance you're going to use. When push comes to shove, it's a caste system." He conjured a controlling host: "I love what you're wearing. Can you maybe button up that shirt one more button? My great-grandmother is here." When hosts try to merge friendship and labor, though, the result can be awkward. Leonhart said, "Even if it starts off well, there's usually a fart-in-church moment, where someone is trying to be cool, as opposed to just owning it for what it is: You paid a shitload of money—enjoy it."

Over time, artists have become more willing to accept proximity. First, they embraced the meet-and-greet, earning extra money on top of a concert ticket in exchange for a photo and some effortful bonhomie. (Scholars of the workplace call this "relational labor.") Privates have extended that concept by several zeros, though the underlying principle remains the same: a man who books Snoop Dogg for a private party is probably a man who would like to smoke a joint with Snoop Dogg. (Snoop avers that he has, indeed, smoked weed while working a bar mitzvah.)

In the taxonomy of paid performances, as in other parts of life, the money tends to vary inversely with dignity. Headlining a regular concert, known to professionals as a "hard ticket," pays the least; a festival, or "soft ticket," pays more, because it is usually flush with corporate sponsorship money. Privates pay the most, with the added bonus that they don't violate "radius clauses," which venues impose to stop bands from playing too many shows near one another. Thus, the modern dream scenario: take a million dollars for a Hamptons holiday party on Tuesday, then play the Beacon Theatre for half that sum on Thursday night.

Ian Hendrickson-Smith is a saxophonist with the Roots, who have played privates around the world, including at Obama's sixtieth birthday on Martha's Vineyard. ("They put me in a tiny plane that was barely a plane. I was terrified," he said.) Hendrickson-Smith also releases albums under his own name, and he has watched the market change. "The largest distributor of actual physical records in the United States was fucking Starbucks," he said. "I used to get some nice checks. Now I put out a record and it gets streamed a ton, but my check from Spotify is, like, sixty-five cents." A 2018 report by the Music Industry Research Association found that the median musician makes less than $35,000 a year, including money that's not from music.

Viewed in that light, private gigs can start to feel like something close to justice. For years, Hendrickson-Smith toured with the late Sharon Jones and her band, the Dap Kings, and they often jetted overseas to play tycoons' weddings. "The second we'd hear the W-word, our price tripled immediately," he said. But he also learned that relying on private money exposed him to a new type of captivity. He once played a private party in New York where the host had hired little people, costumed as Oompa Loompas and as members of Kiss, to serve drinks. "I was mortified," Hendrickson-Smith said. "But I couldn't leave. It was brutal."

There are ways to contain the risks. Adam Harrison, who manages Chromeo, Fitz and the Tantrums, and other acts, politely reminds private clients to limit their requests: "I'm OK doing a callout, but not 'To Gary in sales, who had a great year!'" Moreover, Harrison said, he does not encourage his acts to put aside their values for any gig. "I've had bands not play Saudi Arabia privates," he said. Another longtime manager told me that none of his acts would accept an invitation from the conservative fast food chain Chick-fil-A, except for his one Christian band: "They don't give a fuck. It's right in their wheelhouse." The ideal situation, the manager went on, is when a client is especially wedded to one act—say, the band that was playing on the Starbucks sound system at the moment that a couple met, or a pop star who seems perfectly aligned with a company's brand identity. "When it's a specific thing like that," he said, "everybody smells blood."

You don't have to be a musician to wonder if musicians are held to an unfair standard in an era when painters unabashedly sell work to barons of insider trading, when former presidents (and almost-presidents) get hundreds of thousands of dollars for Wall Street speeches, and when college athletes license their likeness to the highest bidders. Call it an "evolution in the culture," a prominent music producer told me. He brought up Donald Trump, and said, "Look at who almost half the country voted for: a guy who, if you charge less than you can, because you have qualms about playing something strictly for the elite, would look at you and say, 'Loser!' And an amazing number of people would agree."

*   *   *

"So you're writing about the star-fuckers who host these things?" Anthony Scaramucci asked when I called him this spring. He was, in fact, describing himself, but he did not seem offended by my request for an interview. "I'm a wholesale provider of this shit," he said. "I understand this shit."

Long before Scaramucci became a household name for his eleven-day stint in the Trump White House, he was known as a hedge fund manager who hosted a business conference called SALT. To attract attention to the conference, he booked private gigs by Maroon 5, Lenny Kravitz, Will.i.am, Duran Duran, the Chainsmokers, and others who might please a roomful of mostly middle-aged finance types. His conferences tap into the power of aspirational proximity; in other words, he helps well-paid shmegegges get close to their heroes.

"We're in love with fame," he said. "Our entire society is addicted to it." The addiction extends to the wealthiest among us, he went on. "But let me give you the bad news for rich people: They can only go four places. They can go into the art world, or private aircraft and yachting, or charity—naming buildings and hospitals after themselves—or they can go into experiential." He adopted the voice of a big spender: "'I'm super loaded! I have a Rolls-Royce!' Well, fuck that. There's ten thousand of them. But if I tell you, 'You are one of a kind!,' now you're special." As we spoke, he was stuck in midtown traffic, which occasioned a mood of patient contemplation. "You've got to think about it as a pyramid," he said. "The widest part is eating at McDonald's. The narrowest part is 'I paid two hundred million for the Basquiat.' Because that's one of a kind. I'm taking a piece of the immortality that artist created, and I'm owning it. Freud said we're ultimately hysterical because of our own demise. This is why we do these things. I have to prove that I'm really living." He paused to let that sink in, and then returned to the voice of the big spender: "So Andrea Bocelli is going to sing at my daughter's event."

To turn Scaramucci's abstractions into a gig requires a producer who can line up the money and the talent—a mix of diplomat and shrink, who specializes in what's known as "talent buying." Danielle Madeira, a talent buyer and producer in the San Francisco Bay Area, has come to expect that wealthy hosts will have trouble accepting the limits of their power: "I have to explain this to clients—you have agreed to make this offer, but that doesn't mean they accept the offer! It's not like you're buying something at Target."

J. B. Miller, the CEO of Empire Entertainment, an event-production company, conducts due diligence on hosts before making an offer to a star. "I have to provide a lot of biographical material on not just the principals but who is in the room," he told me. Miller recalls a surge of bookings during the dot-com boom. "The underlying business may or may not have ever had a possibility of making it, but when you have artists standing up there under your logo, the world thinks, Wow, look at their stature! They must have so much money."

There is wariness on all sides. When Miller was starting out three decades ago, he booked Aretha Franklin for gigs in Manhattan and the Hamptons, and alongside the Kentucky Derby. Franklin, like many Black artists of her generation, had grown wary of being cheated, so she demanded that her management square up in cash for every gig. "We'd sit down before the show and count it out," Miller said. He also recalled doling out cash to Ray Charles, Etta James, and James Brown. "You'd settle that, and then they'd go down to the stage."

Miller bristles at the question of whether patrons, and artists, might benefit more people by steering that money and talent to occasions that are open to the public. In San Francisco, for example, the late billionaire investor Warren Hellman endowed a free festival, Hardly Strictly Bluegrass, which draws half a million people to big-name concerts in Golden Gate Park. Miller sees no reason that the two kinds of events can't coexist. "When did music cross the Rubicon into a public service?" he asked. "You can certainly see that artist that you love when they come to a town near you. And, if you have the means, you can also have them at other times."

Peter Shapiro, a promoter who owns the Capitol Theatre and the Brooklyn Bowl, argues that this kind of spending is at least a better use of megawealth than other indulgences. "The privates are good for the talent, good for the venue, good for the staff," he said. "A private with great talent means hundreds of your friends can join you. They can't always join you on a yacht or in the Maldives."

*   *   *

On a crisp spring night on the southern tip of Manhattan, Flo Rida was backstage once more. This time, he huddled in a darkened hallway with his dancers and the DJ and Int'l Nephew, their arms laced around one another, as they murmured a prayer. Then they lined up in a loose stack behind the door that separated them from the stage.

On the other side, in a cavernous ballroom bathed in purple light, about four hundred people with matching lanyards were celebrating the twenty-fifth anniversary of a private-equity firm. It was business casual, with the occasional bow tie and ball gown. A sushi buffet ran the length of one wall. The venue, Casa Cipriani, occupies a restored Beaux Arts ferry terminal that also includes a hotel and private club, which offers suites with cashmere-lined walls, easy access to a helicopter pad, and fastidious attention to service. Guests are asked to choose which type of Italian bedding they prefer, cotton or linen.

At the lectern, two of the firm's leaders were holding forth. A gray-haired man in a gray plaid blazer praised his colleagues' delivery of "industry-leading returns for our limited partners," and thanked attendees for various feats, including "five hundred million in proceeds at a 5.5x multiple on investment capital" and enduring "awful six-hour golf rounds with me." As showtime approached, a partner in an elegant black-and-white gown told the crowd, "With pride in our hearts and sushi in our mouths, let's celebrate."

The partygoers had not been told who the headline entertainer would be, and some were quietly hoping for Springsteen. When Flo charged out from backstage, there was a brief vacuum of silence. But he plunged ahead into "Good Feeling," a thumping ode to success, with references to a Gulfstream, a Bugatti, and a Maybach. ("Talk like a winner, my chest to that sun / G5 dealer, U.S. to Taiwan.") The crowd began to fall in, and Flo showed a rowdier mode than he had at the bar mitzvah. "Who wants some shots?" he shouted, holding up bottles of vodka and tequila. There was a nervous titter; a gentleman in a bow tie craned his neck for a look, and then some of the younger guests stepped forward to drink from bottles held in Flo's outstretched hands. The mood in the room started to evolve fast.

I was permitted to attend as long as I promised not to name the firm. It was a private gig, at a private club, for a private-equity firm—an entire arena of American commerce defined by self-conscious exclusivity. I'll call the firm Equity Partners. As the night wore on, Flo developed a call-and-response with the crowd. He'd shout, "What happens at Equity Partners—" and they'd shout back, "Stays at Equity Partners!"

By the time Flo was rhapsodizing about the pole dancer in "Right Round," the formula was in full effect: Flo put his sunglasses on an executive, and the crowd howled, while the man lurched around in awkward ecstasy. When the performers got to "Where Them Girls At," Flo grabbed the roses from the DJ booth and doled them out to giddy recipients. He peeled off his vest and stalked the stage, his naked torso showing tattoos of Ray Charles, James Brown, and Sammy Davis Jr. Before long, there were so many men and women clambering up onstage that the dancers, in their mesh leggings and bikini tops, had to fight to be seen. Flo kept pouring from a bottle of Grey Goose, and people in the crowd kept approaching to tip their heads back, blazers thrown open, lanyards askew.

It was hard to tell which side—Flo or the investors—was more amused by the scene of communion between distant cousins in the family of wealth. When the show was over, the junior analysts staggered off in pairs, while the middle managers hustled to the commuter train. Flo returned to his dressing room, which was bustling with assistants, hangers-on, and aspiring friends. The performers were swapping tales from the night—of "the elderly woman in the front," at stage right, who went bananas during "Wild Ones." "She got her groove back in that exact moment," Oya Baby said. "She was, like, 'Me? I'm wild!'"

It wasn't all that different from Flo's big years; it's just that the audience was smaller and the fee larger. Seven years after his last Top Ten hit, the crowds still get loopy when they hear a song from their high school prom, and some of the erstwhile club kids are now entering middle management, with the power to book the entertainment for the holiday party.

Carts of food arrived—truffle fries, grilled fish, champagne—but Flo was nursing a bottle of Pedialyte, the rehydration secret for middle-aged stardom. The next morning, he was flying off to St. Louis, followed by Miami, Vegas, Arizona, Minnesota, and Vegas again. I wondered how long he planned to keep up his pace. "The thing is, people love to feel loved," he said. "So it doesn't matter if you're doing this gig or that gig. It never gets old." He turned to the side, to oblige one of the event planners with a selfie. The first time we met, he had confessed to the addictive pleasure, as ancient as Caligula, of watching people watch you. And, of course, there was the motivating question that would be familiar to his private audiences: "How much money is enough money?"

———————

In January 2025, David Sacks, who had thrown himself the "Let Him Eat Cake" birthday party, was named to the Trump administration as "AI and Crypto Czar." To mark Trump's inauguration, Sacks hosted a Crypto Ball in Washington, D.C., for which tickets sold at prices between $2,500 and $5,000. Snoop Dogg, one of the event's featured entertainers, had previously implored people not to vote for Trump—saying, in 2019, "He really don't give a fuck about us." Also performing at the Crypto Ball was rapper Soulja Boy, who later faced criticism from fans for accepting the gig. He offered no apologies. His motives, he said, were not political: "They paid me a bag."

THE MECHANICS

How to Keep It

Ghost in the Machine

Can Mark Zuckerberg fix Facebook before it breaks democracy?

— 2018 —

At ten o'clock on a weekday morning in the summer of 2018, Mark Zuckerberg, the chairman and CEO of Facebook, opened the front door of his house in Palo Alto, California, wearing the tight smile of obligation. He does not enjoy interviews, especially after several years of ceaseless controversy. Also, having got his start as a programmer with a nocturnal bent, he has never been a morning person. Walking toward the kitchen, which had a long farmhouse table and cabinets painted forest green, he said, "I haven't eaten breakfast yet. Have you?"

Since 2011, Zuckerberg has lived in a century-old white-clapboard Craftsman in the Crescent Park neighborhood, an enclave of giant oaks and historic homes not far from Stanford University. The house, which cost $7 million, affords him a sense of sanctuary. It's set back from the road, shielded by hedges, a wall, and mature trees. Guests enter through an arched wooden gate and follow a long gravel path to a front lawn with a saltwater pool in the center. The year after Zuckerberg bought the house, he and his longtime girlfriend, Priscilla Chan, held their wedding in the backyard, which encompasses gardens, a pond, and a shaded pavilion. Since then, they have acquired a seven-hundred-acre estate in Hawaii, a ski retreat in Montana, and a four-story townhouse on Liberty Hill in San Francisco. But the family's full-time residence is here, a ten-minute drive from the headquarters of the company.

Occasionally, Zuckerberg records a video from the backyard or the dinner table, as is expected of a man who built his fortune exhorting employees to keep "pushing the world in the direction of making it a more open and transparent place." But his appetite for personal openness is limited. Although Zuckerberg is the most famous entrepreneur of his generation, he remains elusive to everyone but a small circle of family and friends, and his efforts to protect his privacy inevitably attract attention. The local press has chronicled his feud with a developer who announced plans to build a mansion that would look into Zuckerberg's master bedroom. After a legal fight, the developer gave up, and Zuckerberg spent $44 million to buy the houses surrounding his. Over the years, he has come to believe that he will always be the subject of criticism. "We're not—pick your noncontroversial business—selling dog food, although I think that people who do that probably say there is controversy in that, too, but this is an inherently cultural thing," he told me of his business. "It's at the intersection of technology and psychology, and it's very personal."

He carried a plate of banana bread and a carafe of water into the living room, and settled onto a navy blue velvet sofa. Since cofounding Facebook in 2004, his wardrobe had evolved from hoodies and flip-flops to another unchanging uniform, consisting of a gray sweater, indigo jeans, and black Nikes. At thirty-four, Zuckerberg still had very fair skin, a tall forehead, and large eyes, but he was leaner than when he first became a public figure, more than a decade earlier. On the porch, next to the front door, he kept a Peloton stationary bike. Zuckerberg used the machine, but he did not love cycling. A few years earlier, on his first attempt to use a road bike with racing pedals, he forgot to unclip, tipped over, and broke his arm. Except for cycling on his porch, he told me, "I haven't clipped in since."

He and his wife prefer board games to television, and, within reach of the couch, I noticed a game called Ricochet Robots. "It gets extremely competitive," Zuckerberg said. "We play with these friends, and one of them is a genius at this. Playing with him is just infuriating." Dave Morin, a former Facebook employee who is the founder and CEO of Sunrise Bio, a start-up seeking cures for depression, used to play Risk with Zuckerberg at the office. "He's not playing you in a game of Risk. He's playing you in a game of games," Morin told me. "The first game, he might amass all his armies on one property, and the next game he might spread them all over the place. He's trying to figure out the psychological way to beat you in all the games."

Across the tech industry, the depth of Zuckerberg's desire to win is often remarked upon. Dick Costolo, the former CEO of Twitter, told me, "He's a ruthless execution machine, and if he has decided to come after you, you're going to take a beating." Reid Hoffman, the founder of LinkedIn, said, "There are a number of people in the Valley who have a perception of Mark that he's really aggressive and competitive. I think some people are a little hesitant about him from that perspective." Hoffman has been an investor in Facebook since its early days, but for a long time he sensed that Zuckerberg kept his distance because they were both building social networks. "For many years, it was, like, 'Your LinkedIn thing is going to be crushed, so even though we're friendly, I don't want to get too close to you personally, because I'm going to crush you.' Now, of course, that's behind us and we're good friends."

When I asked Zuckerberg about this reputation, he framed the dynamic differently. The survival of any social media business rests on "network effects," in which the value of the network grows only by finding new users. As a result, he said, "there's a natural zero-sumness. If we're going to achieve what we want to, it's not just about building the best features. It's about building the best community." He added, "I care about succeeding. And, yes, sometimes you have to beat someone to something, in order to get to the next thing. But that's not primarily the way that I think I roll."

For many years, Zuckerberg ended Facebook meetings with the half-joking exhortation "Domination!" Although he eventually stopped doing this (in European legal systems, "dominance" refers to corporate monopoly), his discomfort with losing is undimmed. A few years ago, he played Scrabble on a corporate jet with a friend's daughter, who was in high school at the time. She won. Before they played a second game, he wrote a simple computer program that would look up his letters in the dictionary so that he could choose from all possible words. Zuckerberg's program had a narrow lead when the flight landed. The girl told me, "During the game in which I was playing the program, everyone around us was taking sides: Team Human and Team Machine."

*   *   *

If Facebook were a country, it would have the largest population on earth. More than 2.2 billion people, about a third of humanity, log in at least once a month. That user base has no precedent in the history of American enterprise. Fourteen years after it was founded in Zuckerberg's dorm room, Facebook has as many adherents as Christianity.

For much of its first decade, the company reveled in its power. By collecting vast quantities of information about its users, it allowed advertisers to target people with precision—a business model that earned Facebook more ad revenue in a year than all American newspapers combined. Zuckerberg was spending much of his time conferring with heads of state and unveiling plans of fantastical ambition, such as building giant drones that would beam free internet (including Facebook) into developing countries. He enjoyed extraordinary control over his company; in addition to his positions as chairman and CEO, he controlled about 60 percent of shareholder votes, thanks to a special class of stock with ten times the power of ordinary shares. His personal fortune grew to more than $60 billion in far less time than it took most of his peers. Facebook was one of four companies (along with Google, Amazon, and Apple) that dominated the internet; the combined value of their stock was larger than the GDP of France.

Public criticism started mildly. Facebook received complaints about its use of private data and its ability to shape people's behavior. The company's troubles came to a head during the presidential election of 2016, when propagandists used the site to spread misinformation that helped turn society against itself. Some of the culprits were profiteers who gamed Facebook's automated systems with toxic political fictions. In an oft-noted example, at least a hundred websites were traced to Veles, Macedonia, a small city where entrepreneurs, some still in high school, discovered that posting fabrications to pro–Donald Trump Facebook groups unleashed geysers of traffic. Those fake-news sources also paid Facebook directly, to microtarget ads at users who had proved especially susceptible to clicking in the past.

The other culprits, according to U.S. intelligence, were Russian agents who wanted to sow political chaos and help Trump win. In 2018, Robert Mueller, the special counsel named to investigate Russia's role in the election, charged thirteen Russians with an "interference operation" that made use of Facebook, Twitter, and Instagram. The Internet Research Agency, a firm in St. Petersburg working for the Kremlin, drew hundreds of thousands of users to Facebook groups optimized to stoke outrage, including Secured Borders, Blacktivist, and Defend the 2nd. They used Facebook to organize offline rallies, and bought Facebook ads intended to hurt Hillary Clinton's standing among Democratic voters. (One read "Hillary Clinton Doesn't Deserve the Black Vote.") With fewer than a hundred operatives, the IRA used the social network to astonishing effect: Facebook estimated that the content reached as many as 150 million of its users.

At the same time, former Facebook executives, echoing a growing body of research, began to voice misgivings about the company's role in exacerbating isolation, outrage, and addictive behaviors. One of the largest studies, published in 2017 in the *American Journal of Epidemiology*, followed the Facebook use of more than five thousand people over three years and found that higher use correlated with self-reported declines in physical health, mental health, and life satisfaction. At an event that fall, Sean Parker, Facebook's first president, declared himself a "conscientious objector" to social media, saying, "God only knows what it's doing to our children's brains." A few days later, Chamath Palihapitiya, the former vice president of user growth, told an audience at Stanford, "The short-term, dopamine-driven feedback loops that we have created are destroying how society works—no civil discourse, no cooperation, misinformation, mistruth." Palihapitiya, a prominent Silicon Valley figure who worked at Facebook from 2007 to 2011, said, "I feel tremendous guilt. I think we all knew in the back of our minds." Of his children, he added, "They're not allowed to use this shit." (Facebook replied to the remarks in a statement, noting that Palihapitiya had left six years earlier, and adding, "Facebook was a very different company back then.")

In the spring of 2018, Facebook was confronted with an even larger scandal: a researcher with access to Facebook user data had harvested the personal information of 87 million users and sold it to Cambridge Analytica, a consultancy hired by Trump and other Republicans. The firm touted what it called "psychographic" techniques to manipulate voter behavior. Facebook had known of the problem since December of 2015 but had said nothing to users or regulators. The company acknowledged the breach only after the press discovered it.

The Cambridge Analytica revelations touched off the most serious crisis in Facebook's history, and, with it, a public reckoning with the power of Big Tech. By the fall of 2018, Facebook was under investigation by the FBI, the Securities and Exchange Commission, the Department of Justice, and the Federal Trade Commission, as well as by authorities abroad, from London to Brussels to Sydney. Facebook's peers and rivals expressed conspicuously little sympathy. Elon Musk deleted his Facebook pages and those of his companies, Tesla and SpaceX. Tim Cook, the CEO of Apple, told an interviewer, "We could make a ton of money if we monetized our customer," but "we've elected not to do that." At Facebook's annual shareholder meeting, executives struggled to keep order. An investor who interrupted the agenda to argue against

Zuckerberg's renomination as chairman was removed. Outside, an airplane flew a banner that read "YOU BROKE DEMOCRACY."

On July 25, 2018, with pressure building, Facebook's stock price dropped 19 percent, cutting its market value by $119 billion, the largest one-day drop in Wall Street history. A technology writer tweeted that Zuckerberg was losing $2.7 million per second, "double what the average American makes in an entire lifetime." Facebook's user base had flatlined in the U.S. and Canada, and dropped slightly in Europe, and executives warned that revenue growth would decline further, in part because the scandals had led users to opt out of allowing Facebook to collect some data. Facebook depends on trust, and the events of the past two years had made people wonder whether the company deserved it.

Zuckerberg's supporters described his travails as a by-product of success. He was often compared to another Harvard dropout, Bill Gates, who had become a mentor in business and philanthropy. Gates told me, "Somebody who is smart, and rich, and ends up not acknowledging problems as quickly as they should will be attacked as arrogant. That comes with the territory." He added, "I wouldn't say that Mark's an arrogant individual." But, to critics, Facebook was guilty of a willful blindness driven by greed, naïveté, and contempt for oversight.

In a series of conversations over the summer, I talked to Zuckerberg about Facebook's problems, and about his underlying views on technology and society. We spoke at his home, at his office, and by phone. I also interviewed four dozen people inside and outside the company about its culture, his performance, and his decision-making. I found Zuckerberg straining, not always coherently, to grasp problems for which he was plainly unprepared. These are not technical puzzles to be cracked in the middle of the night but some of the subtlest aspects of human affairs, including the meaning of truth, the limits of free speech, and the origins of violence.

Zuckerberg was at the center of a widening debate about the moral character of Silicon Valley and the conscience of its leaders. Leslie Berlin, a historian of technology at Stanford, told me, "For a long time,

Silicon Valley enjoyed an unencumbered embrace in America. And now everyone says, Is this a trick? And the question Mark Zuckerberg is dealing with is: Should my company be the arbiter of truth and decency for two billion people? Nobody in the history of technology has dealt with that."

*   *   *

Facebook's headquarters, at 1 Hacker Way, in Menlo Park, overlooking the salt marshes south of San Francisco, has the feel of a small, prosperous dictatorship, akin to Kuwait or Brunei. The campus is a self-contained universe, with the full range of free Silicon Valley perks: dry cleaning, haircuts, music lessons, and food by the acre, including barbecue, biryani, and salad bars. (New arrivals are said to put on the "Facebook fifteen.") Along with stock options and generous benefits, such trappings have roots in the 1970s, when founders aspired to create pleasant workplaces and stave off the rise of labor unions. The campus, which was designed with the help of consultants from Disney, is arranged as an ersatz town that encircles a central plaza, with shops and restaurants and offices along a main street. From the air, the word "Hack" is visible in gigantic letters on the plaza pavement.

On Zuckerberg's campus, he is king. Executives offered me fulsome praise. David Marcus, who ran Facebook's blockchain project, said, "When I see him portrayed in certain ways, it really hurts me personally, because it's not the guy he is." Even when colleagues spoke anonymously (and candidly), on the whole they liked him personally. "He's not an asshole," a former senior executive told me. "That's why people work there so long."

But there was an unavoidable oddity in Zuckerberg's personal bearing. Before I visited him for the first time, members of his staff offered the kind of advice usually reserved for approaching a skittish bird: proceed gingerly, build a connection, avoid surprises. The advice, I discovered, wasn't entirely necessary; in person, he was more direct than he tended to be in his public pronouncements, which were as arid as corporate pablum. But even after a decade in public life, Zuckerberg was still straining to inject a warm-blooded persona into a reputation for hollowness. His moments of self-reflection were so rare that, following a CNN interview in which he said that he wanted to build a company that "my girls are going to grow up and be proud of me for," the network framed the clip as a news event, with the title "Zuckerberg in rare emotional moment."

I asked Zuckerberg about his aversion to opening up. "I'm not the most polished person, and I will say something wrong, and you see the cost of that," he said. "I don't want to inflict that pain, or do something that's going to not reflect well on the people around me." A few weeks earlier, he had told the podcaster Kara Swisher that he permitted Holocaust deniers on Facebook because he wasn't sure if they were "intentionally getting it wrong." After a furor erupted, he issued a statement saying that he found Holocaust denial "deeply offensive." Zuckerberg told me, "In an alternate world where there weren't the compounding experiences that I had, I probably would have gotten more comfortable being more personal, and out there, and I wouldn't have felt pushback every time I did something. And maybe my persona, or at least how I felt comfortable acting publicly, would shift."

Zuckerberg's exalted status within his own realm made it difficult for him to get genuine, unexpurgated feedback. He had tried, somewhat awkwardly, to puncture his own bubble. In 2013, as a New Year's resolution, he pledged to meet someone new, outside Facebook, every day. In 2017, he traveled to more than thirty states on a "listening tour" that he hoped would better acquaint him with the outside world. David Plouffe, President Obama's former campaign manager, who became the head of policy and advocacy at the Chan Zuckerberg Initiative, the family's philanthropic investment company, attended some events on the tour. Plouffe told me, "When a politician goes to one of those, it's an hour, and they're talking for fifty of those minutes. He would talk for, like, five, and just ask questions."

But the exercise came off as stilted and tone-deaf. Zuckerberg traveled with a professional photographer, who documented him feeding a calf in Wisconsin, ordering barbecue, and working on an assembly line at a Ford plant in Michigan. Online, people joked that the photos made him look like an extraterrestrial exploring the human race for the first time. A former Facebook executive who was involved in the tour told a friend, "No one wanted to tell Mark, and no one did tell Mark, that this really looks just dumb."

Zuckerberg has spent nearly half his life inside a company of his own making, handpicking his lieutenants, and sculpting his environment to suit him. Even Facebook's signature royal blue reflects his tastes. He is red-green color-blind, and he chose blue because he sees it most vividly. Sheryl Sandberg, the longtime chief operating officer, told me, "Sometimes Mark will say, in front of the company, 'Well, I've never worked anywhere else, but Sheryl tells me . . .'" She went on, "He acknowledges he doesn't always have the most experience. He's only had the experience he's had, and being Mark Zuckerberg is pretty extraordinary."

*   *   *

Long before it seemed inevitable or even plausible, Mark Elliot Zuckerberg had an outsized sense of his own potential. It was "a teleological frame of feeling almost chosen," a longtime friend told me. "I think Mark has always seen himself as a man of history, someone who is destined to be great, and I mean that in the broadest sense of the term." Zuckerberg has observed that more than a few giants of history grew up in bourgeois comfort near big cities and then channeled those advantages into transformative power.

In Zuckerberg's case, the setting was Dobbs Ferry, New York, a Westchester County suburb twenty-five miles north of New York City. His mother, Karen Kempner, grew up in Queens; on a blind date, she met a mailman's son, Edward Zuckerberg, of Flatbush, Brooklyn, who was studying to be a dentist. They married and had four children. Mark, the only boy, was the second-oldest. His mother, who had become a psychiatrist, eventually gave up her career to take care of the kids and manage the dental office, which was connected to the family home. Of his father, Zuckerberg told me, "He was a dentist, but he was also a huge techie. So he always had not just a system for drilling teeth but, like, the laser system for drilling teeth that was controlled by the computer." Ed Zuckerberg marketed himself as the Painless Dr. Z, and later drummed up dentistry business with a direct-mail solicitation that declared, "I am literally the Father of Facebook!" (Since 2013, Zuckerberg's parents have lived in California, where Ed practices part-time and lectures on using social media to attract patients.)

In the 1980s and '90s, Ed bought early personal computers—the Atari 800, the IBM XT—and Mark learned to code. At twelve, he set up his first network, ZuckNet, on which messages and files could be shared between the house and his father's dental office. Rabbi David Holtz, of Temple Beth Abraham in Tarrytown, told me that he watched Zuckerberg with other kids and sensed that he was "beyond a lot of his peers. He was thinking about things that other people were not." When I asked Zuckerberg where his drive came from, he traced it to his grandparents, who had immigrated from Europe in the early twentieth century. "They came over, went through the Great Depression, had very hard lives," he said. "Their dream for their kids was that they would each become doctors, which they did, and my mom just always believed that we should have a bigger impact." His eldest sister, Randi, an early Facebook spokesperson, went on to write books and host a radio show; Donna received her PhD in classics from Princeton and edited an online classics journal; Arielle had worked at Google and as a venture capitalist.

When Zuckerberg was a junior in high school, he transferred to Phillips Exeter Academy, where he spent most of his time coding, fencing, and studying Latin. Ancient Rome became a lifelong fascination, first because of the language ("It's very much like coding or math, and so I appreciated that") and then because of the history. Zuckerberg told me, "You have all these good and bad and complex figures. I think Augustus is one of the most fascinating. Basically, through a really harsh approach, he established two hundred years of world peace." For non-classics majors: Augustus Caesar, born in 63 BC, staked his claim to power at the age of eighteen and turned Rome from a republic into an empire by conquering Egypt, northern Spain, and large parts of central Europe. He also eliminated political opponents, banished his daughter for promiscuity, and was suspected of arranging the execution of his grandson.

"What are the trade-offs in that?" Zuckerberg said, growing animated. "On the one hand, world peace is a long-term goal that people talk about today. Two hundred years feels unattainable." On the other hand, he said, "that didn't come for free, and he had to do certain things." In 2012, Zuckerberg and Chan spent their honeymoon in Rome. He later said, "My wife was making fun of me, saying she thought there were three people on the honeymoon: me, her, and Augustus. All the photos were different sculptures of Augustus." The couple named their daughters—Maxima, August, and Aurelia—after Roman emperors.

In 2002, Zuckerberg went to Harvard, where he embraced the hacker mystique, which celebrates brilliance in pursuit of disruption. "The 'fuck you' to those in power was very strong," the longtime friend said. In 2004, as a sophomore, he embarked on the project whose origin story is now well known: the founding of Thefacebook.com with four fellow-students ("the" was dropped the following year); the legal battles over ownership, including a suit filed by twin brothers, Cameron and Tyler Winklevoss, accusing Zuckerberg of stealing their idea; the disclosure of embarrassing messages in which Zuckerberg mocked users for giving him so much data ("they 'trust me.' dumb fucks," he wrote); his regrets about those remarks, and his efforts, in the years afterward, to convince the world that he has left that mind-set behind.

During Zuckerberg's sophomore year, in line for the bathroom at a party, he met Priscilla Chan, who was a freshman. Her parents, who traced their roots to China, had grown up in Vietnam and arrived in the

U.S. as refugees after the war, settling in Quincy, Massachusetts, where they washed dishes in a Chinese restaurant. Priscilla was the eldest of three daughters, and the first member of her family to go to college. "I suddenly go to Harvard, where there's this world where people had real and meaningful intellectual pursuits," she told me. "Then I met Mark, who so exemplified that." She was struck by how little Zuckerberg's background had in common with her own. "Fifty percent of people go to college from the high school I went to. You could learn how to be a carpenter or a mechanic," she said. "I was just, like, 'This person speaks a whole new language and lives in a framework that I've never seen before.'" She added, "Maybe there was some judgment on my part: 'You don't understand me because you went to Phillips Exeter,'" but, she said, "I had to realize early on that I was not going to change who Mark was." After Harvard, Chan taught in a primary school and eventually became a pediatrician. In 2017, she stopped seeing patients to be the day-to-day head of the Chan Zuckerberg Initiative. When I asked Chan about how Zuckerberg had responded at home to the criticism of the past two years, she talked to me about *sitzfleisch*, the German term for sitting and working for long periods of time. "He'd actually sit so long that he froze up his muscles and injured his hip," she said.

*   *   *

After his sophomore year in college, Zuckerberg moved to Palo Alto and never left. Even by the standards of Silicon Valley, Facebook's first office had a youthful feel. Zuckerberg carried two sets of business cards. One said "I'm CEO . . . bitch!" Visitors encountered a graffiti mural of a scantily clad woman riding a Rottweiler. In Adam Fisher's *Valley of Genius*, an oral history of Silicon Valley, an early employee named Ezra Callahan muses, "'How much was the direction of the internet influenced by the perspective of nineteen-, twenty-, twenty-one-year-old well-off white boys?' That's a real question that sociologists will be studying forever."

Facebook was fortunate to launch when it did: Silicon Valley was recovering from the dot-com bust and was entering a period of near-messianic ambitions. The internet was no longer so new that users were scarce, but still new enough that it was largely unregulated; first movers could amass vast followings and consolidate power, and the coming rise of inexpensive smartphones would bring millions of new people online. Most important, Facebook capitalized on a resource that most people hardly knew existed: the willingness of users to subsidize the company by handing over colossal amounts of personal information for free.

In Facebook, Zuckerberg had found the instrument to achieve his conception of greatness. His onetime speechwriter Katherine Losse, in her memoir, *The Boy Kings*, explained that the "engineering ideology of Facebook" was clear: "Scaling and growth are everything, individuals and their experiences are secondary to what is necessary to maximize the system." Over time, Facebook devoted ever-greater focus to what is known in Silicon Valley as "growth hacking," the constant pursuit of scale. Whenever the company talked about "connecting people," that was, in effect, code for user growth.

Then, in 2007, growth plateaued at around fifty million users and wouldn't budge. Other social networks had maxed out at around that level, and Facebook employees wondered if they had hit some unavoidable limit. Zuckerberg created a special Growth Team, which had broad latitude to find ways of boosting the numbers. Among other fixes, they discovered that, by offering the site in more languages, they could open huge markets. Alex Schultz, a founding member of the Growth Team, said that he and his colleagues were fanatical in their pursuit of expansion. "You will fight for that inch, you will die for that inch," he told me. Facebook left no opportunity untapped. In 2011, the company asked the Federal Election Commission for an exemption to rules requiring the source of funding for political ads to be disclosed. In filings, a Facebook lawyer argued that the agency "should not stand in the way of innovation."

Sandy Parakilas, who joined Facebook in 2011 as an operations manager, paraphrased the message of his orientation session as "We believe in the religion of growth." He said, "The Growth Team was the coolest. Other teams would even try to call subgroups within their teams the 'Growth X' or the 'Growth Y' to try to get people excited."

To gain greater reach, Facebook had made the fateful decision to become a "platform" for outside developers, much as Windows had been in the realm of desktop computers a generation before. The company had opened its trove of data to programmers who wanted to build Facebook games, personality tests, and other apps. After a few months at Facebook, Parakilas was put in charge of a team responsible for making sure that outsiders were not misusing the data, and he was unnerved by what he found. Some games were siphoning off users' messages and photographs. In one case, he said, a developer was harvesting user information, including that of children, to create unauthorized profiles on its own website. Facebook had given away data before it had a system to check for abuse. Parakilas suggested that there be an audit to uncover the scale of the problem. But, according to Parakilas, an executive rejected the idea, telling him, "Do you really want to see what you'll find?"

Parakilas told me, "It was very difficult to get the kind of resources that you needed to do a good job of insuring real compliance. Meanwhile, you looked at the Growth Team and they had engineers coming out of their ears. All the smartest minds are focused on doing whatever they can possibly do to get those growth numbers up."

New hires learned that a crucial measure of the company's performance was how many people had logged in to Facebook on six of the previous seven days, a measurement known as L6/7. "You could say it's how many people love this service so much they use it six out of seven days," Parakilas, who left the company in 2012, said. "But if your job is to get that number up, at some point you run out of good, purely positive ways. You start thinking about 'Well, what are the dark patterns that I can use to get people to log back in?'"

Facebook engineers became a new breed of behaviorists, tweaking levers of vanity and passion and susceptibility. The real-world effects were striking. In 2012, when Chan was in medical school, she and Zuckerberg discussed a critical shortage of organs for transplant, inspiring Zuckerberg to add a small, powerful nudge on Facebook: if people indicated that they were organ donors, it triggered a notification to friends, and, in turn, a cascade of social pressure. Researchers later found that, on the first day the feature appeared, it increased official organ donor enrollment more than twentyfold nationwide.

Sean Parker later described the company's expertise as "exploiting a vulnerability in human psychology." The goal: "How do we consume as much of your time and conscious attention as possible?" Facebook engineers discovered that people still acclimating to social media found it nearly impossible not to log in after receiving an email saying that someone had uploaded a picture of them. Facebook also discovered its power to affect political behavior; during the 2010 midterm elections, Facebook prodded users to vote simply by feeding them pictures of friends who had already voted, and by giving them the option to click on an "I Voted" button. The technique boosted turnout by 340,000 people—more than four times the number of votes separating Trump and Clinton in key states in the 2016 race. It became a running joke among employees that Facebook could tilt an election just by choosing where to deploy its "I Voted" button.

These powers of social engineering could be put to dubious purposes. In 2012, Facebook data scientists used nearly 700,000 people as guinea pigs, feeding them happy or sad posts to test whether emotion is contagious on social media. (They concluded that it is.) When the findings were published in the *Proceedings of the National Academy of Sciences*, they caused an uproar among users, many of whom were horrified that their emotions may have been surreptitiously manipulated. In an apology, one of the scientists wrote, "In hindsight, the research benefits of the paper may not have justified all of this anxiety."

Facebook was, in the words of Tristan Harris, a former design ethicist at Google, becoming a pioneer in "persuasive technology." He explained,

"A hammer, in your hand, is non-persuasive—it doesn't have its own ways of manipulating the person that holds it. But Facebook and Snapchat, in their design features, are persuading a teenager to wake up and see photo after photo after photo of their friends having fun without them, even if it makes them feel worse." In 2015, Harris delivered a talk at Facebook about his concern that social media was contributing to alienation. "I said, 'You guys are in the best position in the world to deal with loneliness and see it as a thing that you are amplifying and a thing that you can help make go the other way,'" he told me. "They didn't do anything about it." He added, "My points were in their blind spot."

*   *   *

As Facebook grew, Zuckerberg and his executives adopted a core belief: even if people criticized your decisions, they would eventually come around. In one of the first demonstrations of that idea, in 2006 Facebook introduced the News Feed, a feature that suddenly alerted friends whenever a user changed profile pictures, joined groups, or altered a relationship status. (Until then, users had to visit a friend's page to see updates.) Users revolted. There was a street protest at the headquarters, and hundreds of thousands of people joined a Facebook group opposing the change. Zuckerberg posted a tepid apology ("Calm down. Breathe. We hear you."), and people got used to the feed.

"A lot of the early experience for me was just having people really not believe that what we were going to do was going to work," Zuckerberg told me. "If you think about the early narratives, it was, like, 'Well, this was just a college thing.' Or 'It's not gonna be a big deal.' Or 'OK, other people are using it, but it's kind of a fad. There's Friendster and there's MySpace, and there will be something after,' or whatever." He added, "I feel like it really tests you emotionally to have constant doubt, and the assertion that you don't know what you are doing."

In 2006, Zuckerberg made his most unpopular decision at the fledgling company. Yahoo was offering a billion dollars to buy Facebook and, as Matt Cohler, a top aide at the time, recalls, "Our growth had stalled out." Cohler and many others implored Zuckerberg to take the offer, but he refused. "I think nearly all of his leadership team lost faith in him and in the business," Cohler said. Zuckerberg told me that most of his leadership "left within eighteen months. Some of them I had to fire because it was just too dysfunctional. It just completely blew up. But the thing that I learned from that is, if you stick with your values and with what you believe you want to be doing in the world, you can get through. Sometimes it will take some time, and you have to rebuild, but that's a pretty powerful lesson."

Even as Zuckerberg stumbled, he was learning to expect that he could eventually prevail over one critic or another. In 2007, Facebook botched a matter of privacy: it started giving advertisers a chance to buy into a program called Beacon, which would announce to a user's friends what that user was browsing for, or buying, online. Users could opt out, but many had no idea that the feature existed until it revealed upcoming holiday gifts, or, in some cases, exposed extramarital affairs. Zuckerberg apologized ("We simply did a bad job with this release, and I apologize for it," he wrote), and Beacon was withdrawn.

Despite the apology, Zuckerberg was convinced that he was ahead of his users, not at odds with them. In 2010, he said that privacy was no longer a "social norm." That year, the company found itself in trouble again after it revised its privacy controls to make most information public by default. The Federal Trade Commission cited Facebook for "engaging in unfair and deceptive practices" with regard to the privacy of user data. The company signed a consent decree pledging to establish a "comprehensive privacy program" and to evaluate it every other year for twenty years. In a post, Zuckerberg offered a qualified apology: "I think that a small number of high profile mistakes . . . have often overshadowed much of the good work we've done."

Facebook had adopted a buccaneering motto, "Move fast and break things," which celebrated the idea that it was better to be flawed and first than careful and perfect. Andrew Bosworth, one of Zuckerberg's longest-serving lieutenants and a member of his inner circle, told me, "A failure can be a form of success. It's not the form you want, but it can be a useful thing to how you learn." In Zuckerberg's view, skeptics were often just fogies and scolds. "There's always someone who wants to slow you down," he said in a commencement address at Harvard in 2017. "In our society, we often don't do big things because we're so afraid of making mistakes that we ignore all the things wrong today if we do nothing. The reality is, anything we do will have issues in the future. But that can't keep us from starting."

Zuckerberg's disregard for criticism entered a more emphatic phase in 2010, with the release of the movie *The Social Network*, an account of Facebook's early years written by Aaron Sorkin and directed by David Fincher. Some of the film was fictionalized. It presented Zuckerberg's motivation largely as a desire to meet girls, even though, in real life, he was dating Priscilla Chan for most of the time period covered in the movie. But other elements cut close to the truth, including the depiction of his juvenile bravado and the early feuds over ownership. Zuckerberg and Facebook had chosen not to be involved in the production, and the portrayal was unflattering. Zuckerberg, played by Jesse Eisenberg, is cocksure and cold, and the real Zuckerberg found the depiction hurtful. "First impressions matter a lot, and for a lot of people that was their introduction to me," he told me. "My reaction to this, to all these things, is primarily that I perceive it through the employees." His concern was less about how people would think of him, he said, than about "how is our *company*, how are our employees—these people I work with and care so much about—how are they going to process this?"

Shortly before the movie came out, Facebook executives debated how to respond. Zuckerberg settled on a stance of effortful good cheer, renting a movie theater to screen it for the staff. Years later, Facebook executives still mentioned what they call, resentfully, "the movie." Sandberg, one of Zuckerberg's most ardent defenders, told me, "From its facts to its essence to its portrayal, I think that was a very unfair picture. I still think it forms the basis of a lot of what people believe about Mark."

Zuckerberg proved willing to make sharp turns to achieve his aims. When users started moving from desktop computers to phones, Facebook, in 2011, swerved toward mobile technology. He told employees that he would kick them out of his office if their ideas did not account for the transition. "Within a month, you literally can't meet with Mark if you're not bringing him a mobile product," Bosworth recalled.

Zuckerberg made a series of other decisions that solidified his confidence in his instincts. In 2012, he paid a billion dollars for Instagram, the photo-sharing service, which at the time had only thirteen employees. Outside the industry, the start-up appeared wildly overpriced, but it proved to be one of the best investments in the history of the internet. (Within six years, Instagram was valued at more than a hundred times what Zuckerberg paid for it, and, even more important, it was popular with young people, a cohort with declining interest in Facebook.) That spring, Facebook went public on the Nasdaq, at a valuation of $104 billion. There were technical glitches on the day of the listing, and many people doubted that the company could earn enough money to justify the valuation. *The Wall Street Journal* called the IPO a "fiasco," and shareholders sued Facebook and Zuckerberg. "We got a ton of criticism," he recalled. "Our market cap got cut in half. But what I felt was, we were at a sufficient skill and complexity that it was going to take a couple years to work through the problem, but I had a strong conviction that we were doing the right thing." (In the first six years after the I.P.O., the value of Facebook stock more than quadrupled.)

In 2014, as the company evolved from a start-up to a behemoth, it changed its motto, "Move fast and break things," to the decidedly less glamorous "Move fast with stable infrastructure." Still, internally, much of the original spirit endured, and the push for haste began to take a steeper toll in the offline world. Zuckerberg directed employees to accelerate the release of Facebook Live, a video-streaming service, and expanded its team of engineers from twelve to more than a hundred. But when the product emerged two months later, so did unforeseen issues: the service let users flag videos as inappropriate, but it didn't give them a way to indicate where in a broadcast the problem appeared. As a result, Facebook Live videos of people committing suicide, or engaged in criminal activity, started circulating before reviewers had time to race through, find the issues, and take the videos down. A Chicago man named Antonio Perkins was fatally shot on Facebook Live and the video was viewed hundreds of thousands of times.

The incident might have served as a warning to slow down, but, instead, the next day, Bosworth sent around a remarkable internal memo justifying some of Facebook's "ugly" physical and social effects as the trade-offs necessary for growth: "Maybe it costs a life by exposing someone to bullies. Maybe someone dies in a terrorist attack coordinated on our tools. And still we connect people. The ugly truth is that we believe in connecting people so deeply that anything that allows us to connect more people more often is *de facto* good."

After the memo leaked to BuzzFeed, Bosworth said that he had been playing devil's advocate, and Zuckerberg issued a statement: "Boz is a talented leader who says many provocative things. This was one that most people at Facebook including myself disagreed with strongly. We've never believed the ends justify the means."

*   *   *

Zuckerberg was also experimenting with philanthropy. In 2010, shortly before the release of *The Social Network*, he made a high-profile gift. Appearing onstage at *The Oprah Winfrey Show* along with Chris Christie, the governor of New Jersey, and Cory Booker, then-mayor of Newark, he announced a hundred-million-dollar donation to help Newark's struggling public school system. The project quickly encountered opposition from local groups that saw it as out of touch, and eight years later it's generally considered a failure. (Ras Baraka, Newark's mayor, said of the donation, "You can't just cobble up a bunch of money and drop it in the middle of the street and say, 'This is going to fix everything.'")

For all the criticism, the project produced some measurable improvements. A Harvard study found greater gains in English than the state average, and a study by MarGrady Research, an education-policy group, found that high school graduation rates and overall student enrollment in Newark have risen since the donation. Zuckerberg emphasizes those results, even as he acknowledges flaws in his approach. "Your earning potential is dramatically higher if you graduate from high school versus not. That part of it, I think, is the part that worked and it was effective," he said. "There were a bunch of other things that we tried that either were much harder than we thought or just didn't work." Strategies that helped him in business turned out to hurt him in education reform. "I think in a lot of philanthropy and government-related work, if you try five things and a few of them fail, then the ones that fail are going to get a lot of the attention," he said.

In 2015, Zuckerberg and Chan pledged to spend 99 percent of their Facebook fortune "to advance human potential and promote equality for all children in the next generation." They created the Chan Zuckerberg Initiative, a limited-liability company that gives to charity, invests in for-profit companies, and engages in political advocacy. In contrast to a traditional foundation, an LLC could lobby and give money to politicians, without as strict a legal requirement to disclose activities. In other words, rather than trying to win over politicians and citizens in places like Newark, Zuckerberg and Chan could help elect politicians who agreed with them, and rally the public directly by running ads and supporting advocacy groups. (A spokesperson for CZI said that it had given no money to candidates; it supported ballot initiatives through a 501(c)(4) social welfare organization.) "The whole point of the LLC structure is to allow a coordinated attack," Rob Reich, a codirector of Stanford's Center on Philanthropy and Civil Society, told me. The structure was gaining popularity in Silicon Valley but had been criticized for allowing wealthy individuals to orchestrate large-scale social agendas behind closed doors. Reich said, "There should be much greater transparency, so that it's not dark. That's not a criticism of Mark Zuckerberg. It's a criticism of the law."

In 2016, Zuckerberg announced, onstage and in a Facebook post, his intention to "help cure all disease in our children's lifetime." (That was partly bluster: CZI was working on a slightly more realistic agenda, to "cure, prevent or manage all diseases.") The theatrics irritated some in the philanthropy world who thought that Zuckerberg's presentation minimized the challenges, but, in general, scientists applauded the ambition. When I asked Zuckerberg about the reception of the project, he said, "It's funny, when I talk to people here in the Valley, you get a couple of reactions. A bunch of people have the reaction of 'Oh, that's obviously going to happen on its own—why don't you just spend your time doing something else?' And then a bunch of people have the reaction of 'Oh, that seems almost impossible—why are you setting your sights so high?'"

Characteristically, Zuckerberg favored the optimistic scenario. "On average, every year for the last eighty years or so, I think, life expectancy has gone up by about a quarter of a year. And, if you believe that technological and scientific progress is not going to slow, there is a potential upside to speeding that up," he said. "We're going to get to a point where the life expectancy implied by extrapolating that out will mean that we'll basically have been able to manage or cure all of the major things that people suffer from and die from today. Based on the data that we already see, it seems like there's a reasonable shot."

I asked Bill Gates, whose private foundation is the largest in the U.S., about Zuckerberg's objectives. "There are aspirations and then there are plans," he said. "And plans vary in terms of their degree of realism and concreteness." He added that Zuckerberg's long-range goal is "very safe, because you will not be around to write the article saying that he overcommitted."

*　　　　*　　　　*

As Facebook expanded, so did its blind spots. The company's financial future relied partly on growth in developing countries, but the platform became a catalyst of violence in fragile parts of the globe. In India, the largest market for Facebook's WhatsApp service, hoaxes triggered riots, lynchings, and fatal beatings. (Local officials in India resorted to shutting down the internet sixty-five times in 2017.) In Libya, people took to Facebook to trade weapons, and armed groups relayed the locations of targets for artillery strikes. In Sri Lanka, after a Buddhist mob attacked Muslims over a false rumor, a presidential adviser told a reporter, "The germs are ours, but Facebook is the wind."

Nowhere was the damage starker than in Myanmar, where the Rohingya Muslim minority had been subject to brutal killings, gang rapes, and torture. In 2012, around one percent of the country's population had access to the internet. Three years later, that figure had reached 25 percent. Phones often came preloaded with the Facebook app, and Buddhist extremists seeking to inflame ethnic tensions with the Rohingya mastered the art of misinformation. Wirathu, a monk with a large Facebook following, sparked a deadly riot against Muslims in 2014 when he shared a fake report of a rape and warned of a "Jihad against us." Others gamed Facebook's rules against hate speech by fanning paranoia about demographic change. Although Muslims made up no more than 5 percent of the country, a popular graphic on Facebook cautioned that "when Muslims become the most powerful" they will offer "Islam or the sword."

Beginning in 2013, a series of experts on Myanmar met with Facebook officials to warn them that the network was fueling attacks on the Rohingya. David Madden, an entrepreneur based in Myanmar, delivered a presentation to officials at the Menlo Park headquarters, pointing out that the company was playing a role akin to that of the radio broadcasts that spread hatred during the Rwandan genocide. In 2016, C4ADS, a Washington-based nonprofit, published a detailed analysis of Facebook usage in Myanmar, and described a "campaign of hate speech that actively dehumanizes Muslims." Facebook officials said that they were hiring more Burmese-language reviewers to take down dangerous content, but the company repeatedly declined to say how many had actually been hired. By 2018, the situation had become dire: almost a million Rohingya had fled the country, and more than a hundred thousand were confined to internal camps. The United Nations investigator in charge of examining the crisis, which the U.N. had deemed a genocide, said, "I'm afraid that Facebook has now turned into a beast, and not what it was originally intended." When pressed on the issue, Zuckerberg repeatedly said that Facebook was "hiring dozens" of additional Burmese-language content reviewers.

More than three months later, I asked Jes Kaliebe Petersen, the CEO of Phandeeyar, a tech hub in Myanmar, if there had been any progress. "We haven't seen any tangible change from Facebook," he told me. "We don't know how much content is being reported. We don't know how many people at Facebook speak Burmese. The situation is getting worse and worse here."

I saw Zuckerberg the following morning, and asked him what was taking so long. He replied, "I think, fundamentally, we've been slow at the same thing in a number of areas, because it's actually the same problem. But, yeah, I think the situation in Myanmar is terrible." It was a frustrating and evasive reply. I asked him to specify the problem. He said, "Across the board, the solution to this is we need to move from what is fundamentally a reactive model to a model where we are using technical systems to flag things to a much larger number of people who speak all the native languages around the world and who can just capture much more of the content."

I told him that people in Myanmar are incredulous that a company with Facebook's resources has failed to heed their complaints. "We're taking this seriously," he said. "You can't just snap your fingers and solve these problems. It takes time to hire the people and train them, and to build the systems that can flag stuff for them." He promised that Facebook would have "a hundred or more Burmese-speaking people by the end of the year," and added, "I hate that we're in this position where we are not moving as quickly as we would like." A few weeks after our conversation, Facebook announced that it was banning Myanmar's army chief and several other military officials.

Over the years, Zuckerberg had come to see his ability to reject complaints as a virtue. But, by 2016, that stance had primed the company for a crisis. Tristan Harris, the design ethicist, said, "When you're running anything like Facebook, you get criticized all the time, and you just stop paying attention to criticism if a lot of it is not well founded. You learn to treat it as naive and uninformed." He went on, "The problem is it also puts you out of touch with genuine criticism from people who actually understand the issues."

* * *

The 2016 election was supposed to be good for Facebook. That January, Sheryl Sandberg told investors that the election would generate "ad spend" comparable to the Super Bowl and the World Cup. Facebook offered to "embed" employees, for free, in presidential campaign offices to help them use the platform effectively. Clinton's campaign said no. Trump's said yes, and Facebook employees helped his campaign craft messages. Although Trump's language was openly hostile to ethnic minorities, inside Facebook his behavior felt, to some executives, like just part of the distant cesspool of Washington. Americans always seemed to be choosing between a hated Republican and a hated Democrat. Trump's team used Facebook to launch a voter-suppression effort targeting three Democratic constituencies—white liberals, young women, and African Americans—sending them videos precisely tailored to discourage them from turning out for Clinton. Theresa Hong, the Trump campaign's digital-content director, later told an interviewer, "Without Facebook we wouldn't have won."

After the election, Facebook executives fretted that the company would be blamed for the spread of fake news. Zuckerberg's staff gave him statistics showing that the vast majority of election information on the platform was legitimate. At a tech conference a few days later, Zuckerberg was defensive. "The idea that fake news on Facebook—of which, you know, it's a very small amount of the content—influenced the election in any way, I think, is a pretty crazy idea," he said. To some at Facebook, Zuckerberg's defensiveness was alarming. When I asked Zuckerberg about his "pretty crazy" comment, he said that he was wrong to have been "glib." He told me, "Nobody wants any amount of fake news. It is an issue on an ongoing basis, and we need to take that seriously." But he still bristled at the implication that Facebook may have distorted voter behavior. "I find the notion that people would only vote some way because they were tricked to be almost viscerally offensive," he said. "Because it goes against the whole notion that you should trust people and that individuals are smart and can understand their own experience and can make their own assessments about what direction they want their community to go in."

Shortly after the election, Mark Warner, the ranking Democrat on the Senate Intelligence Committee, contacted Facebook to discuss Russian interference. "The initial reaction was completely dismissive," he told me. But, by the spring, he sensed that the company was realizing that it had a serious problem. "They were seeing an enormous amount of Russian activity in the French elections," Warner said. "It was getting better, but I still don't think they were putting nearly enough resources behind this." Warner, who made a fortune in the telecom business, added, "Most of the companies in the Valley think that policymakers, one, don't get it, and, two, that ultimately, if they just stonewall us, then we'll go away."

Facebook moved fitfully to acknowledge the role it had played in the election. After Robert Mueller obtained a search warrant, Facebook agreed to give his office an inventory of ads linked to Russia and the details of who had paid for them. Russian operatives had published about eighty thousand Facebook posts, reaching 126 million Americans. But after the Cambridge Analytica news broke, Zuckerberg and Facebook were paralyzed. For five days, Zuckerberg said nothing. His personal Facebook profile had nothing fresher than a photo of him and Chan baking hamantaschen for Purim.

When I asked him about it later, he conceded, "I feel like we've let people down and that feels terrible." But he also suggested that the misinformation problem was overblown: "The average person might perceive, from how much we and others talk about it, that there is more than ten times as much misinformation or hoax content on Facebook than the academic measures that we've seen so far suggest." He was still unconvinced that the spread of misinformation had an impact on the election. He said, "I still think that's the kind of thing that needs to be studied."

In conversation, Zuckerberg is, unsurprisingly, highly analytical. When he encounters a theory that doesn't accord with his own, he finds a seam of disagreement—a fact, a methodology, a premise—and hammers at it. It's an effective technique for winning arguments, but one that makes it difficult to introduce new information. Over time, some former colleagues say, his deputies have begun to filter out bad news from presentations before it reaches him. A former Facebook official told me, "They only want to hear good news. They don't want people who are disagreeing with them. There is a culture of 'You go along to get along.'"

I once asked Zuckerberg what he reads to get the news. "I probably mostly read aggregators," he said. "I definitely follow Techmeme"— a roundup of headlines about his industry—"and the media and political equivalents of that, just for awareness." He went on, "There's really no newspaper that I pick up and read front to back. Well, that might be true of most people these days—most people don't read the physical paper— but there aren't many news websites where I go to browse." A couple of days later, he called me and asked to revisit the subject. "I felt like my answers were kind of vague, because I didn't necessarily feel like it was appropriate for me to get into which specific organizations or reporters I read and follow," he said. "I guess what I tried to convey, although I'm not sure if this came across clearly, is that the job of uncovering new facts and doing it in a trusted way is just an absolutely critical function for society."

Zuckerberg and Sandberg have attributed their mistakes to excessive optimism, a blindness to the darker applications of their service. But that explanation ignores their fixation on growth, and their unwillingness to heed warnings. Zuckerberg resisted calls to reorganize the company around a new understanding of privacy, or to reconsider the depth of data it collects for advertisers.

James P. Steyer, the founder and CEO of Common Sense Media, an organization that promotes safety in technology and media for children, visited Facebook's headquarters in the spring of 2018 to discuss his concerns about a product called Messenger Kids, which allowed children under thirteen to make video calls and send messages to contacts that a parent approves. He met with Sandberg and Elliot Schrage, at the time the head of policy and communications. "I respect their business success, and like Sheryl personally, and I was hoping they might finally consider taking steps to better protect kids. Instead, they said that the best thing for young kids was to spend more time on Messenger Kids," Steyer told me. "They still seemed to be in denial. Would you 'move fast and break things' when it comes to children? To our democracy? No, because you can damage them forever."

To some people in the company, the executives seemed concentrated not on solving the problems or on preventing the next ones but on containing the damage. Tavis McGinn, a former Google pollster, started working at Facebook in the spring of 2017, doing polls with a narrow focus: measuring the public perception of Zuckerberg and Sandberg. During the next six months, McGinn conducted eight surveys and four focus groups in three countries, collecting the kinds of measurements favored by politicians and advertisers. Facebook polled reactions to the company's new stated mission to "bring the world closer together," as well as to items on Zuckerberg's social media feed, including his writings, photographs, and even his casual banter during a backyard barbecue broadcast on Facebook Live.

In September, McGinn resigned. In interviews with the tech press, he said he had grown disheartened: "I couldn't change the values. I couldn't change the culture." He concluded that measuring the "true social outcomes" of Facebook was of limited interest to senior staffers. "I think research can be very powerful, if people are willing to listen," he said. "But I decided after six months that it was a waste of my time to be there." (McGinn, who signed a nondisclosure agreement with Facebook, declined my requests for comment.)

*   *   *

In 2018, Zuckerberg agreed to testify before Congress for the first time about Facebook's handling of user data. As the hearing approached, it acquired the overtones of a trial. In barely two years, the mood in Washington had shifted. Internet companies and entrepreneurs, formerly valorized as the vanguard of American ingenuity and the astronauts of our time, were being compared to Standard Oil and other monopolists of the Gilded Age. *The Wall Street Journal* published an article that began, "Imagine a not-too-distant future in which trustbusters force Facebook to sell off Instagram and WhatsApp." It was accompanied by a sepia-toned illustration in which portraits of Zuckerberg, Tim Cook, and other tech CEOs had been grafted onto overstuffed torsos meant to evoke the robber barons.

Tim Wu, a Columbia Law School professor and the author of a book inspired by Brandeis's warning about the "curse of bigness," told me, "Today, no sector exemplifies more clearly the threat of bigness to democracy than Big Tech." He added, "When a concentrated private power has such control over what we see and hear, it has a power that rivals or exceeds that of elected government."

Shortly before Zuckerberg was due to testify, a team from the Washington law firm of WilmerHale flew to Menlo Park to run him through mock hearings and to coach him on the requisite gestures of humility. Even before the recent scandals, Bill Gates had advised Zuckerberg to be alert to the opinions of lawmakers, a lesson that Gates had learned in 1998, when Microsoft faced accusations of monopolistic behavior. Gates testified to Congress, defiantly, that "the computer-software industry is not broken, and there is no need to fix it." Within months, the Department of Justice sued Microsoft for violating federal antitrust law, leading to three years of legal agony before a settlement was reached. Gates told me that he regretted "taunting" regulators, saying, "Not something I would choose to repeat." He encouraged Zuckerberg to be attentive to D.C. "I said, 'Get an office there—now.' And Mark did, and he owes me," Gates said. (In 2017, Facebook spent $11.5 million on lobbying in Washington, ranking it between the American Bankers Association and General Dynamics among top spenders.)

On April 10, when Zuckerberg arrived at the Senate hearing, he wore a somber blue suit, and took a seat before more than forty senators. Cameras caught an image of his notes, which outlined likely questions and answers, including the prospect that a senator might ask him to step down from the company. His answer, in shorthand, would be: "Founded Facebook. My decisions. I made mistakes. Big challenge, but we've solved problems before, going to solve this one. Already taking action."

As it turned out, nobody asked him to resign—or much of anything difficult. Despite scattered moments of pressure, the overwhelming impression left by the event was how poorly some senators grasped the issues. In the most revealing moment, Orrin Hatch, the eighty-four-year-old Republican from Utah, demanded to know how Facebook makes money if "users don't pay for your service." Zuckerberg replied, "Senator, we run ads," allowing a small smile.

To observers inclined to distrust Zuckerberg, he was evasive to the point of amnesiac—he said, more than forty times, that he would need to follow up—but when the hearing concluded, after five hours, he had emerged unscathed. Wall Street, watching closely, rewarded him by boosting the value of Facebook's stock by $20 billion. A few days later, on the internal Facebook message board, an employee wrote that he planned to print up T-shirts reading "Senator, we run ads."

*　　　　*　　　　*

Over time, a consensus took hold in Washington that regulators were unlikely to succeed in breaking up Facebook. The FTC would almost

certainly fine the company for violations, and might consider blocking it from buying big potential competitors, but, as a former FTC
commissioner told me, "in the United States you're allowed to have a
monopoly position, as long as you achieve it and maintain it without
doing illegal things."

But Facebook was encountering tougher treatment in Europe, where
antitrust laws are stronger and the history of fascism makes people
especially wary of intrusions on privacy. In 2017, after an investigation
of Google's search engine, the European Union's top antitrust regulator,
Margrethe Vestager, accused the company of giving an "illegal advantage" to its shopping service and fined it $2.7 billion, at that time the
largest fine ever imposed by the E.U. in an antitrust case. The following
year, she added another $5 billion fine for the company's practice of
requiring device makers to preinstall Google apps.

In Brussels, Vestager was a high-profile presence—nearly six feet
tall, with short black-and-silver hair. She grew up in rural Denmark,
the eldest child of two Lutheran pastors, and, when I spoke to her, she
talked about her enforcement powers in philosophical terms. "What
we're dealing with, when people start doing something illegal, is exactly
as old as Adam and Eve," she said. "Human decisions very often are
guided by greed, by fear of being pushed out of the marketplace, or of
losing something that's important to you. And then, if you throw power
into that cocktail of greed and fear, you have something that you can
recognize throughout time."

Vestager told me that her office had no open cases involving Facebook, but she expressed concern that the company was taking advantage
of users, beginning with terms of service that she called "unbalanced."
Imagine, she said, if a brick-and-mortar business asked to copy all your
photographs for its unlimited, unspecified uses. "Your children, from
the very first day until the confirmation, the rehearsal dinner for the
wedding, the wedding itself, the first child being baptized. You would
never accept that," she said. "But this is what you accept without a blink
of an eye when it's digital."

In Vestager's view, a healthy market should produce competitors to Facebook that position themselves as ethical alternatives, collecting less data and seeking a smaller share of user attention. "We need social media that will allow us to have a nonaddictive, advertising-free space," she said. "You're more than welcome to be successful and to dramatically outgrow your competitors if customers like your product. But, if you grow to be dominant, you have a special responsibility not to misuse your dominant position."

*　　　*　　　*

The cult of growth had led to the curse of bigness: every day, a billion things were being posted to Facebook. At any given moment, a Facebook "content moderator" was deciding whether a post in, say, Sri Lanka met the standard of hate speech or whether a dispute over Korean politics had crossed the line into bullying. Zuckerberg sought to avoid banning users, preferring to be a "platform for all ideas." But he needed to prevent Facebook from becoming a swamp of hoaxes and abuse. His solution was to ban "hate speech" and impose lesser punishments for "misinformation," a broad category that ranged from crude deceptions to simple mistakes.

Facebook tried to develop rules about how the punishments would be applied, but each idiosyncratic scenario prompted more rules, and over time they became byzantine. According to Facebook training slides leaked in 2017, moderators were told that it was permissible to say "You are such a Jew" but *not* permissible to say "Irish are the best, but really French sucks," because the latter was defining another people as "inferiors." Users could not write "Migrants are scum," because it was dehumanizing, but they could write "Keep the horny migrant teenagers away from our daughters." The distinctions were explained to trainees in arcane formulas such as "Not Protected + Quasi Protected = Not Protected."

But that calculus of content was reaching its limits. Facebook had long resisted requests to ban the conspiracy theorist Alex Jones, who promoted the lie that parents of children killed in the Sandy Hook school massacre were paid actors with an anti-gun agenda. In response to complaints, Facebook tweaked the algorithm so that Jones's messages would be shown to fewer people, while feeding his fans articles that fact-checked his assertions, but he remained on Facebook. In July 2018, the parents of Noah Pozner, a child killed at Sandy Hook, published an open letter addressed "Dear Mr Zuckerberg," in which they described "living in hiding" because of death threats from conspiracy theorists, after "an almost inconceivable battle with Facebook to provide us with the most basic of protections." In their view, Zuckerberg had "deemed that the attacks on us are immaterial, that providing assistance in removing threats is too cumbersome, and that our lives are less important than providing a safe haven for hate."

Facebook took down some of Jones's videos and suspended him temporarily. Eventually, only after Apple stopped distributing Jones's podcasts, Facebook shut down four of Jones's pages on the grounds of hate speech and bullying. I asked Zuckerberg why Facebook had wavered in its handling of the situation. He was prickly about the suggestion: "I don't believe that it is the right thing to ban a person for saying something that is factually incorrect."

Jones seemed a lot more than factually incorrect, I said.

"OK, but I think the facts here are pretty clear," he said, homing in. "The initial questions were around misinformation." He added, "We don't take it down and ban people unless it's directly inciting violence." He told me that when Apple announced its ban, Facebook was still gathering information. Zuckerberg said, "When they moved, it was, like, OK, we shouldn't just be sitting on this content and these enforcement decisions. We should move on what we know violates the policy. We need to make a decision now."

Facebook's free speech dilemmas have no simple answers—even the fiercest critic of Alex Jones might be unnerved by the company's extraordinary power to silence a voice when it chooses, or, for that matter, to amplify others, to pull the levers of what we see, hear, and experience. Zuckerberg was hoping to erect a scalable system, an orderly decision tree that accounts for every eventuality and exception, but the boundaries of speech are a bedeviling problem that defies mechanistic fixes. The Supreme Court, defining obscenity, landed on "I know it when I see it." Facebook was making do with a Rube Goldberg machine of policies and improvisations, and opportunists were relishing it. Senator Ted Cruz, Republican of Texas, seized on the ban of Jones as a fascist assault on conservatives. In a moment that was rich even by Cruz's standards, he quoted Martin Niemöller's famous lines about the Holocaust, saying, "As the poem goes, you know, 'First they came for Alex Jones.'"

For the moment, the company was proclaiming its growing powers of fact-checking. "We now have over twenty thousand people and we are able to review reports in fifty languages, twenty-four hours a day," Sandberg told the Senate Intelligence Committee. But many people in Silicon Valley believed that, ultimately, Sandberg and Facebook's board of directors had to find ways of balancing or curbing Zuckerberg's power, if only to prevent his idiosyncratic vision from leading the company into other mistakes. "I know a couple of guys who are color-blind," a prominent executive told me, "and their wives lay their clothes out for them in the morning if they don't want to go out every day looking like Bozo the Clown. Sheryl and the board are expected to lay the clothes out for Mark." He went on, "If you have blind spots, then you rely on the people around you to tell you where they are."

*   *   *

In one of our conversations, I asked Zuckerberg whether he finds it insulting when people speculate that he lacks emotions. "Insulting?" he asked, and then paused for several seconds to consider. "I don't find it insulting. I don't think it's accurate. I mean, I definitely care a lot. There's a difference between letting emotions drive impulsive decisions and caring." He went on, "Ultimately, I think the reason that we built this successful thing is because we just solve problem after problem after problem, and typically you don't do that by making impulsive, emotional decisions."

The caricature of Zuckerberg is that of an automaton with little regard for the human dimensions of his work. The truth is something else: he decided long ago that no historical change is painless. Like Augustus, he is at peace with his trade-offs. Between speech and truth, he chose speech. Between speed and perfection, he chose speed. Between scale and safety, he chose scale. His life thus far has convinced him that he can solve "problem after problem after problem," no matter the howling from the public it may cause.

At a certain point, the habits of mind that served Zuckerberg well on his ascent will start to work against him. To avoid further crises, he will have to embrace the fact that he's now a protector of the peace, not a disrupter of it. Facebook's colossal power of persuasion has delivered fortune but also peril. Like it or not, Zuckerberg is a gatekeeper. The era when Facebook could learn by doing, and fix the mistakes later, is over. The costs are too high, and idealism is not a defense against negligence.

In some sense, the "Mark Zuckerberg production"—as he called Facebook in its early years—has only just begun. At the time of this writing, Zuckerberg is not yet thirty-five, and the ambition with which he built his empire could well be directed toward shoring up his company, his country, and his name. The question is not whether Zuckerberg has the power to fix Facebook but whether he has the will; whether he will kick people out of his office—with the gusto that he once mustered for growth—if they don't bring him ideas for preventing violence, or protecting privacy, or mitigating the toxicity of social media. He succeeded, long ago, in making Facebook great. The challenge before him now is to make it good.

———————

In July 2019, the Federal Trade Commission fined Facebook $5 billion, the largest penalty ever imposed on a company for violating consumer privacy. The financial effect was immaterial; in 2021, Facebook's valuation surpassed $1 trillion; that year, it changed its name to Meta, reflecting Zuckerberg's interest in "building the metaverse," where human beings interact in virtual reality. The strategy did not succeed; in 2022, citing various factors, Meta embarked on mass layoffs, shedding a fifth of its workforce in less than three years.

Zuckerberg's politics appeared to change sharply. Before the 2020 election, he and Chan had donated $400 million to promote safe voting during the pandemic. But Trump repeatedly criticized that donation, claiming it was a form of election interference that aided Democrats. When Trump ran again in 2024, he warned that if Zuckerberg "does anything illegal this time he will spend the rest of his life in prison." By then, Zuckerberg was taking pains to project a personal evolution. He stopped funding progressive causes, posted videos of himself wearing camouflage or practicing martial arts, grew out his hair, donned a gold chain, and told friends he was a libertarian. He publicly praised Trump's recovery from an assassination attempt as "badass," and visited Mar-a-Lago, where he reportedly promised changes to his businesses.

In 2025, Zuckerberg posted a video in which he embraced Trump's criticism of content moderation as "censorship" and announced an end to the third-party fact-checking once intended to curb disinformation in politics and violence in places such as Myanmar. He promoted a Republican operative to his policy chief and named Dana White, a Trump ally who heads the Ultimate Fighting Championship, to Meta's board of directors. By 2025, Zuckerberg's net worth had surpassed $200 billion, ranking him the world's second or third richest person, depending on daily stock performance. Meta's audience continued to grow; more than 3.3 billion people use at least one of its apps every day.

The Greenwich Rebellion

How country-club Republicans learned to ignore
their neighbors and love Trump

— 2020 —

Prescott Bush, the father and grandfather of future presidents, was the eight-time club champion on the golf course at the Round Hill Club, one of eight country clubs in Greenwich, Connecticut. Bush was a staunch believer in standards; he required his sons to wear a jacket and tie for dinner at home. He was tall, restrained, and prone to righteousness; friends called him a "Ten Commandments man." In the locker room at Round Hill, someone once told an off-color joke in front of his fourteen-year-old son, George H. W. Bush, and Prescott stormed out, saying, "I don't ever want to hear that kind of language in here again."

In Greenwich, which had an unusually high number of powerful citizens, even by the standards of New York suburbs, Prescott Bush cast a large shadow; he was an investment banker, the moderator of the town council, and, from 1952 to 1963, a United States senator. In Washington, he was President Eisenhower's golf partner, and the embodiment of what Ike called "modern Republicanism." Prescott wanted government lean and efficient, but, like Nelson Rockefeller, the New York governor whose centrism inspired the label Rockefeller Republican, he was more liberal than his party on civil rights, birth control, and welfare. He denounced his fellow-Republican Joseph McCarthy for creating "dangerous divisions among the American people" and for demanding that Congress follow him "blindly, not daring to express any doubts or disagreements." Bush could be ludicrously aristocratic—his grandchildren called him Senator—but he believed, fundamentally, in the duty of government to help people who did not enjoy his considerable advantages. He supported increasing the federal minimum wage and immigration quotas, and he beseeched fellow-senators, for the sake of science, education, and defense, to "have the courage to raise the required revenues by approving whatever levels of taxation may be necessary."

Long after Bush died in 1972, his family stayed central to the community of Greenwich Republicans. His son Prescott Jr., known as Pressy, served as the chairman of the Republican Town Committee; alumni of the Bush administrations still live around town. Each year, the highest honor bestowed by the Connecticut Republican Party is the Prescott Bush Award.

When Donald Trump ran for president, he was hardly a natural heir to the Greenwich Republican tradition. In the 1980s, he bought a mansion on the town's waterfront, but he did not often observe the prim Yankee ethic inscribed on the Greenwich coat of arms: *fortitudine et frugalitate*—courage and thrift. Locals were embarrassed by the house's gilded décor, and, after he and his wife Ivana divorced, she sold it. When George H. W. Bush called for a "kinder, gentler nation," Trump responded, "If this country gets any kinder or gentler, it's literally going to cease to exist." In early 2016, even before Trump was asserting his right to "locker-room talk," he was denounced in *Greenwich Time*, the town's daily newspaper, by Leora Levy, a prominent local fundraiser. "He is vulgar, ill-mannered and disparages those whom he cannot intimidate," she wrote. Levy—who went on to win the Prescott Bush Award—was lending her support to Prescott's grandson Jeb Bush, the former governor of Florida.

But not everyone in Greenwich was excited about Jeb. Jim Campbell was the chairman of the Republican Town Committee. The Campbells, like the Bushes, had deep roots in town. Jim prepped at Exeter and graduated from Harvard and Harvard Law School, before working in Europe and returning home as a real estate executive. On a fall evening, Campbell attended a reception for Jeb Bush at the Belle Haven Club, a private tennis-and-boating club overlooking Long Island Sound. Jeb was expansive and mild, which struck Campbell as precisely wrong for the political moment: "He gave a whole talk about a woman named Juanita in South Florida, and how 'immigration is love,' and I just looked at the people I came with and said, 'Does he think he's already the nominee? He's running in a tough Republican primary, and just because we're at the Belle Haven Club doesn't mean we're all voting for him.'"

At home one night, watching television, Campbell happened on a Trump rally in Iowa. "I'm not a hard-core conservative—I'm a Republican from Greenwich," Campbell said. "But I listened, and he had that line that he would use: 'Folks, we either have a country or we don't.' And I felt the chill—like Chris Matthews with the little Obama zing up the leg. I'm, like, 'Oh, my God, this is a really good line.'" To Campbell, Trump was describing immigration in ways that resonated: "Could somebody finally say that we're allowed to enforce the law at the border without being called a racist? I lived in Switzerland for ten years. Do you think I was allowed to go around without a passport?"

Campbell tapped out a text message to a friend: "Trump live - can't turn the channel. Unbelievable. I don't think any R can beat him." Campbell watched the rally for forty-five minutes. "He was mesmerizing," he said. Not long afterward, he saw a Republican debate in which Trump described the invasion of Iraq as a mistake. For Campbell, the acknowledgment came as a catharsis. "Of course it was a big, fat mistake," he told himself. "He says everything I think."

In early 2016, Campbell attended a dinner for Republicans at the Delamar Greenwich Harbor, a Mediterranean-themed boutique hotel that is popular with local finance executives. After a dinner speaker mocked the notion of building a wall and imposing tariffs, Campbell raised his hand: "I said, 'With all due respect, why is it that we're not allowed to support a candidate who supports the things that you just ticked off?'" Campbell knew that his question would cause a stir, but he had decided that it was time "to let everybody know who I was supporting." When the event was over, he discovered that he was not alone: "I had four guys make a beeline for me, Wall Streeters, all saying, 'What can we do? Can I sign up? Are you organizing?'"

In February 2016, with Jeb still vying for the nomination, Campbell endorsed Trump. "I just think there's a lot of people supporting Donald and don't want to say so," he told a local reporter. That spring, as Connecticut Republicans prepared to vote in their primary, political observers predicted that John Kasich, the moderate governor of Ohio, would prevail in towns and cities from Greenwich to Fairfield—a stretch of American bounty known as the Gold Coast. Instead, Trump largely dominated the region.

Four years later, Trump signs remained scarce in Greenwich (population 62,600), but his supporters were easy to find. There was the first selectman—the local equivalent of mayor—and the chairman of the Greenwich finance board, as well as an ardent backer who served in the state House of Representatives. Some local Republicans helped fund Trump's inauguration, and some joined his White House, including Linda McMahon, the former professional wrestling executive who headed the Small Business Administration, and Hope Hicks, Trump's longtime communications adviser. (She once captained the Greenwich high school lacrosse team.) Others in town had abandoned their objections to Trump. Leora Levy, who had called him vulgar in the local paper, took to applauding his "leadership" and quoting him on social media, where she adopted some of his rhetorical style. "AMERICA WILL NEVER BE A SOCIALIST COUNTRY!!!" she posted. "WE ARE BORN FREE AND WILL STAY FREE!!!" In 2019, Trump nominated her to be the ambassador to Chile.

*   *   *

How did America's country-club Republicans, the cultural descendants of Prescott Bush, learn to love Donald Trump? They didn't have much in common with the clichéd image of his admirers: anxious about losing status to minorities, resentful of imperious elites, and marooned in places where life expectancy had fallen. But the full picture has never been that simple. As early as May 2016, exit polls and other data showed that Trump supporters earned an average of $72,000 a year, while supporters of Hillary Clinton earned $11,000 less. Two-thirds of Trump's supporters had incomes higher than the national median—sometimes, as in Greenwich, much higher.

I grew up in Greenwich, on Round Hill Road, not far from the club where Prescott Bush stormed out of the locker room. My great-grandparents Albert and Linda Sherer moved to town from Chicago in 1937. Albert was a Republican who worked in advertising for the National Biscuit Company, and Linda raised their two children. They were renters until 1968, when they bought a white Colonial with a wide lawn. The house passed down through the generations, and when I was ten years old my parents moved the family from Brooklyn to Greenwich, into a world of uncountable advantages. In 1994, I graduated from Greenwich High School, which is the rare public school that has a championship water polo team and an electron microscope. (It was a donation, obtained by an award-winning science teacher.)

People around town have never much cared for caricatures of the place—the starchy patricians, the chinless wonders, the history of exclusion—even when there is truth in them. For decades, many African Americans and Jews were prevented from buying homes. In 1975, protesters came to town with signs reading "Cocktail bigots" and "Share the summer," because Greenwich barred nonresidents from a public beach—a restriction that lasted until the state Supreme Court overturned it in 2001. Nobody pretends that bigotry has vanished, but these days the town has more diversity than outsiders expect. Thirty-eight percent of its public school students are minorities, mostly Latino;

in some elementary schools, at least half the students qualify for free or reduced-price lunch. Many of their parents work in local service jobs, bearing high rents and expenses in order to access some of the country's best public schools. Frank Farricker, a real estate developer and a Democratic activist, said, "I tell everybody that Greenwich only discriminates on the basis of one color: green."

The seacoast of Fairfield County has always been one of America's most affluent places, but in recent decades it has sprinted ahead of the rest of the country. In 2016, according to federal estimates, it was the wealthiest metropolitan area in the United States, outstripping the oil country of Midland, Texas, and the technology hub of San Francisco. Even though a string of tycoons have fled Connecticut in search of lower taxes, the latest *Forbes* ranking of the world's billionaires lists fifteen of them in the "Greater Greenwich Area," led by Ray Dalio, the founder of the hedge fund Bridgewater, who is worth an estimated $18 billion.

From afar, it is easy to misread the politics of the place: like much of America's coasts, the Gold Coast has swung left, culturally and politically, since the days of Prescott Bush. The largest share of voters in Greenwich today are unaffiliated; Republicans still hold an edge over Democrats, but the margin is less than four thousand registered voters. In 2016, nobody was surprised that Clinton beat Trump in Greenwich, 57 percent to 39. But that portrait—of liberal cosmopolitans appalled by Trump—obscures a potent element of American politics: the executive class of the Republican Party. Its members are wealthier, more conservative, and more politically active than their forebears, in ways that have helped Trump reach the White House, survive impeachment, and fortify his bid for reelection during the anguish of the coronavirus pandemic. Understanding how he retained the overwhelming support of Republicans required an accounting of not only what he promised Americans at the bottom but also what he provides Americans at the top.

The story of Trump's rise is often told as a hostile takeover. In truth, it is something closer to a joint venture, in which members of America's elite accepted the terms of Trumpism as the price of power. Long before anyone imagined that Trump might become president, a generation of unwitting patrons paved the way for him. From Greenwich and places like it, they launched a set of financial, philanthropic, and political projects that have changed American ideas about government, taxes, and the legitimacy of the liberal state.

The former congressman Christopher Shays is a moderate Republican who was elected eleven times to represent the Gold Coast, from 1987 to 2009. Now conservatives mock him as a RINO—a Republican in name only. "When Sean Hannity calls someone like me a RINO, I want to punch him in the nose," Shays told me. "I got elected as a Republican for thirty-four effing years, and Hannity has never gotten elected for anything." When Shays talks to former staff and constituents in Connecticut, he has come to recognize the delicate language of accommodation: "I was talking to a guy I know well, after some pathetic thing that Trump did, and his response was 'Yes, but he's selecting the right Supreme Court justices.' I started to laugh at him, because I know for a fact that's a minor issue for him." Shays believes that many Americans quietly share Trump's desire to reduce immigration and cut social welfare programs for the poor. "He's saying what people think, and they appreciate that," Shays said. "But not many are going to admit that's why they support him."

When it comes to the essential question—will Trump get reelected?—the answer rests heavily on a persistent mystery: How many Americans plan to vote for him but wouldn't say so to a pollster? In Greenwich, Edward Dadakis, a corporate insurance broker who has been involved with Republican politics for fifty years, told me that many of his friends are "below the radar screen." He went on, "In a sense, I'm one of them. I'm out there in the public domain, so people know where I stand, but in 2016, for the first election ever, I did not put a bumper sticker on my car." He worries how strangers will react. He said, "I still have two 'Make America Great Again' hats at home, wrapped in plastic."

*   *   *

The southern panhandle of Connecticut is cradled between the gray-blue waters of Long Island Sound and the wooded border of New York State. In politics and in culture, it's a mashup of New England and New York, a place settled by Puritans who agonized over what the historian Missy Wolfe calls "the proper balance between their flock's economic success and the level of success that they deemed would offend God." Long after the Puritans were gone, the tension remained in a seesaw-ing battle between the Brahmin and the buccaneer, service and profit, restraint and greed. For much of the twentieth century, the Brahmin had the advantage.

In 1927, Owen D. Young, a Greenwich resident who was the first chairman of General Electric, gave a speech at Harvard Business School, in which he scolded businessmen who "devise ways and means to squeeze out of labor its last ounce of effort and last penny of compensation." He encouraged them instead to "think in terms of human beings—one group of human beings who put their capital in, and another group who put their lives and labor in a common enterprise for mutual advantage." Rick Wartzman, a longtime head of the Drucker Institute and a histo-rian of corporate behavior, told me, "This really was beyond rhetoric. We were much more of a 'we' culture than an 'I' culture." On Young's watch, G.E. became one of the first American companies to give workers a pension, profit-sharing, life insurance, medical coverage, loans, and housing assistance.

Greenwich was home to a community of progressive journalists and authors, including Lincoln Steffens, Anya Seton, and Munro Leaf. But it was most popular with executives—at General Electric, Tex-aco, U.S. Tobacco—who were fleeing high income taxes in New York. Other residents served as their investment bankers, a cohort that was, by today's standards, almost unrecognizably buttoned-down. By and large, local Republicans had come to accept the expansion of govern-ment under Franklin D. Roosevelt and were concerned mainly with avoiding excesses and insolvency. Showing off your money was déclassé. At Morgan Stanley, executives competed to see who could wear the cheapest watch. "Some of the wealthiest people went around dressed like gardeners," a friend of mine who grew up in Darien recalled.

One of America's most powerful capitalists, Reginald Jones, who became G.E.'s chairman and CEO in 1972, lived in a modest brick Colonial in Greenwich. His daughter, Grace Vineyard, told me, "He asked my mom, 'Do you want anything more?' And she said, 'Why would we want anything more?'" Leo Hindery worked for Jones as a junior executive. "I earned fifteen thousand six hundred dollars when I got out of Stanford, and Reg's salary was two hundred thousand dollars," Hindery said. "G.E. was the preeminent company in America, and the CEO was making twelve or thirteen times what I did." According to the Economic Policy Institute, that ratio wasn't unusual: in 1965, the CEO of an average large public company earned about twenty times as much as a front-line worker. Today, that figure is 278 times.

*　　　*　　　*

The moderate consensus was always shakier than it looked, and by the mid-1960s it was gyrating out of control. In 1955, William F. Buckley Jr. had established his magazine *National Review* on the principle that government exists only "to protect its citizens' lives, liberty and property. All other activities of government tend to diminish freedom and hamper progress." It was the opening shot of the modern conservative movement, though, on the whole, liberal intellectuals did not regard it as a serious challenge. In 1963, John Kenneth Galbraith, the liberal economist and adviser to the Kennedys, mocked the modern conservative for being engaged in "one of man's oldest, best financed, most applauded, and, on the whole, least successful exercises in moral philosophy. That is, the search for a truly superior moral justification for selfishness."

In Greenwich, however, some people were seized by the new conservatism. J. William Middendorf II was a Harvard-educated investment banker who had served on the town council with Prescott Bush, his friend and neighbor. "I sold him a piece of land at the foot of my property," Middendorf told me. When he retired to his porch in the evening, he could hear the Bushes singing Yale songs in their backyard. But beneath the similarities, Middendorf had adopted a strikingly different ideology; he had become, in his words, a "disciple" of the libertarian movement, enthralled by Friedrich Hayek and Joseph Schumpeter. He condemned Eisenhower's moderates for regarding government as "a working tool that should be used to shape society." Instead, he wrote, "I believe that society is shaped by individuals."

Middendorf wanted to push libertarianism into mainstream politics, and he found a vehicle in Barry Goldwater, the fiery Arizona senator. Goldwater, the heir to a department store fortune in Phoenix, ran for president in 1964, fueled by what he described as "my resentment against the New Deal." Goldwater's campaign was a backlash against liberalism—the antiwar movement, civil rights, welfare—but also against moderate Republicans. Nelson Rockefeller was a "cardboard candidate," Middendorf told me. "He could speak for an hour, but I honestly could not remember a single word he ever said." Middendorf became Goldwater's campaign treasurer, raising money from other well-to-do dissidents of the East Coast establishment. "He was obviously out of the mainstream, and we had an uphill battle," he said.

They prevailed that summer at the Republican National Convention in San Francisco. Rockefeller made a desperate last attempt for relevance: from the lectern, he denounced the advent of a "radical" right-wing element within the party, in the hope that the moderates would rise up and resist. Instead, the hall erupted in boos. Jackie Robinson, the Black baseball star and an avatar of integration among Republicans, heard the catcalls and felt, as he said later, like "a Jew in Hitler's Germany." Middendorf, who was also in attendance, received Rockefeller's denunciation as an affirmation. "He was talking about me and my friends," he wrote in *Potomac Fever*, his political memoir.

In the general election, Goldwater lost—spectacularly—to Lyndon Johnson. But his brand of libertarian, antitax absolutism found a fervent audience among American executives who were confronting an alarming change: after a quarter century of relentless growth, American profits were declining. Japan and Western Europe, finally rebuilt after the Second World War, were formidable new competitors; the Arab oil shock of 1973 triggered the longest recession since the 1930s. Moreover, the environmental and consumer protection movements had hastened new regulations, on products ranging from flammable fabrics to cigarettes and bank loans.

Executives felt besieged. "They decided regulation was mostly to blame," the historian Rick Perlstein writes in *Reaganland*. In Perlstein's telling, "the denizens of America's better boardrooms, who had once comported themselves with such ideological gentility, began behaving like the legendary Jacobins of the French Revolution. They declared war without compromise." Back home in Greenwich, Middendorf—who went on to work in the Nixon, Ford, and Reagan administrations—gloried in having vanquished the moderates. He wrote, "We created the conditions that put conservative Republicans back in power after more than thirty years of domination by the liberal eastern establishment—the so-called 'Country Club' Republicans."

*   *   *

A short drive from the Round Hill Club, in a Georgian manor overlooking a lake, lived Lee and Allie Hanley, who were early converts to the conservative movement. Lee had graduated from St. Paul's and from Yale, where he played polo, squash, and soccer, and he had taken over Hanley Co., his family's brick-and-oil business. He was a bon vivant, with a fondness for salmon-colored slacks, and a ready checkbook for political ventures. "Very warm and engaging," a Greenwich friend said. "A collector of curiosities, a Renaissance man at sort of a superficial level. More of a gut player who wanted to be in the game." Allie was a devout Christian with a keen interest in politics. The 1980 Republican primary was shaping up to be a contest between the old Republican

Party and the new—the local son, George H. W. Bush, a Washington insider known around town as Poppy, versus Ronald Reagan, the conservative governor of California. On that question, the Hanleys broke with their neighbors in Greenwich. "For us, it was never Bush country," Allie told me. "It was always Reagan country."

Roger Stone, who was Reagan's campaign director for the Northeastern states, recalled that most people in Greenwich recoiled from his candidate: "They thought, Reagan, oh, my God, he's another Goldwater. He has no chance in the general election. He's a cowboy-movie actor." (Stone, who later became a Trump confidant, spoke to me before he was convicted of lying to Congress during Robert Mueller's investigation.) "Hanley was the only high WASP we had," Stone continued. "All the 'right' people were for Poppy."

The Hanleys, hoping to spread their enthusiasm in Greenwich, agreed to host a reception at their home. But when they met Reagan to discuss the plans over lunch at the Pierre Hotel, Allie saw a problem. "He had on a brown tie, and it was ghastly," she told me. "When you go to a different part of the country, the most important thing you need to do is dress like they do. They feel more comfortable talking to you. So I ran to Bloomingdale's, and I bought four ties." When the Reagans turned up for the party, Allie said, "Here's a gift for you! Go upstairs and freshen up." Reagan came back down a few minutes later, and the offending tie had been replaced by her gift. "He wore it on all the posters after that," she said.

Stone and Lee Hanley adopted an approach that uncannily prefigured Trump's electoral strategy: they built a coalition of conservative elites and the white working class. Hanley introduced Stone to small-business owners in Greenwich, many of them Italian American—"mining for Catholic votes," as Stone called it. "Lee was very well connected with the merchants in town—the grocer, the butcher," Stone said. "He could talk to anybody. He was not stuffy like some WASPs." Hanley told Stone before one visit, "We're going to have to drink some espresso, but we can get them." The strategy worked; in the Connecticut primary, Reagan beat Bush in the Bush-family stronghold of the southern panhandle. In 1984, Reagan rewarded Hanley by nominating him to the board of the Corporation for Public Broadcasting. Two years later, he became the chairman.

In the next three decades, Hanley and other wealthy conservatives— Richard Scaife, John Olin, the Koch brothers—helped train a generation of Republicans in Congress to adhere to ideological orthodoxy. Hanley made a string of historic political investments. He saved Regnery, America's most prominent conservative book publisher, with a crucial infusion of cash. He helped found the Yankee Institute for Public Policy, the Connecticut affiliate of a network of think tanks that advocate for low taxes and small government. He became the principal backer of a political consulting firm formed by Stone and two other young Reaganites, Charlie Black and Paul Manafort. "We had the credentials and the potential business and all that, but we didn't have any money," Black told me. "Lee was a good friend, so we approached him." Black, Manafort & Stone, as they called themselves, became pioneering lobbyists, known for their brazen use of what Manafort described as "influence peddling." Clients included Rupert Murdoch's News Corp. and a young real estate developer named Donald Trump.

By the end of the century, the courtly politics of Prescott Bush were gone, a change accelerated by the decisions of his son George H. W. Bush. George had inherited his father's restraint—at school in Greenwich, he was nicknamed Have-Half, for his willingness to share—and also the family tradition of public service. But running for president in 1988, Bush unleashed his brawling campaign manager Lee Atwater on the governor of Massachusetts, Michael Dukakis. Atwater vowed to "strip the bark off the little bastard." In the most searing moment, a political action committee linked to the Bush campaign paid for a television ad blaming Dukakis for the case of Willie Horton, a convict who had committed rape during a furlough from a Massachusetts prison. The ad crudely exploited white fears, showing pictures of Horton, who was African American, while a narrator spoke of kidnapping, rape, and murder. Atwater denied any involvement in the ad, but Bush recognized the power of the rhetoric, and took to mentioning Horton almost daily on the stump. Atwater boasted that he would make Horton "Dukakis's running mate."

Not long before Atwater died, in 1991, he apologized to Dukakis for the "naked cruelty" of that campaign. But the Willie Horton strategy was the forerunner of a more savage era in American politics—of Swift Boat attacks on a war hero; of the racist birther fiction against America's first Black president—and it pushed candidates to avoid looking weak by advancing tough-on-crime policies that both parties now view as devastating for low-income and minority Americans.

In the end, Bush was "a gentleman, but he was a politician, too," his biographer Jon Meacham wrote. For all Bush's decency, he had decided early on that, in order to serve, he needed to win. In a tape-recorded diary entry near the end of the 1988 campaign, Bush told himself, "The country gets over these things fast. I have no apologies, no regrets, and if I had let the press keep defining me as a wimp, a loser, I wouldn't be where I am today."

*   *   *

In the early years of this century, the economic divisions that would come to define America in the age of Trump became evident on the lush back roads of Greenwich, in a sign so subtle that it was easy to miss. Many of the new estates going up were no longer surrounded by the simple stone walls, stacked to the height of a farmer's hip, that crossed the New England landscape. Instead, the builders introduced a more imposing barrier: tall, stately walls of chiseled stone, mortared in place.

The fashion for higher walls had little to do with safety; Greenwich has one of the lowest crime rates in America. To Frank Farricker, who served on the town's planning-and-zoning commission, they symbol-ized power and seclusion. "Instead of building two or three feet high, people got into six-footers—the 'Fuck you' walls," he said. When nearby municipalities noticed the trend, they treated it like an invasive species; they rewrote zoning rules to prevent the spread of what stonemasons took to calling "Greenwich walls."

The walls were products of one of the most extraordinary accumulations of wealth in American history. In much of the country, the corporate convulsions of the 1970s had entailed layoffs, offshoring, and declining union power, but on Wall Street they inspired a surge of creativity. Since the 1700s, Wall Street had focused mostly on funneling American savings into new businesses and mortgages. But in the last two decades of the twentieth century, financiers and economists opened vast new realms of speculation and financial engineering—aggressive methods to bet on securities, merge businesses, and cut expenses using bankruptcy laws. U.S. stock markets grew twelvefold, and most of the gains accrued to the wealthiest Americans. By 2017, Wall Streeters were taking home 23 percent of the country's corporate profits—and home, for many of them, was Connecticut.

The internet allowed financiers to work from anywhere, so some escaped New York's higher taxes by relocating their offices closer to where they lived. Newspapers took to calling Greenwich the "Hedge Fund Capital of the World." The dealmakers earned vastly more than the industrial executives they had replaced. In 2004, *Institutional Investor* reported that the top twenty-five hedge fund managers earned an average of $207 million a year.

Nine of those top managers lived or worked in Greenwich, led by Edward Lampert, who in 2004 earned an estimated $1.02 billion after orchestrating the merger of Kmart and Sears. Lampert was not one to dress like a gardener; just offshore, he docked his yacht, a 288-foot vessel that he had named *Fountainhead*, for Ayn Rand's individualist fable. (Trump has said that he identifies with the book's hero, Howard Roark, a designer of skyscrapers who declares, "I do not recognize anyone's right to one minute of my life. . . . No matter who makes the claim, how large their number, or how great their need.") So much individual wealth accumulated in southern Connecticut that tax officials took to monitoring the quarterly payments of a half-dozen of the richest taxpayers, because their personal earnings would affect how much the entire state was able to spend on public services.

Around town, Morgan Stanley executives no longer competed to wear the cheapest wristwatch. (A recent chairman and CEO, James Gorman, was celebrated on watch enthusiast blogs for a rare Rolex that can sell for $17,000.) Jack Welch, who succeeded Reginald Jones at G.E., retired in 2001 with a record severance package of more than $400 million. One of Jones's friends, the investor Vincent Mai, was dismayed that many business leaders put short-term interests ahead of long-term vision. "The culture changed into grabbing as much as you can, as quickly as you can," Mai, the founder and chairman of the Cranemere Group, told me. "Restraint just seems to have gone out the window."

The money physically redrew Greenwich, as financiers built estates on a scale once favored by Gilded Age railroad barons. The hedge fund manager Steven A. Cohen paid $14.8 million in cash for a house, then added an ice rink, an indoor basketball court, putting greens, a fairway, and a massage room, ultimately swelling the building to 36,000 square feet—larger than the Taj Mahal. In a final flourish, Cohen obtained special permission to surround his estate with a wall that exceeded the town's limits on height. It was nine feet tall.

*   *   *

When the tide began to turn against Wall Street, you could follow it from my family's front door. Up and down Round Hill Road, neighbors became known for one imbroglio after another. If you took a right turn out of our driveway, you could wander by the stone Colonial house of Walter Noel, a money manager with a gracious Nashville accent, who funneled billions of his clients' dollars to the grifter Bernie Madoff. (Noel claimed that he, too, was duped.) If you turned left, you reached

the estate of the hedge fund manager Raj Rajaratnam, who once celebrated his birthday by flying in Kenny Rogers to sing "The Gambler"
over and over, until Rogers finally refused. In 2009, Rajaratnam was
arrested as part of a stock-cheating case that the FBI called Operation
Perfect Hedge. He was given a sentence of eleven years in prison, the
longest ever for insider trading. Eventually, so many neighbors were
ensnared in financial scandals that a local blogger nicknamed our street
Rogues Hill Road.

In truth, nobody was shocked that the vast new fortunes of the Gold
Coast contained the seeds of financial catastrophe. In the run-up to the
2008 crisis, William Wechsler was a managing director at Greenwich
Associates, a consulting firm, where he saw financiers taking ever-larger
risks. Historically, the bylaws of the New York Stock Exchange had
required trading firms, such as Goldman Sachs, to be private partnerships. "When it was time for you to go, you sold your share to the next
generation," Wechsler told me. "It was culturally acceptable to get to
a certain level of success and retire happy." But, by 1999 the rules had
changed, the big banks had become public companies, and investors
expected large returns. Hedge funds and other firms made huge bets in
pursuit of dramatic windfalls. Instead of directing most of their capital
to funding businesses that hired people and made things, the financiers
in New York and Connecticut had become an economy unto themselves. "Every year that goes by, more and more of the added value in
our society goes toward capital, and less and less toward labor," Wechsler
told me. "What you end up with is a very unstable society."

On top of that, Wall Street was hiring lobbyists to dismantle regulations that protected the country from an economic fiasco. In some
cases, Greenwich residents led the big banks that lobbied for destructive
changes. John Reed was a co-chairman of Citigroup, and William B.
Harrison Jr. was the chief executive of JPMorgan Chase. Their banks
were two of the largest contributors to Senator Phil Gramm, the Texas
Republican who engineered a ban on the regulation of over-the-counter
derivatives. Later, the government's official autopsy of the collapse called

that ban "a key turning point in the march toward the financial crisis," because "derivatives rapidly spiraled out of control and out of sight."

As the economy quaked, the shock waves reverberated through politics. The Tea Party movement raged against Obama, taxes, and social welfare programs, helping Republicans to greater gains in the 2010 midterms than in any congressional election in six decades. Even in Greenwich, where people are not quick to hoist placards, Tea Party activists protested in front of Town Hall, and the first selectman Peter Tesei, the town's top elected official, joined in. "Liberty has contracted today because the role of government has expanded," he told the crowd. (Tesei, like many of his ideological allies, later pledged to support Trump.)

The sentiment was a familiar one—even the Romans resented their taxes—but Greenwich was not traditionally known for absolutism on the subject. In the 1980s, Lowell Weicker, a Greenwich Republican who had served as first selectman and gone on to the U.S. Senate, became known in Washington for blocking Reagan's attempts to cut spending on health and education. In 1991, after Weicker became governor, he imposed Connecticut's personal income tax, which was so unpopular that protesters cursed and spat at him. In a speech that fall, he said, "Respect—if not reelection—comes from speaking the truth."

But to some in the current generation, especially Greenwich's new concentration of libertarians, a fiercer resistance to taxes and to government was a matter of moral principle. Cliff Asness, a billionaire who runs AQR Capital Management, was among the most vocal. When Governor Andrew Cuomo of New York discussed raising taxes on hedge funds, Asness tweeted that he was a "flat out lying demagogue," who was trying to run a "gulag not a state." Around town, the expectation that a person of substantial means might pay substantial taxes no longer held sway. That became especially clear in 2013 when Thomas Foley, a Greenwich private-equity investor, ran for governor. He owned a yacht, a number of vintage cars, two British fighter jets, and a house that *Greenwich Time* likened to "the Hogwarts castle." But, on tax returns that he showed reporters, he had claimed so many investment losses and alimony payments that his federal taxes amounted to $673 that year. (Foley lost the race.)

Charles Rossotti, a Republican businessman who served as the commissioner of the IRS from 1997 to 2002, has estimated that sophisticated tax ploys and shelters cause ordinary citizens to pay an extra 15 percent in taxes each year. Brooke Harrington, an economic sociologist at Dartmouth, told me, "Some of that shortfall just never gets made up. Those are roads that don't get improved, public transport that doesn't get built, schools that don't get fixed." Connecticut has the richest one percent of any state, but, according to several studies of crumbling infrastructure, its roads are among the worst in the country.

Harrington said, "For an earlier generation, even if your heart wasn't in it, you'd say, 'I've got to join the local charity board, to project that I deserve this wealth.'" The current generation, instead of focusing on the local charity board, prefers targeted private philanthropy, bypassing public decisions on whom to help and how. "The underlying massive change is that wealth no longer needs to justify itself—it is self-justifying," Harrington said. "I look back, and I think, That's when we gave up on being a 'we.'"

*   *   *

In the political ferment brought on by the Tea Party and the resistance to Obama, conservative donors expanded their influence. The Hanleys became funders of Turning Point USA, a nonprofit founded in 2012 that promotes conservatism in high schools and colleges. More important, Allie Hanley helped its founder, Charlie Kirk, meet other donors. "Allie Hanley opened the entire southern corridor for us," he wrote later. Kirk became a conservative celebrity and the chairman of Students for Trump, a campus political network. Over time, Turning Point faced multiple controversies. Some student governments sought to ban it for interfering in their elections; staff and members were discovered making racist comments. In 2019, a video showed Riley Grisar, the head of a Turning Point chapter in Nevada, saying "white power," with his arm wrapped around a woman who said, "Fuck the niggers." (Grisar was removed from the organization.)

Lee Hanley used his fortune to elevate candidates on the right wing of the Republican Party. In 2014, he donated some $357,000; the money went to prominent figures such as Ted Cruz, but also to oddball outsiders like Chris McDaniel, a Mississippi state lawmaker and former talk radio host who was trying to unseat the incumbent senator, Thad Cochran. McDaniel lost, but his campaign themes were a preview of politics to come; before Trump was popularizing anti-immigrant rhetoric, McDaniel was pledging to block increases in residency permits and work visas. (When McDaniel ran for the Senate again, in 2018, he embraced a blunter racial message, arguing to preserve a Confederate emblem on the state flag.)

But none of Hanley's political investments would pay off as well as an obscure project for which Steve Bannon, Trump's former strategist, calls him one of the nation's "unsung heroes." Not long after Mitt Romney lost to Obama in 2012, Hanley commissioned a pollster named Patrick Caddell to investigate why conventional Republican candidates were underperforming. Caddell had made his name advising Jimmy Carter, but he had broken with Democrats and begun appearing frequently on Fox News. As he and Hanley discussed the project, both suspected that the electoral returns suggested a deep frustration with the status quo. "I said, 'I think something's happening in the country,'" Caddell recalled. "Lee said, 'You know, I think something may be, too. I want you to go out and just find out.'" Caddell's polls quickly suggested that the "level of discontent in this country was beyond anything measurable."

In 2013, Hanley asked Caddell to show his findings to Bannon, and to another patron, the hedge fund billionaire Robert Mercer. They huddled over the data during a conservative conference in Palm Beach. The numbers, Caddell told them, indicated a public appetite for a populist challenger who could run as an outsider, exposing corruption and rapacity. He called it the Candidate Smith project—the search for a political savior along the lines of *Mr. Smith Goes to Washington*.

When Trump took an early lead in 2015, most of the political and financial world ignored him. Jeffrey Sonnenfeld, a professor at the Yale School of Management, attended a salon that summer at the Connecticut home of Larry Kudlow, the business commentator who went on to lead Trump's National Economic Council. "It was a lot of very deep-pocketed Republicans from Greenwich and New York," Sonnenfeld told me. "Not one person had a pleasant thing to say about Trump." Sonnenfeld urged them to take Trump's chances seriously, but a fellow-guest, who worked for a super PAC supporting Ted Cruz in the primaries, disagreed. "She said, 'I'm a lifelong expert on the psychographics of women's voter behavior, and I can tell you that Donald Trump will never get 2 percent of Republican women voters,'" Sonnenfeld told me. "She got wild applause. That was Kellyanne Conway." (Conway, now a senior adviser to Trump, called this a "specious, self-serving claim," adding, "I don't know 'Professor' So-and-So.")

But Caddell and Hanley concluded that Trump was the closest thing they would find to a Candidate Smith. He had none of Reagan's optimism, but he had name recognition, money, and a preternatural sense of how a billionaire could surf the rage kicked up by the financial crisis. Their conviction persuaded Mercer to invest in Trump, and other wealthy donors followed. As Election Day approached, Charlie Glazer, a Greenwich money manager who had served as George W. Bush's ambassador to El Salvador, began talking to friends, "rationalizing why we should all vote for Trump," one recalls.

For some, it was a plainly calculated choice. Thomas Peterffy, a billionaire who at the time owned the largest estate in Greenwich, donated to Trump but never pretended to admire him. "When the choice is between two ideologies, then it's a luxury to dwell on the personalities of the candidates," he told me. "It's a luxury that we cannot afford." Peterffy, who made his fortune as a pioneer in digital trading, said that the choice was between "a high degree of government regulation or a diminished amount of government regulation, because, basically, that's how the U.S. will get to socialism—increasing government regulation."

When the votes were counted, Trump's greatest support in Greenwich was not in the middle-class sections of downtown. It was in two of the wealthiest precincts—the Tenth and Eleventh Districts, which sprawl across the lush northern backcountry, encompassing the Round Hill Club, where Prescott Bush once reigned, and the estate of Steven Cohen, the investor with the nine-foot wall. Cohen, whose hedge fund closed in 2014, after pleading guilty to insider trading, donated a million dollars to support the inauguration. Peterffy chipped in $150,000. Glazer joined the transition.

Hanley didn't live to see it. He died in Greenwich, four days before the 2016 election. Bannon wishes that more people knew about his high-impact, low-profile contribution to the origins of the Trump movement. "Lee Hanley is like, when you read the history of the American Revolution or the Civil War—all these great events—you find out about these individuals in back that never won any credit, but, if it was not for them, the victory would not be achieved," he told a conservative audience in 2017. "He had a real love of the hobbits, of the deplorables, and he put his money where his mouth was."

*   *   *

Every town in America has its story of what changed after the 2016 election. In Greenwich, the Trump era started almost instantly. In December, a town employee reported to police that Christopher von Keyserling, a well-known member of the town council, had touched her groin after saying, "I love this new world. I no longer have to be politically correct." Lynn Mason, the accuser, warned him not to touch her again, to which he allegedly replied, "It would be your word against mine, and nobody will believe you." After the town government contacted von Keyserling about the complaint, he said that Mason had overreacted to a "little pinch," according to court records. He was charged with misdemeanor sexual assault. (In 2021, a jury convicted him, and von Keyserling was sentenced to ninety days of house arrest.)

The combination of Trump and the von Keyserling incident caused an immediate reaction in Greenwich: women signed up to run for office, and more than fifty won seats on the town council. "A lot of us just woke up," Joanna Swomley, a retired lawyer who entered the race, said. "We were horrified." Swomley organized a local chapter of Indivisible, a progressive network, to heighten public engagement. It worked. In 2017, Greenwich Democrats won control of the town finance board for the first time in recorded history; the next year, they won seats in the state legislature that no Democrat had occupied since Herbert Hoover was in the White House.

But the blue wave quickly subsided. In 2019, Republicans reclaimed control of the finance board, and elected as first selectman a local businessman and state lawmaker named Fred Camillo, who had voted for Trump. At the voting booths, Swomley sensed a change in the atmosphere. "I was holding a Democrat's sign, and a Republican yelled out, 'Oh, hell no!' It was not the embarrassment, the quietness that you saw in 2017. It was 'I am going to own this. I like this.'"

Claire Tisne Haft, a *Greenwich Time* columnist who lives in town with her husband and three kids, was appalled by Trump, and she assumed that her neighbors were, too. She got her first indication to the contrary at a dance recital for her daughter, when another mother told her how excited she was to "see what Trump can do." Not long afterward, Tisne Haft and her husband had dinner with friends, and the conversation turned to politics. "We realized halfway through the meal that we had to adjust our tone," she told me.

In March 2019, a seemingly unrelated bit of news helped illuminate Trump's local support. That month, a powerful Greenwich attorney named Gordon Caplan, the co-chairman of the law firm Willkie Farr & Gallagher, was indicted for paying $75,000 for a test proctor to fix his daughter's ACT exam. Caplan was one of fifty-three defendants in the college admissions scandal, a list dotted with addresses in Greenwich,

Atherton, and Bel Air. In phone calls recorded by the FBI, Rick Singer, the consultant behind the scam, had explained to Caplan that his daughter would never know that her family had cheated on her behalf: "She will think that she's really super smart and she got lucky on a test." Caplan uttered one of the scandal's indelible expressions: "To be honest, I'm not worried about the moral issue here." Caplan pleaded guilty and served a month in prison.

In a column after the scandal broke, Tisne Haft wrote that the case brought up "a whole lot of uncomfortable in a town like Greenwich." It exposed how far some of America's most powerful and prosperous people will go to give their families an advantage in a life already full of them—an ethos that ran through Trump's career.

Tisne Haft sensed that some people in town had become so cynical about the workings of power that they had lost their moral footing. "A friend said, 'You know those kids whose parents gave libraries to their colleges? How is that so different than pushing the boundaries of the truth about your kid?'" Tisne Haft told me. "I just had to look at this person and say, 'Hang on. Someone Photoshopped a kid's head onto a picture.' I feel like we jumped off a cliff there somewhere and didn't notice."

The admissions case reminded me of the rationale I kept hearing for looking past Trump's behavior toward women, minorities, immigrants, war heroes, the FBI, democracy, and the truth, not to mention his request that Ukraine "do us a favor" by investigating his political opponents: a conviction that, ultimately, nothing matters more than cutting taxes and regulations and slowing immigration. Places like Greenwich take pride in their commitment to civility and decency, but Caplan's indifference to the "moral issue," as he put it, bespoke the kind of quiet compromises that a person makes in the privacy of a phone call, or a voting booth.

*   *   *

Even before the 2020 campaign was under way—before the rise and fall of Elizabeth Warren and Bernie Sanders, before the virus that upturned every assumption about the race—it was clear that the essential fault line in American politics was inequality. At times, this anger showed up on the Gold Coast. In 2017, activists staged a bus tour of Greenwich, called "Lifestyles of the Rich and Shameless," which stopped outside the homes (or, more often, the walls) of local financiers. They left oversized cardboard "tax bills," charging the owners for what the tour's organizers called "the havoc they've wreaked on our economy." At the time, Connecticut was considering cutting four thousand state jobs, to relieve a $1.7 billion budget deficit. The activists' final stop was at the office of the libertarian Cliff Asness, where they erected a giant inflatable pig, chomping on a cigar.

As of 2019, America's four hundred richest individuals owned about $3 trillion in wealth—more than all Black households and a quarter of all Latino households combined, according to the Institute for Policy Studies. In calmer moments, Americans have tended to regard our largest fortunes as a kind of national spectacle and, for some, a source of inspiration. But more and more polls underscored the findings of a survey by NBC News and *The Wall Street Journal*, in which 70 percent of Americans described themselves as angry "because our political system seems to only be working for the insiders with money and power."

Amid this populist outrage, some prominent citizens of Greenwich joined the ranks of business leaders who said that capitalism must change in order to survive. Ray Dalio, the town's richest resident, took to calling income inequality a "national emergency"; his family philanthropy donated to Connecticut public schools. In 2019, the hedge fund manager Paul Tudor Jones urged a Greenwich audience to recognize that workers had been shortchanged, though he hastened to reassure attendees: "It wasn't because good people did bad things. It was unfortunately just a natural, unchecked movement." Alan Barry, the town's commissioner of human services, told me that he applauded the concern but disagreed with the notion that inequality was unforeseeable. "Stated policies combined to create this," he said. "Now you're turning around and saying, 'Whoa, we've got runaway capitalism.'"

The targets of broad American antipathy tend not to look inward for its source. "It's all this rapid technological change that results in income inequality," Peterffy told me. "It suddenly increases productivity, and we need fewer workers to produce the same amount of goods and services." One remedy, he said, is direct payments to citizens, and he has become an advocate for replacing all government benefits with a universal basic income: "It is much, much cheaper to give the people money and not restrict business in any way." I asked Peterffy, who built a fortune worth an estimated $14 billion, if he thought America could have avoided radical inequality by not permitting people like him to amass so much money. "Well, it would have decreased my incentive to work as hard as I did," he said. "The number of times I nearly went bankrupt, if I would have had an easier way out, I probably would've chosen that." In 2017, Peterffy sold his Greenwich estate; he moved to Florida, which has no state income tax.

If you are among the Greenwich elite, whether you love Trump or hate him, it is easy to count the ways that he has oriented his administration to help people like you. When Trump introduced his tax bill, he called it a gift to "the folks who work in the mail rooms and the machine shops of America." That was absurd. The bill cut the corporate tax rate by 14 percent, and most of the windfall went to investors in the form of dividends and stock buybacks. Trump pledged to "eliminate tax breaks and complex loopholes" favored by the rich. Though he limited the deductions for state and local taxes, wealthy citizens were compensated by new tax breaks, including some specifically for the commercial real estate industry and for wealthy heirs. On average, Trump gave households in the top one percent a $48,000 tax cut, while those in the bottom 20 percent received $120, according to the Institute on Taxation and Economic Policy, a nonpartisan think tank. As the 2020 campaign got under way, Jim Campbell, the Republican organizer who had embraced Trump early in 2016, told me, "I don't know anyone who voted for Donald Trump in 2016 and won't vote for him again. In Greenwich, he'll probably pick up some votes."

In the spring of 2020, when the pandemic paralyzed New York City, the effects echoed through the suburbs; the city of Stamford reported that a crematory had caught fire after wiring melted from overuse. As in other parts of the country, some people resented the requirements for social distancing. After Greenwich closed its beaches and parks, Thomas Byrne, who held Prescott Bush's old job as moderator of the Greenwich town council, told the local media that the government's measures were "the greatest assault on our freedom in my lifetime," adding, "Why we don't have a revolution in the streets escapes me."

Not everyone was ready to stand on principle, though. As stock markets sank, the investor Cliff Asness reconsidered his objections to government aid. On social media, he made a series of "economic suggestions that kind of hurt me to admit," he wrote. "We need, and I don't think I've ever said this before, fiscal help. We need fiscal relief for individuals and small (and maybe large) businesses." Anticipating the charge of hypocrisy, he wrote, "Yes, I'm losing libertarian bonafides here. I'm ok with that." When Trump eventually signed a relief bill in March, it included a tax deduction, mostly for hedge funds and real estate businesses, that was worth an average of $1.7 million for each of America's 43,000 wealthiest taxpayers and cost the Treasury about $90 billion in the first year.

In various ways, the virus confronted Americans with the result of a generation's worth of political decisions. Even on the Gold Coast, the virus exposed cracks in the economic foundation; in Greenwich, municipal employees scrambled to provide emergency meal deliveries to some seven hundred families a week. Alan Barry, the town official, told me, "Greenwich represents two Americas. The haves and have-nots are literally separated and do not mix."

Most of all, the virus seemed to magnify the central issue running through America's discussions of wealth and fairness: How, exactly, would a fractured country define its understanding of the public good? Who were Americans ready to help? And who were we willing to ignore?

Few people in Greenwich had more reason to consider these questions than Michael Mason, who served as the chairman of the town finance board, a sterile-sounding job with vast authority over daily life. He presided over discussions on how much to spend on special education, on poverty programs, and on the teaching of English as a second language. In April 2020, despite public protests from parents and students, Mason cast the deciding vote in favor of deep cuts to the town's education budget, citing the economic effects of the pandemic.

Mason is tall, with parted silver hair and an earnest zeal for discussions of budgets and civic minutiae. His father flew a plane in the Second World War, and his two older brothers fought in Vietnam. Mason grew up in town, worked in the family aviation business, and volunteered as a fireman, before owning a branch of Million Air, a company that serves the private-jet industry.

He is also perhaps the town's earliest Trump supporter. He attended the campaign announcement in which Trump descended a golden escalator and promised to build a wall against "rapists" from Mexico. "I'm friends with the family," he told me. He met Trump's sons Don Jr. and Eric through a conservation club for hunters in Chappaqua, New York. They invited him to the convention, in case they needed votes to thwart a challenge from within the party. "I'm not going to run south under political pressure," Mason said. Later, he joined them for private celebrations on Election Night and Inauguration Day.

Mason knew that the president's "culture" upset many people in Greenwich. But, he said, "his policies over the last three years have gained more attention and probably more support." He predicted that the trauma of the pandemic would persuade some voters that Trump was right to want to cut immigration and lure back industries from abroad. "He had policies that he wanted to change on our borders, on immigration. I certainly think people in this country now are worried about that."

With the economy in crisis, Mason suspected that Trump would succeed in turning any rebound into a political asset. "There are people in the town right now—I guarantee you—who are saying, 'Wow, this happened to me in '08. My 401(k) went from X down to Y,'" he said. "What is Donald Trump telling you? 'We're going to do everything we need to so it does not take ten years to get you back where it was.' I haven't heard Joe Biden say that."

Eventually, we wound our way to the inevitable question: How did he make his peace with Trump? The behavior toward women and immigrants? The separation of children from parents at the border? The "shithole" countries? Mason listened calmly. "I have no control over that," he said. "What I have control over is what I worry about—the health and safety of my family, financial security of my family." I pressed him, but he didn't budge. "I've been empowered to care about the financial administrative affairs of a municipality with sixty thousand people sleeping at night," he said. "I care about them."

As Americans reckoned with the origins of our political moment—the Trump years, the fury on all sides, the fraying of a common purpose—we tended to focus on the effects of despair among members of the working class who felt besieged by technology, globalization, immigration, and trade. But that ignored the effects of seclusion among members of the governing class, who helped disfigure our political character by demonizing moderation and enfeebling the basic functions of the state. We—or they, depending on where you stand—receded behind gracious walls.

On the ground where I grew up, some of America's powerful people championed a version of capitalism that liberates wealth from responsibility. They embraced a fable of self-reliance (except when the fable was untenable), a philosophy of business that leached more wealth from the real economy than it created, and a vision of politics that forgave cruelty as the price of profit. In the long battle between the self and service, we settled, for the time being, firmly on the self. To borrow a phrase from a neighbor in disgrace, we stopped worrying about "the moral issue here."

Roger Stone and Paul Manafort, who were pardoned by Trump in 2020, returned to the business of political consulting. In 2022, Trump loyalists in

Greenwich won a majority of seats on the Republican Town Committee. They accused old-guard Republicans of, as one put it, "turning Greenwich into San Francisco," and focused on removing mentions of transgender rights and DEI from local schools and government. After two years, the moderate wing, which accused the Trump loyalists of spreading "conspiracy theories and unhinged rhetoric," regained control of the local party committee. But Trump's support in Greenwich remained stable. In the 2024 election, he received 41 percent of all votes in town, his highest performance since he entered politics.

Trump's return to the White House elevated the status of early defectors from the establishment. Linda McMahon, who helped found the America First Policy Institute in the years Trump was out of office and facing criminal prosecution, was nominated to be his secretary of education. Allie Hanley, who, with her late husband, funded the Mr. Smith Project, joined the Advisory Council for Turning Point USA, which had grown into a pillar of Republican politics. Its founder, Charlie Kirk, was present in the Capitol Rotunda at Trump's second inauguration.

Ruling-Class Rules

How to thrive in the power elite—while declaring it your enemy

— 2024 —

As a young man in the 1980s, Tucker Swanson McNear Carlson set out to claim his stake in the establishment. His access to money and influence started at home. His stepmother, Patricia, was an heir to the Swanson frozen food fortune. His father, Dick, was a California TV anchor who became a Washington fixture after a stint in the Reagan administration. For fortunate clans like the Carlsons, it was "A Wonderful Time," to borrow the title of a volume of contemporaneous portraits of "the life of America's elite," which included "the Cabots sailing off Boston's North Shore, and Barry Goldwater on the range in Arizona."

As a teenager, Carlson attended St. George's School, beside the ocean in Rhode Island, one of sixteen American prep schools that the sociologist E. Digby Baltzell described as "differentiating the upper classes from the rest of the population." Carlson dated (and later married) the headmaster's daughter. His college applications were rejected, but the headmaster exerted influence at his own alma mater, Trinity College, and Carlson was admitted. He did not excel there; he went on to earn what he described as a "string of Ds." After college, he applied to the CIA, and when he was rejected there, too, his father offered some rueful advice: "You should consider journalism. They'll take anybody." Soon, Carlson was writing for the *Policy Review*, a periodical published by the

Heritage Foundation, followed by *The Weekly Standard*, *Esquire*, and *New York*, while also becoming the youngest anchor on CNN.

But, in 2005, Carlson's CNN show was canceled, and, after a period of wandering—including a failed program on MSNBC, a cha-cha on *Dancing with the Stars*, and an effort to build a right-wing answer to *The New York Times*—he found success at Fox News. There, he developed a dark new mantra. "American decline is the story of an incompetent ruling class" he told his audience in 2020. "They squandered all of it in exchange for short-term profits, bigger vacation homes, cheaper household help." It was an audacious message from a man with homes in Maine and Florida, a reported income of $10 million a year, and Washington roots so deep that the Mayflower Hotel honored his standing order for a bespoke, off-menu salad. (Iceberg, heavy on the bacon.) But Carlson framed his advantages as proof of credibility; he told an interviewer, "I've always lived around people who are wielding authority, around the ruling class." His origins helped give fringe ideas—such as the conspiracy theory that George Soros is trying to "replace" Americans with migrants—the ring of inside truth. His eventual firing from Fox in 2023 only fortified his persona as a dissident member of the power elite.

In declaring war on the upper class that made him, Carlson joined a long, volatile lineage of combatants against the elite. From the beginning, the United States has had a vexed relationship to distinctions of status—a by-product of what Frances Trollope called our "fable of equality." Americans tend to root for the adjective ("elite Navy SEALs") and resent the noun ("the Georgetown elite").

What's different these days is that so many of the attacks come from inside the palace walls. Senator Josh Hawley, a Missouri Republican, grew up comfortably (his father was a bank president), graduated from Stanford and from Yale Law School, taught at a British school for "gifted boys," and met his wife when they both clerked for Chief Justice John Roberts. But he ignores these credentials when he criticizes what he calls "the people at the top of our society." As a religious conservative, he believes that his values leave him disadvantaged, writing in 2019, "Our cultural elites look down on the plain virtues of patriotism and self-sacrifice." The Florida congressman Matt Gaetz—the son of a wealthy health care entrepreneur who for years served as the head of the state senate—called his rival Kevin McCarthy "the most elite fundraiser in the history of the Republican caucus." This was instantly understood to be an insult.

Even as the ruling class has become a preoccupation of the right, it remains a concern on the left. Senator Bernie Sanders had such an abundant audience for his latest book, *It's OK to Be Angry About Capitalism,* that his royalties nearly matched his salary for representing Vermont. Alexandria Ocasio-Cortez, who entered Congress denouncing the "tippy-top of the one percent," has become a target of activists further to her left, who accuse her of turning into an "Establishment liberal." Critiques of the elite now emanate from so many angles that it's difficult to know who remains to be critiqued.

Nobody in American public life has a more unsettled relationship to status than Donald Trump. For years, as he elbowed his way into Manhattan and Palm Beach, he touted the exclusivity of his golf courses ("the most elite in the country") and hotels ("the city's most elite property"), and he promoted Trump University with the message "I want you to become part of an elite wealth building team that works under my direction." (He later agreed to a $25 million settlement with former students who described Trump U. as a scam.) None of his elite talk endeared him to what he called "the tastemakers," who dismissed him as a boorish trespasser. Even after he turned his Mar-a-Lago estate into a private club, he still resented those who had sniffed at him, telling an interviewer, in a tone rarely employed after the age of twelve, "I have a better club than them."

When Trump first ran for president in 2016, he adopted the expected criticism of "media elites," "political elites," and "elites who only want to raise more money for global corporations." But after he took office he didn't seem to want to do away with the idea of an elite; he just wanted his own people to be on top. During a 2017 speech in Arizona, he told the crowd, "You know what? I think we're the elites."

The term is now invoked so ubiquitously that it can seem to crumble through our fingers. As George Orwell wrote about a frequent accusation of the 1940s, "The word Fascism has now no meaning except in so far as it signifies 'something not desirable.'" But, if our elites are undesirable, what would a better elite look like? What, exactly, are elites for?

*   *   *

At the turn of the twentieth century, the Italian economist Vilfredo Pareto, living as a wealthy recluse in Switzerland, was at work on some of the earliest statistical research into what we now call income inequality. By his count, 20 percent of the population of Italy owned about 80 percent of the land. He found a similar ratio in another, more eccentric area: 20 percent of the pea pods in his garden yielded 80 percent of the peas. Pareto took to describing these imbalances as a "natural law," known as the "80/20 rule."

Pareto wanted a pithy term for his concept, but "ruling class" was out—it had been popularized by his archrival, the scholar Gaetano Mosca. Instead, he adopted *élite*, a French word derived from the Latin *eligere*, which means "to choose." Pareto intended it to be neither a pejorative nor a compliment; he believed that there were elite scholars, elite shoe shiners, and elite thieves. Under capitalism, they would tend to be plutocrats; under socialism, they would be bureaucrats.

His formulation suggests several varieties of elite influence. There is the cultural power wielded by scholars, think tanks, and talkers; the administrative power radiating from the White House and the Politburo; the coercive power resident in the police and the military. (Security forces constitute the strongest branch of elites in much of the world but the weakest in America.) Looming over them is economic power, which has occupied a fluctuating position in the West—worshipped, except when it is scorned.

In ancient Athens, wealthy citizens supported choruses, schools, and temples, on pain of being sentenced to exile or death. In the late Middle Ages, philosophers proposed that, instead of banishing the rich, society should exploit their bounty. The Tuscan humanist Poggio Bracciolini argued in *On Avarice* that in times of public need the prosperous elite could be made to serve as a "private barn of money."

This idea prevailed for centuries. During the American bank crisis of 1907, a group of tycoons that included John D. Rockefeller and J. P. Morgan put up personal funds to bail out the financial markets. But that crisis also marked the end of an era: it spurred the creation of the Federal Reserve, which relieved the economic elite of an "onus they had carried since medieval times," according to Guido Alfani, the author of *As Gods Among Men*, a history of wealth in the West. Freed of that responsibility, the rich of the early twentieth century became both more entrenched and more extraneous, attracting criticism from regulators, muckrakers, and the growing ranks of organized labor. Alfani notes a pattern that unfolds "repeatedly and systematically across history": when economic elites become ingrown, impenetrable, and "insensitive to the plight of the masses," societies tend to become unstable.

To prevent that kind of instability, Pareto believed, the upper echelons of power must stay open to new contestants, in a process that he called the "circulation of elites." Hugo Drochon, a historian of political thought at the University of Nottingham, told me, "Pareto's metaphor was the river. If it is not moving anymore, and it's becoming crystallized, then you are more likely to have a revolt, because of forces rising up."

That risk—of a stagnant, crystallized ruling class—inspired the sociologist C. Wright Mills, who explored the American implications in his 1956 book, *The Power Elite*. The elites "accept one another, understand one another, marry one another, tend to work and to think if not together at least alike," he wrote. Once ensconced, they rarely lost power, he warned; they simply swapped seats, moving among industry, academia, media, and public office. Mills laid the foundation for the idea of a "military-industrial complex," which Dwight Eisenhower popularized in a 1961 speech. (According to some historians, Eisenhower wanted to add "scientific" or "congressional" to that complex, but it was nixed.)

An invective was born. Scholars on the left used it against conservatives who opposed the rise of Black and women's studies. Conservatives, tapping into the decline of public trust in authority since Vietnam and Watergate, turned the government, the media, Wall Street, and the Ivy League into the swamp, the fake news, the globalists, and the ivory tower. The elite became whoever is peering down on us, judging us, manipulating us.

A century after Pareto laid down the concept, he is rarely read, but Branko Milanovic, a former economist at the World Bank, believes that this is a mistake. In his book *Visions of Inequality*, a history of thinking on the distribution of wealth, Milanovic notes that Pareto's era "strongly resembles current capitalist societies." Pareto was writing at a time when vast, entrenched inequality in Europe and America fueled calls for radical upheaval. He was initially sympathetic to demands for change, but he came to see socialist leaders as a new elite and was courted by the Fascists. He ran unsuccessfully for office, his wife ran off with the cook, and, eventually, he lived as a hermit in a villa with dozens of cats.

His "disappointments may have darkened his frame of mind," Milanovic writes, but they unlocked his insights. "History is the graveyard of elites," Pareto wrote, in perhaps his most oft-quoted—and oft-misunderstood—observation. What he was predicting was not an end to the elite but, rather, its constant regeneration.

*   *   *

These days, the feuding hierarchies—of capital, authenticity, virtue, victimhood—generate separate corps of recruits for the ruling class. Who would fare better in the ongoing cultural contest of Who's the Elite? John Fetterman or Ron DeSantis? Ibram X. Kendi or Britney Spears? Chris Rock or Kid Rock?

Even identifying who is eligible for the elite has grown more complicated. Conservatives venerate the building of wealth and political power but see themselves as persecuted by intellectuals and bureaucrats. DeSantis, in his memoir, *The Courage to Be Free*, defines elites as those who "control the federal bureaucracy, lobby shops on K Street, big business, corporate media, Big Tech companies, and universities." But in a feat of rhetorical gerrymandering he excludes Supreme Court Justice Clarence Thomas, arguing that, although Thomas occupies the "commanding heights of society," he "rejects the group's ideology, tastes, and attitudes."

Thomas, for his part, focuses his ire on academia, lambasting "know-it-all elites" and declaring that he prefers "Walmart parking lots to the beaches"—though he evidently makes exceptions for certain beaches. Last year, ProPublica reported that for decades Thomas has taken undisclosed luxury vacations, paid for by the Republican donor Harlan Crow, including tropical sojourns on Crow's superyacht and visits to the secretive California retreat Bohemian Grove, where Thomas befriended the Koch brothers. (Another tycoon helped fund the forty-foot RV in which Thomas visits those Walmart parking lots.)

Some of the combatants' definitions of "elite" are almost perfectly opposed. In recent writings, Bernie Sanders blasted the "billionaire class, the corporate elites, and the wealthy campaign donors"; Marc Andreessen, the billionaire venture capitalist and campaign donor, enumerated "enemy" ideas that block the advance of technology, including "the nihilistic wish, so trendy among our elites, for fewer people, less energy, and more suffering and death."

Amid the competing accusations, you may find yourself quietly wondering: Am I in the ruling class? For Americans, that tends to be a touchy question. When Paul Fussell, a historian and a social critic, was writing his 1983 satire, *Class: A Guide Through the American Status System*, he noticed that people he mentioned it to responded as if he had said, "I am working on a book urging the beating to death of baby whales using the dead bodies of baby seals."

Fussell, undeterred, catalogued the markers of the upper class: frequent house guests ("implying as it does plenty of spare bedrooms to lodge them in and no anxiety about making them happy"); tardiness ("proles arrive punctually"); and, as in the case of the young Tucker Carlson, rumpled bow ties. ("If neatly tied, centered, and balanced, the effect is middle-class," Fussell wrote.) He composed lists, including one that delineated the "only six things" that can be made of black leather without causing "class damage to the owner." (Belts, shoes, handbags, gloves, camera cases, and dog leashes.) He ended the book with a system for evaluating the class valence of the goods on display in your house: "New Oriental rug or carpet: subtract 2 (each). Worn Oriental rug or carpet: add 5 (each)."

Forty years after Fussell's *Class*, its most striking feature is its prescience. Before we could see the full contours of our new Gilded Age, Fussell sensed that the middle class was "sinking," pulled down by "unemployment, a static economy, and lowered productivity." A generation whose parents had clambered out of the working class was amusing itself to distraction in a world of proliferating screens and cheap consumption—"prole drift," Fussell called it. The class divide was widening once more, and the greatest gap was the one separating Americans who could protect themselves with money from those who could not. Fussell quoted the working-class father of a man killed in Vietnam: "You bet your goddam dollar I'm bitter. It's people like us who give up our sons for the country."

These days, some of the signifiers have changed; there are fewer takers for a tastefully worn rug. In New York City, the press has documented the rise of private kitchen staff, rotating teams of nannies, and in-home laundresses who will devote half an hour to ironing a single shirt. When a foray outside the home becomes unavoidable, the Aman hotel offers the private refuge of a members-only club, which charges a $200,000 initiation fee and $15,000 in annual dues.

Yet the deepest drive is not for stuff but for the social rank that stuff conveys. The musician Moby, who sold twelve million copies of his album *Play*, once said that he kept courting success in the music business not to make more money but to "keep being invited to parties." In the 2022 book *Status and Culture*, the journalist W. David Marx argues that we are hardwired to pursue status, because it delivers a steady accretion of esteem, benefit, and deference. In ancient Rome, elites were permitted to recline at dinner, while children sat and slaves stood. More recently, the champion golfer Lee Trevino remarked, "When I was a rookie, I told jokes, and no one laughed. After I began winning tournaments, I told the same jokes, and all of a sudden, people thought they were funny."

Status can be frustratingly ephemeral. As you get closer to the top of a pyramid, the steps get crowded. Just ask the senators who peer longingly down Pennsylvania Avenue toward the Oval Office, knowing that they are contestants in a zero-sum game. "For every person who goes up," Marx writes, "someone must go down."

* * *

Jockeying in a hierarchy, no matter how lofty, occasionally swerves toward the physical. Not long before becoming president, Joe Biden offered to take Trump out "behind the gym" and beat him senseless; Trump, asserting that he had a "much better body," insisted he'd win. In a Senate hearing in 2023, Markwayne Mullin, of Oklahoma, told an invited witness, the president of the Teamsters union, "If you want to run your mouth, we can be two consenting adults—we can finish it here."

Their taunts barely registered above the din of other elite standoffs in recent years: Kanye West vs. Taylor Swift, Chrissy Teigen vs. Alison Roman, Lauren Boebert vs. Marjorie Taylor Greene. Each dispute has its own esoteric stakes, but, taken together, they make up a perpetual American undercard, feeding our cravings for entertainment. Peter Turchin, an emeritus professor at the University of Connecticut, calls this an age of "intraelite conflict."

He explains it as a game of musical chairs: each year, we get fresh graduates from Stanford and the Ivy League, bored hedge fund executives, restless tycoons—all angling for seats. Year by year, their numbers accumulate, but the chairs do not, and the losers become "frustrated elite aspirants." Eventually, one of them will cheat—by faking a kid's college résumé, trading on an inside tip, or trying to overthrow an election. Others will catch on and begin to wonder if they're the last suckers in the bunch. Things fall apart.

That's the pattern that Turchin explores in *End Times: Elites, Counter-Elites, and the Path of Political Disintegration*. Trained as a theoretical biologist, he now mines a vast historical data set, called CrisisDB, for insights into how societies encounter chaos. The crux of his findings: a nation that funnels too much money and opportunity upward gets so top-heavy that it can tip over. In the dispassionate tone of a scientist assessing an ant colony, Turchin writes, "In one-sixth of the cases, elite groups were targeted for extermination. The probability of ruler assassination was 40 percent."

In fifteenth-century England, he notes, a long spell of prosperity minted more nobles than society could absorb, and they took to brawling over land and power. The losers were beheaded on muddy battlefields. During the three grisly decades of the Wars of the Roses, three-quarters of England's elites were killed or driven out by "downward social mobility"—an estimate that scholars reached by studying the declining imports of French wine. Eventually, Turchin writes, "the most violent were killed off, while the rest realized the futility of prolonging the struggles and settled down to peaceful, if not glamorous, lives."

In America's case, history holds two examples with wildly different outcomes. In the early nineteenth century, old-line Southern elites, who profited from slavery and from exports of cotton, faced competition from Northern elites, who made their money in mining, railroads, and steel. They battled first in politics—some ran for office, others funded candidates—but the elites proliferated faster than politics could accommodate them. Between 1800 and 1850, the number of America's millionaires soared from half a dozen to roughly a hundred. During the Civil War, the North's tycoons prospered, the South's went into decline, and the country suffered incalculable damage.

Half a century later, America was riven once more. In the 1920s, suspected anarchists bombed Wall Street, killing thirty people; coal miners in West Virginia mounted the largest insurrection since the Civil War. But this time American elites, some of whom feared a Bolshevik revolution, consented to reform—to allow, in effect, greater public reliance on those "private barns of money." Under Franklin D. Roosevelt (Groton, Harvard), the U.S. raised taxes, took steps to protect unions, and established a minimum wage. The costs, Turchin writes, "were borne by the American ruling class." Between 1925 and 1950, the number of American millionaires fell—from sixteen hundred to fewer than nine hundred. Between the 1930s and the 1970s, a period that scholars call the Great Compression, economic inequality narrowed, except among Black Americans, who were largely excluded from those gains.

But by the 1980s the Great Compression was over. As the rich grew richer than ever, they sought to turn their money into political power; spending on politics soared. The 2016 Republican presidential primary involved seventeen contestants, the largest field in modern history. Turchin calls it a "bizarre spectacle of an elite aspirant game reaching its logical culmination." It was a lineup of former governors, sitting senators, a former CEO, a neurosurgeon, the offspring of political and real estate dynasties—all competing to convince voters that they despised the elite. Their performances of solidarity with the masses would have impressed the Castros.

When Trump reached the White House in 2017, he ushered in allies with similar credentials: Wilbur Ross (Yale), Steven Mnuchin (Yale), Steve Bannon (Harvard Business), Mike Pompeo (Harvard Law), Jared Kushner (Harvard). Though Bannon, the chief strategist, had earned his fortune at Goldman Sachs and in Hollywood, he billed himself as an outsider and sounded every bit the disheveled count from the Middle

Ages. "I want to bring everything crashing down," he liked to say, "and destroy all of today's establishment."

Turchin ends his book with a sobering vision. Using data to model scenarios for the future, he concludes, "At some point during the 2020s, the model predicts, instability becomes so high that it starts cutting down the elite numbers." He likens the present time to the run-up to the Civil War. America could still relearn the lessons of the Great Compression—"one of the exceptional, hopeful cases"—and act to prevent a top-heavy society from toppling. When that has happened in history, "elites eventually became alarmed by incessant violence and disorder," he writes. "And we are not there—yet."

*　　　*　　　*

In the summer of 2023, the tussling between two noted American elites entered the realm of burlesque. For years, Elon Musk and the Facebook cofounder Mark Zuckerberg had privately grumbled about each other. Zuckerberg yearned for the innovator's cred that Musk enjoyed, and Musk lamented that he was not (yet) as wealthy as Zuckerberg. In public, Musk mocked Zuckerberg's understanding of AI as "limited" and said that Facebook "gives me the willies." In June 2023, after Musk, the owner of Twitter, purged its staff and plunged it into turmoil, Zuckerberg's company announced plans for a "sanely run" alternative. Musk responded by proposing a "cage match," and Zuckerberg, who had been training in Brazilian jujitsu, replied on Instagram, "Send Me Location." Soon, Musk and Zuck—worth a combined $335 billion—were posing for sweaty gym photos. The Italian government discussed hosting the fight at the Colosseum, and tech bros divided into rival fandoms.

Eventually, Musk put off the fight—he acknowledged that he was out of shape—and Zuck declared that it was "time to move on." But even interrupted, the billionaire cage match showcased some of the rivalries and insecurities already at work in the next 80/20 society. The gentry of new technologies have displaced the industrial and media barons of an earlier age, but the new hierarchies are still in flux. In Silicon Valley, it's common to hear the prediction that artificial intelligence will yield a world of two broad classes: those who tell the AI what to do and those whom the AI tells what to do.

Technology won't spare us a ruling class—and, in any case, it's hard to envision a thriving society in which no one is allowed to aspire to status. But instead of continuing to exhaust the meaning of "the elite," we would be better off targeting what we really resent—inequality, immobility, intolerance—and attacking the barriers that block the "circulation of elites." Left undisturbed, the most powerful among us will take steps to stay in place, a pattern that sociologists call the "iron law of oligarchy."

Democracy is meant to insure that the elite continue to circulate. But no democracy can function well if people are unwilling to lose power— if a generation of leaders, on both the right and the left, becomes so entrenched that it ages into gerontocracy; if one of the two major parties denies the arithmetic of elections; if a cohort of the ruling class loses status that it once enjoyed and sets out to salvage it.

Which brings us back to Tucker Carlson. When he tells the story of America's elites, he often scorns them as "mediocre" and "stupid." But he frames his own failures—the strings pulled on his behalf, the rejected applications, the canceled shows—as jaunty diversions on the path to success. To be fair, we are all bad at estimating our own abilities. (In a study of college professors, 94 percent rated themselves "above-average.") But Carlson is not just overlooking his history of falling short; he is trying to rebrand it as righteousness. In his broadcasts, first on Fox and later on X, he specialized in giving voice to fellow frustrated elite aspirants: former general Michael Flynn, former representative Tulsi Gabbard, and, of course, Donald Trump, the last of whom toyed with naming Carlson as his running mate in the 2024 campaign.

Together, these counter-elites conjure a pervasive conspiracy—of immigrants, experts, journalists, and the FBI. It's a narrative of vengeful self-pity, a pining for the wonderful times gone by. Carlson's old friends in the ruling class occasionally wonder how much of his shtick he really believes, and how much he simply grieves for having lost the game of musical chairs to faster, shrewder, more capable elites. The latter, at least, would make his desperation understandable: he *is* being replaced.

———————————

The 2024 presidential campaign intensified the public contest over who is, and is not, the "elite." In July, when President Biden was under pressure to drop out of the campaign, he said on MSNBC's Morning Joe: *"I'm getting so frustrated by the elites. Now I'm not talking about* you *guys. The elites in the party." Trump continued to train his supporters' ire on powerful, if vaguely defined, enemies. Scholars who analyzed speeches by presidential nominees back to 1992 found that Trump, in 2024, invoked the specter of an unspecified "they" more frequently than any candidate before him.*

Trust Issues

A disgruntled wealth manager exposes her clients' tax secrets

— 2023 —

For the very rich, private wealth managers are in a separate class from other retainers, even from the trusted pilots, chefs, and attendants who maintain their lifestyles. Guarding the capital—the "corpus," as it's known in the business—puts you in contact with a family's most closely held secrets. Managers handle delicate tasks; one professional in the Cayman Islands described the sensitivity of making a financial plan for an out-of-wedlock child that "has to be kept totally private from the wife." Others specialize in keeping clients out of the news by minimizing public transactions. The most devoted liken themselves to clergy or consiglieri, and tend to get prime seats at the kids' weddings and the patriarch's deathbed.

Marlena Sonn entered the wealth-management industry in 2010, and found a niche working with what she called "progressive, ultra-high-net-worth millennials, women, inheritors, and family offices." She sought to create a refuge from jargon and bro culture. "Women and young people are talked down to," she told me. "A level of respect for people is refreshing."

Sonn didn't come from money. She was born in Queens, to parents from South Korea, who she says were determined to see her "fulfill the American Dream—go to Ivy League schools and become a doctor or a lawyer." As a student at Barnard College, she was drawn to the punk and goth scenes and to progressive politics. After school, she moved to San Francisco, campaigned for a higher minimum wage, and planned on a career in activism. But in 2005, while working at a nonprofit, she developed an unexpected fascination with her retirement account. She took to listening to analyst calls with CEOs, buying stocks on E-Trade, and watching exultantly as some of her picks spiked in value. Within a few years, she had left the nonprofit world for finance. "That was where the real levers of power were," she said, adding, "My parents were so relieved."

She started out at a small firm in lower Manhattan, working as a receptionist and studying at night to become a financial planner. Once she was certified, she signed up clients who wanted to "align their wealth with their values." Her new role obligated her to master a shifting vocabulary of noblesse oblige. "They keep changing the name," she said. "It went from 'socially responsible investing' to 'ESG'"—environmental, social, and governance. "Now it's what we call 'impact investing.'" What firms like hers offered was not charity; it was capitalism with progressive characteristics. "We would work out tax-efficient strategies to move clients out of legacy positions and into a new portfolio that was more simpatico with their conscience," she said. For clients who had investments in "offender industries," such as fossil fuels or private prisons, she could help them sell the stock and plant trees in the Amazon, structuring the trades to minimize the cost in taxes.

In the spring of 2013, a lawyer told her about a potential client who might benefit from Sonn's expertise: a young woman in line to inherit part of an iconic American fortune. The lawyer was cagey about specifics, but eventually identified the prospect as Kendalle P. Getty, a granddaughter of the oil tycoon J. Paul Getty. In the 1950s, Getty was declared the richest living American.

Sonn and Kendalle met for dinner at a restaurant in Williamsburg, Brooklyn, and discussed her situation. Kendalle had become an heir in a roundabout way. Her father, Gordon Getty, a composer and a philanthropist in San Francisco, worth an estimated $2.1 billion, had four sons with his wife, Ann. Secretly, he also fathered three daughters in Los Angeles during an extramarital affair. The full extent of his offspring became publicly known in 1999, after the girls' mother asked a court to recognize them as his legal descendants. On the day the story broke, Gordon was vacationing with his wife aboard a friend's yacht in the Mediterranean; he released a statement acknowledging that he was the girls' father, and proclaimed, "I love them very much."

Gordon cut his daughters in on the Getty fortune using a trust fund—in essence, an imaginary legal lockbox that can shelter assets from taxes, creditors, and ex-spouses. Though trusts have been around since the Middle Ages, they have recently experienced a surge of innovation and popularity, as wealthy people pursue ever stronger ways to avoid publicity and taxes. The trust that Gordon created was named Pleiades, for a set of sisters in Greek myth who had dalliances with Olympian gods and were immortalized as stars in the night sky. It was arranged to grow until Gordon's death, at which time the sisters would gain control of a pile of assets that Sonn estimated would be worth about a billion dollars.

Over dinner with Kendalle, Sonn felt "an instantaneous meeting of the minds." Despite the differences in their backgrounds, the two women shared political views and an irreverent posture toward the money around them. Kendalle, a multimedia artist, identified herself on Instagram as a "bastard princess," and advertised support for "environmental conservation, animal welfare, human rights, and reforming the way the justice system handles gendered violence, racial inequities and bias, and transphobia." She seemed eager to pull money out of the petroleum investments that had built the Gettys' wealth and repurpose it, in a spirit that Sonn likened to reparations.

While her father was living, Kendalle had a nest egg of about $5 million, administered by Goldman Sachs. She moved a million of it to Sonn, who agreed to invest it for an annual fee of one percent of the assets—a standard industry rate. Their relationship flourished.

Kendalle soon transferred the rest of her assets from Goldman to Sonn, and introduced her to one of her sisters, Alexandra S. Getty. Known as Sarah, she split her time between Los Angeles, New York, and Japan, and identified herself on social media as an "artist, webtoon creator, boxer, runner, and vegan." Sarah hired Sonn, and within a year the sisters asked her to help run their trust fund, too. As her duties expanded, Sonn assisted Sarah with insurance and real estate. She helped Kendalle manage art projects, pay bills, and navigate family dynamics. The three bantered by texts punctuated with "LOL," "Okee Dokee," and "Love you."

For nearly eight years, Sonn served the Getty sisters as an adviser and a confidante, until the relationship underwent a spectacular rupture. In a lawsuit filed in 2022, Kendalle's lawyers accused Sonn of "unjust enrichment," saying that she "coerced" her client into promising a bonus worth millions of dollars. In a countersuit, Sonn accused the Gettys and their advisers of retaliating for her opposition to a "dubious tax avoidance scheme" that could save them as much as $300 million. Robert Leberman, the administrator of the trust, and one of the defendants in Sonn's suit, denied her allegations against the family. In a statement, he said that Sonn's firing had been "non-retaliatory and warranted," and that the suit was a "sad example of overreaching by someone now seeking to take advantage of a position of trust."

As it moved through the courts, Sonn's complaint, which contained portions of family emails and texts, marked the rarest of indiscretions from a financier who serves the superrich. Wealth managers like to say, "A submerged whale does not get harpooned." In this case, one of their own was allowing one of America's richest clans to heave into view.

*   *   *

The arc of an American fortune, it is often said, goes from "shirtsleeves to shirtsleeves in three generations." Other cultures have similar admonitions. The Japanese version is bleak: "The third generation ruins the house." The Germans dwell on the mechanics: "Acquire it, inherit it, destroy it."

And yet, in recent times, the fortunes of many prominent American clans have soared. Between 1983 and 2020, the net worth of the Kochs, who prospered in fossil fuels and became right-wing megadonors, grew twenty-five-fold, from $3.9 billion to $100 billion. The Mars family fortune, which began in the candy business, grew by a factor of thirty-six, to $94 billion. The Waltons, of Walmart, expanded their fortune forty-four-fold, to $247 billion. The financial triumph of such clans helps explain how the imbalance of wealth in the United States has risen to levels unseen in a century. In 1978, the top 0.1 percent of Americans owned about 7 percent of the nation's wealth; today, according to the World Inequality Database, it owns 18 percent.

A century ago, American law handled the rare pleasure of a giant inheritance with suspicion. Instead of allowing money to cascade through generations, like a champagne tower, the state siphoned off some of the flow through taxes on estates, gifts, and capital gains. As the Supreme Court Justice Oliver Wendell Holmes wrote in 1927, "Taxes are what we pay for civilized society." But since the late 1970s, American politics has taken a more accommodating approach to dynastic fortunes—slashing rates, widening exemptions, and permitting a vast range of esoteric loopholes for wealthy taxpayers. According to Emmanuel Saez and Gabriel Zucman, economists at the University of California, Berkeley, the average tax rate on the top 0.01 percent has fallen by more than half, to about 30 percent, while rates for the bottom 90 percent have climbed slightly, to an average of 25 percent.

Some advisers to ultrarich families describe the current era as a golden age of tax avoidance. In 2022, Marvin Blum, a Texas lawyer and accountant, gave a seminar for fellow-accountants who were figuring out how to profit from the influx of wealth that needed protecting. Blum told his colleagues, "Conditions for leaving large sums have never been better," noting that "Congress has not closed an estate-planning loophole in over thirty years." In a report from 2021, the Treasury Department estimated that the top one percent of taxpayers are responsible for 28 percent of the nation's unpaid taxes, amounting to an annual shortfall of more than $160 billion.

When it comes to taxes, there have always been advantages in certain lines of work. If your money comes from complex investments, it is easier to avoid taxes than if your employer regularly reports your income to the Internal Revenue Service. The same is true of tips and cash, which is how many low-income workers receive their wages. But the wealthiest Americans have access to ever more creative dodges—most of them legal, some illegal, and some on the murky border in between.

That lucrative maneuvering is the realm of specialized attorneys, accountants, and money managers, many of whom work for family offices: in-house financial teams that typically include a dozen or so full-time attendants. Family offices, which have roots in nineteenth-century operations that served John D. Rockefeller and a handful of his peers, have proliferated in the past two decades, to at least ten thousand worldwide. They tend to have no public presence—Gordon Getty's family office is known, inconspicuously, as Vallejo Investments—but by some estimates family offices in America and abroad now control about $6 trillion in assets, a larger sum than is managed by all the world's hedge funds.

Critics of global inequality call this stratum of business the "wealth-defense industry," and have pushed Congress to impose taxes, eliminate loopholes, and restore narrower limits on American inheritance. The cultural outrage has grown lately. A series of disclosures, beginning in 2016 with a leak from the law firm Mossack Fonseca, have revealed spectacular extremes of high-priced tax maneuvering—which, among other consequences, brought down the leader of Iceland and embarrassed the prime minister of the U.K. In that year's presidential election, Donald Trump bragged that he was "smart" for not paying taxes, provoking fury among opponents and agreement among supporters. By 2019, Senator Elizabeth Warren, of Massachusetts, was calling for people with fortunes of more than $50 million to give up two cents on every additional dollar—a formula repeated so often that crowds at her events began chanting, "Two cents! Two cents!"

Scholars of wealth and taxes say that the golden age of elite tax avoidance has contributed to the turbulence in American politics, by hardening social stratification; reducing public resources for education, health, and infrastructure; and eroding trust in America's mythologies of fairness and opportunity. Edward McCaffery, a tax professor at the USC Gould School of Law, said, "Tax, which is supposed to be a cure, is in fact one of the problems. This is a pattern that recurs throughout history. Capital keeps getting more and more unequal, until there's a crash."

But Tom Handler, a Chicago tax lawyer who specializes in ultrawealthy clients, told me that the political pressure on the one percent has only generated more business for him and his peers. "Most of the high-net-worth client base, they're running for cover," he said. "So income tax planning has gone up, estate tax planning has gone up, asset protection has gone up." Handler's clients feel "vilified," he said. "Other than the very liberal, highly educated, intellectual elite, they don't feel guilty at all. They're angry."

For people born to the most elevated classes, the fight over a few points' difference in tax rates can feel existential. Brooke Harrington, a Dartmouth sociology professor whose book *Capital Without Borders* examines the tools of tax avoidance, told me that families like the Kochs, the Waltons, and the Gettys have escaped the old adages about generational decline thanks to a "perpetual-motion machine of wealth creation." Often, she said, "the advisers' job is protecting the fortune from the family. Without clever wealth management and attorneys, the Getty fortune would've gone up in smoke."

*   *   *

What the Vanderbilt name represented in the Gilded Age, or the names Musk and Bezos might in our time, Getty was to postwar America: a reigning symbol of what money can do. The family fortune began in 1903, when a couple of flinty, frugal Minnesotans named George and Sarah Getty struck oil in Oklahoma. The trade was so profitable that their son, J. Paul Getty, became a millionaire by the age of twenty-three—at which point he announced his retirement. He saw "no reason why I should exert myself further to make more," he wrote in a memoir called *My Life and Fortunes*. He would focus instead on "enjoying myself," and in that pursuit he acquired Hollywood friends, such as Charlie Chaplin and Gloria Swanson, and abundant hangers-on.

His parents, devout Methodists, disapproved. They told him that a rich man must "keep his money working to justify its existence." Paul dutifully returned to the family business, but when his father died in 1930, the will contained a harsh surprise: the estate, some $15 million, had been bequeathed almost entirely to Sarah. Paul complained to his mother, who agreed to sell him her share of the company as a Christmas present. She codified the deal with a formal offer, noting that it would expire if "not accepted by you in writing on or before noon of 30 December." But even as they reached an agreement, she worried that her son might squander the fortune, so she locked up some of it in what accountants call a "spendthrift trust," which gives the beneficiary limited access to the funds.

Her worries turned out to be misplaced. For Paul, the insult of the will stirred a strain of thrift, ambition, and suspicion that would develop into compulsion. Claus von Bülow, a top lieutenant at Getty Oil, later described Paul's attitude: "Dad was going to eat his words." (Von Bülow became famous himself when he was convicted of trying to kill his wife, Martha, an heiress to a utilities fortune; he was subsequently acquitted.) Paul put nearly all his energy and profits back into the company and the trust. His biggest bet, on the oil prospects of a region between Saudi Arabia and Kuwait, became a bonanza. Within fifty years, the trust had grown a thousandfold, to $4 billion.

He vowed to create a "Getty dynasty," but this was more a financial concept than a familial one. He had five divorces, and five sons, from whom he was so distant that he did not bother to attend their weddings. The alimony and child support he sent did not suggest the magnitude of his wealth. When in 1957 *Fortune* crowned him the richest American, his sons were shocked. He was more interested in larger expressions of legacy. "I feel no qualms or reticence about likening the Getty Oil Company to an empire—and myself to a 'Caesar,'" he wrote.

Even compared with other wealthy skinflints, Paul was strikingly parsimonious. He installed a pay phone at Sutton Place, his seventy-two-room mansion in the English countryside, to avoid paying for guests' long-distance calls. His last wife, a singer named Teddy Getty, had to beseech him to pay for maternity clothes, pointing out that he could deduct them from his taxes as an expense for her performing career. In one emphatic letter, she wrote, "SO HERE AGAIN YOU HAVE LOST NOTHING." When their son, Timmy, was treated for a brain tumor, Paul declined to visit, and complained to Teddy that the doctors "grossly overcharged you." He wrote, "Some doctors like to charge a rich person 20 times more than their regular fee."

Getty took a similarly dim view of taxes. When he donated art works, he would value them at higher prices than he had paid and take a hefty deduction. He invited twelve hundred people to a mansion-warming party at Sutton Place and declared it a business expense. His tactics became so aggressive that President John F. Kennedy personally leaked details of Getty's taxes to *Newsweek*, revealing that in a recent year Getty had paid a total of $504 in federal income tax. Getty was undeterred; in his 1965 book, *How to Be Rich*, he condemned an "insane hodgepodge of Federal, state, county and city levies that make life a fiscal nightmare for everyone." Elsewhere, he derided government spending on "nonproductive and very frequently counterproductive socialistic schemes."

Nothing exhibited his relationship to money more than his management of a family tragedy. In 1973, his sixteen-year-old grandson, John Paul Getty III, who had left school to be a painter in Rome, was kidnapped by Calabrian gangsters, who stashed him in the mountains and demanded $17 million for his safe return. The grandfather, by then known as Old Paul, suspected that it was a charade orchestrated by family members to extract money. He eventually relinquished that theory, but insisted he would never pay a ransom. "I have fourteen other grandchildren," he told the press, "and if I pay one penny now, I'll have fourteen kidnapped grandchildren."

After three months, the kidnappers, growing impatient, cut off the boy's right ear and mailed it to a newspaper to broadcast their warning. They reduced their demand to about $3 million, but threatened to cut off other body parts, too, if they got no reply. Ultimately, Old Paul consented to pay $2.2 million of the requested sum—the maximum, according to his biographer John Pearson, that advisers had told him was tax deductible. He loaned his son the rest of the ransom money, about $800,000, at 4 percent interest.

When Old Paul died, in 1976, he was living in England but trying to avoid British taxes by claiming to be a resident of California—even though he had not been to California in a quarter century. After his death, members of the family feuded in court, and forced the sale of Getty Oil to Texaco. Eventually, four factions of the family agreed to divvy up the trust into portions of $750 million apiece, and to pay a tax bill of a billion dollars. One of the lawyers likened it to "an elaborate treaty negotiation among warring nations."

Even the dismembered parts of the realm were vast. One son, Paul Jr., instantly became the sixth-richest man in Britain; the interest payments alone paid him a million dollars a week. Most of Old Paul's personal estate—his art, property, land—was insulated from taxes almost entirely, thanks to a final gesture to keep the money out of the government's hands: he bequeathed it to a museum trust that would carry on his name forever.

*   *   *

The Getty Center, on a sun-drenched hilltop in the Santa Monica Mountains, is one of America's most visited art museums. Its walls and walkways are made of pale travertine, mined from an ancient quarry east of Rome. It's the same quarry that yielded the stone you find in the Trevi Fountain and the Colosseum, a material, as the museum puts it, "historically associated with public architecture." This is a telling bit of sleight of hand: *public* architecture belongs to the public, a concession that Old Paul Getty fought his whole life to avoid. On a nearby stretch of coastline, with panoramic views of the Pacific, its sister museum, the Getty Villa, occupies a re-created Roman country house that is more popular with the public than with architects. Joan Didion once described it as "a palpable contract between the very rich and the people who distrust them least."

But this kind of prominence should not be mistaken for happiness. Through the years, Old Paul's protectors have suggested that he was the greatest victim of his own stinginess. "The only person he was ever mean with was himself," Robina Lund, a lover and a longtime aide, once said. In 1963, a BBC documentary called *The Solitary Billionaire* featured him dining alone at a seventy-foot banquet table and performing exercises in a three-piece suit, hoisting a barbell over his head, beside a wall decorated with a Renoir. "The money is the root of the problem with the Gettys," Gordon's confidant William Newsom once said, according to Russell Miller's book *The House of Getty*. "It is a ludicrous, preposterous amount of money, enough to make you wonder if anybody in the world should have that much. It taints everything."

Marlena Sonn thought that she could help the Getty sisters expunge that taint, she told me one morning in November 2022. We met in a conference room of a co-working space in a converted pencil factory in Brooklyn. In a black-and-white dress and chunky glasses, with salt-and-pepper hair falling to her shoulders, she betrayed little sign of the erstwhile punk and activist. I wondered whether, working for the Gettys, she imagined herself as a sleeper cell, there to dismantle the system. "No," she said. "I thought we could reform it."

In the past century, the Gettys, like many American clans, have moved from a business of bare-knuckle extraction into more genteel labors; younger branches of the family extend into acting, conservation, and influence work. In 2021, Ivy Love Getty, an artist-model and a great-granddaughter of the oil tycoon, was married in San Francisco in a ceremony officiated by House Speaker Nancy Pelosi.

But, Sarah Getty told me, her "crazy family history" and abrupt transformation into an heir gave her little preparation for managing a fortune. "In exchange for the love I didn't receive in my life, I got money," she said. "So, at first, I always felt misery and guilt, and I didn't know what to do with it." Sonn was twice her age, capable and solicitous. "Our relationship was very much like mother-daughter, because my mother wasn't very present in my life," she said. Sonn called her "babe," and they "would do things for fun, not just for work," Sarah said.

Sonn had been in the job less than two years when she caught a glimpse of how complex the inner workings of the family might be. In March 2015, Kendalle and Sarah's half-brother Andrew Getty died at his home in the Hollywood Hills—suffering, the Los Angeles County coroner's office found, from methamphetamine intoxication, heart disease, and bleeding linked to an ulcer. Sonn flew to San Francisco to help handle the fallout. Andrew's death, she said, required a reshuffling of more than $200 million, as his share of a trust was redistributed among his siblings.

Sonn assisted Kendalle and Sarah as they navigated the complications of their new wealth. To oversee the Pleiades Trust, Gordon's family office had helped establish a corporate entity for each of the sisters, named for their initials: ASG Investments and KPG Investments. The sisters were the presidents, and Sonn became vice president. Four times a year, Kendalle and Sarah received a dense book of several hundred pages, detailing investment decisions. "What do we do with this five million, and what do we do with that five million?" Sonn recalled. "They were asked to make decisions pretty much on the spot."

For the next several years, Sonn consulted on investment strategies, interviewed money managers, and sometimes voted in Sarah's stead. One of her primary duties was monitoring the important matter of location; Sonn said that she was enlisted in "maintaining the appearance" that Kendalle and Sarah neither resided nor transacted trust business in California, in order to minimize their exposure to state income tax, which ranges up to 13 percent. Across the family fortune, she said, "that's a lot of tax on billions of dollars." While their grandfather had sought to duck taxes by claiming California residency, Sonn was helping the granddaughters attempt that maneuver in reverse. Among other tactics, she helped Kendalle and Sarah buy real estate in New York, which could fortify their claim to dividing residency across multiple states. And she kept track of the time that each spent in California. "For Sarah, she was in Japan, then she was in New York, then she's in California. For Kendalle, she was back and forth between L.A. and New York, and also traveling. So there's this game of counting their days," she said.

The delicate arbitrage of state taxes is governed less by the constraints of the physical world than by the dream palace of accounting innovation. The original Getty trusts were established in California, but advisers had moved Gordon's to Nevada in 1995. In an effort to spur the local economy, Nevada had taken to promoting itself as the "Delaware of the West," with no taxes on income, inheritances, or capital gains. The financial upside bordered on the supernatural. Consider a typical Nevada trust scenario: as a planner at a family office, you put the maximum sum allowed, tax-free, into a trust; under current laws, that's a meaty $12.9 million. By simply entering a long-term trust, that sum becomes immune to the 40 percent tax that applies to ordinary assets at the turn of every generation. After seventy-five years, your $12.9 million will balloon to approximately $502 million, according to calculations by the Northern Trust Institute, a wealth-management firm based in Chicago. That's more than quadruple the growth it would experience outside the trust.

To enjoy the financial advantages of Nevada, the Gettys did not have to move there. The Pleiades Trust was officially administered from a small office complex a block from the Reno-Tahoe airport: Airport

Gardens, which shared a parking lot with a private investigator and a hobby shop selling electric trains. In all the years Sonn worked with Kendalle and Sarah, they had never, as far as she was aware, set foot in Airport Gardens.

One particular ritual was sacrosanct: four times a year, to maintain the claim that their trust was not run from California, they boarded jets to some locale beyond the state border, before casting their official votes on investment decisions. "It would be a different place every quarter," Sonn said. "New York, Seattle. Once a year, it would be in Nevada, usually in Las Vegas, because none of the family members wanted to go to Reno." Buried in the details of California law was a statute that said that, as long as they could make the case that they never did the "major portion" of their business in California, they might each be able to dodge tens of millions of dollars in taxes on the inheritance.

*   *   *

The question of how much to leave your kids has been with us since the Ice Age. At an archaeological site called Sungir, east of Moscow, which holds the remains of hunter-foragers from at least thirty thousand years ago, researchers found the bones of children buried with spears, art, and furs adorned with thousands of beads, painstakingly carved from mammoth tusks. Archaeologists calculate that shaping each bead took as long as forty-five minutes, so the kids' finery represented years' worth of labor by someone else—in effect, a prehistoric trust fund.

For the one in five American households that receive any family money at all, it can fortify a sense of identity and solidarity. And, in normal quantities, it narrows inequality, by helping low-income families pay for homes and education. (The average American bequest today is around $46,000, according to the Survey of Consumer Finances.) But when inheritance patterns reach extremes, they wreak social and political havoc. In ancient Greece, the Spartans developed rules that consolidated property into a narrow class of heirs, while the growing

population of people left behind were reclassified as *hypomeiones*—
inferiors. By the third century BCE, tensions between the groups had
pushed Spartan politics into violent convulsions over land, debt, and
power.

The concept of a trust—the holding of property for the benefit
of another—developed in the fourteenth century, among English
landowners who were called up to the Crusades. To avoid transferring
assets to their wives, since women were restricted from owning land,
they entrusted control temporarily to male friends and relatives. Trusts
proved immensely popular. "Nobles figured out very quickly that it
was a great way to dodge taxes," Brooke Harrington, the Dartmouth
sociologist, said. "Property taxes were due only if the owner of a property died, so, if you kept playing hot potato with the deed, effectively
the owner never died." In 1682, to curb gaming of the law, England's
Lord Nottingham established a "rule against perpetuities," which set
the maximum length of a trust at the lifespan of the beneficiary plus
twenty-one years.

That term limit endured for centuries, not only in England but eventually in the United States, where a resistance to inherited nobility
was among the founding ideals. Thomas Jefferson believed that steep
inheritance taxes would encourage an "aristocracy of virtue and talent,"
which he regarded as "essential to a well ordered republic." Thomas Paine
wanted taxes on the largest estates to approach "the point of prohibi-
tion." Even some of America's greatest entrepreneurs saw inheritance
as a handicap—a "misguided affection," as Andrew Carnegie put it.
William K. Vanderbilt, a descendant of Cornelius, observed, evidently
from experience, that inherited wealth was "as certain a death to ambition as cocaine is to morality."

Theodore Roosevelt took steps toward a progressive tax on inheritances, in the belief that a "man of great wealth owes a peculiar obligation to the State, because he derives special advantages from the mere
existence of government." A 10 percent estate tax went into effect in
1916; the Great Depression and the New Deal fueled calls for higher

levies, and by 1941 the top rate had climbed to 77 percent, where it remained for decades.

Ever since then, Americans have groped for a balance between the instinct to bequeath and the dangers of excess. Running for president in 1972, George McGovern proposed that nobody should be allowed to receive more than half a million dollars in inheritance and gifts. People hated the idea. His spokesman, Richard Dougherty, identified the concern: "Every slob in the street thinks that if he hits the lottery big, he may be able to leave half a million to his family."

In the 1990s, conservatives, pressing to eliminate the estate tax, condemned it as a "death tax," and insisted that it imperiled family farms. The evidence was always elusive; in the early 2000s, Neil Harl, a prominent economist at Iowa State University, searched for family farms that had been killed by the tax, and concluded, "It's a myth." But the effort never really had much to do with farmers; according to a 2006 study by the nonprofit groups Public Citizen and United for a Fair Economy, the campaign against the estate tax was quietly financed by eighteen ultrawealthy dynasties, including the founding families of Gallo wine and Campbell's soup.

The campaign succeeded spectacularly. In 1976, about 139,000 American households were eligible for the estate tax; by 2020, it had been loosened and punctured by so many exemptions that only 1,275 households nationwide had to pay. Gary Cohn, Trump's economic adviser in the first term, who helped engineer the most recent loosening of the provision, was heard to tell members of Congress, "Only morons pay the estate tax."

*   *   *

So how, exactly, do the well-to-do find a way around taxes? There are functional concerns and ethical ones. The line between avoidance and evasion is not mysterious. It's perfectly legal to avoid taxes by honestly reporting losses and deducting expenses, and it's perfectly illegal to evade them with lies (by understating income or bartering to avoid sales, among many other techniques). The more intriguing terrain is where most Americans dwell, between avoidance and acquiescence. Researchers who study IRS data can chart our behavior on a continuum, from "flagrantly defiant" (people who cheat even at great risk) through "strategic" (calculators of costs and benefits) to "conflicted" (moral agonists) and "pathologically honest" (bless their hearts).

The simplest way to avoid income taxes is to avoid "income." If you run a company, alert the press that your salary is a dollar a year; then, for walking-around money, summon your banker to provide a "portfolio loan," which uses your stock as collateral. Because it's a loan, you'll owe no taxes on the cash. Better yet, if you cling to your winning stocks until you die, the moment that your soul departs your body it will take your capital gains obligations with it. Whatever taxes you would have had to pay on the rising value of the stock vanish into a loophole known as the "stepped-up basis"—or, as admirers call it, the "angel of death."

The angel of death loophole, a vestige of a time when paper records made it difficult to pinpoint how much an asset had grown, endures today as a giveaway to the rich, estimated to cost the Treasury as much as $54 billion a year. If Jeff Bezos died tomorrow, a hundred billion dollars of gains on his Amazon stock would go untaxed. This tidy routine—skip the income, live off loans, and avoid capital gains until you go—can run forever. Edward McCaffery, of USC, calls it "buy, borrow, die."

The wealth-management industry prefers a gentler vocabulary; it makes fewer mentions of money and taxes than of creating "meaningful legacies" and of fending off "wealth attrition" and "dilution." In 2021, ProPublica deployed leaked tax data to investigate some of the most meaningful legacies of recent years: $205 million for the son of the opioid-maker Mortimer Sackler; $570 million in trust income for William Wrigley Jr., the great-grandson of the chewing gum magnate. If you're strategic enough, even less iconic brands can produce a dynasty.

Just ask the princely tribes endowed by Family Dollar, Public Storage, and Hot Pockets microwave pastries.

Managers like to hail the forethought of "first-generation wealth creators" and "patriarchs and matriarchs." But the industry's most important concept involves no venture at all; it is simply endurance. When Chuck Collins, a great-grandson of the meatpacker Oscar Mayer, told a fellow-heir that he planned to give away the corpus in his trust, she invoked the goose that lays the golden egg. "You don't barbecue the goose," she said. In 2014, not long after the French economist Thomas Piketty warned of the reemergence of "hereditary aristocracy," a trade magazine for the wealth-management industry carried an illustration of a medieval knight, bearing a sword and a mace, guarding overflowing bags of cash. The caption read, "Armour for your assets." Like any combatants, wealth managers gather intelligence: a tax lawyer told me that his firm had used the Freedom of Information Act to obtain a copy of an internal IRS handbook, which lists the thresholds that agents use to determine if a discount is suspiciously large.

To understand the quietest corners of the tax-avoidance world, I called Bob Lord, a lawyer in Arizona whose tax practice once helped clients find loopholes. Lord, who was born in 1956 and raised in Maryland, entered the business in the 1980s, just as the drive for deregulation was triggering an obscure but seismic change in state law. In 1983, South Dakota became the first U.S. state to abolish the ancient "rule against perpetuities," clearing the way for what became known as "dynasty trusts," which can shield assets from inheritance taxes for centuries. Other states raced to catch up. Nevada set its limit at 365 years, Alaska at a thousand. South Dakota barred any limit at all, reverting to the legal conditions akin to feudal England. "We had this crazy competition where states are trying to outdo each other in giving cushy tax situations," Lord said. "They think that by attracting rich people and their businesses they're going to do better than taxing those rich people."

Lord was struck by how much the distribution of wealth had changed in his lifetime. "I played a lot of golf as a kid," he said. "My parents belonged to Woodmont, the premier Jewish club. And I remember these tremendously wealthy people—they would drive a Mercedes, maybe fly first class—but they didn't have the kind of wealth people have today." Eventually, he found it impossible to abide the inequality that his advice helped create: "We have this insanely rich country, but we have people living horribly because of a terrible distribution of wealth." In 2013, he started analyzing tax issues for the Institute for Policy Studies, a liberal think tank, and he is now a senior adviser to the Patriotic Millionaires, a group of wealthy advocates for more stringent taxes on themselves. "If we hadn't allowed all of this avoidance to take place over the last four or five decades, where would we be now?" he said. "I worry about what's going to happen two or three decades from now if nothing is done. We will have families with wealth in the trillions."

To have any hope of joining the trillionaire club, an aspiring family should avail itself of levers installed out of reach of lesser Americans. Owning Thoroughbreds can allow you to write off millions in pleasant investment losses each year. The same goes for auto racing and cattle ranching. And don't forget the private-jet loophole created by Trump's tax law, which allowed family offices to soak up "excess business losses" by upgrading the Gulfstream.

But perhaps nothing has contributed more to the latest revival of dynastic fortunes than a spate of innovation around trusts, known by such recondite acronyms as SLATs, CRUTs, and BDITs. (The opacity is no accident. The late U.S. senator Carl Levin, a critic of finance abuses, accused the industry of deflecting attention with MEGOs—"My Eyes Glaze Over" schemes.) The most coveted are GRATs, or grantor-retained annuity trusts. The recipe requires only two steps: have your lawyer set up a trust on paper with your heirs as beneficiaries, and fill it with assets that you strongly suspect will rise in value—say, the stock of your company about to go public. As soon as the assets grow faster than interest rates, voilà! Your heirs receive almost all the difference, and it's tax-free. It doesn't count as a gift, because the trust is, technically, an annuity, which pays you back over two or three years. Best of all, there's nothing to stop you from setting up a new GRAT every month. Sheldon Adelson, the late casino owner, sometimes had at least ten at once; in one three-year period, according to Bloomberg, he used them to escape $2.8 billion in taxes. The benefits of the GRAT are obvious, Tom Handler, the tax lawyer, told me: it's cheap, simple, and easy to repeat. "Even unsophisticated clients can understand that one."

Like many tax-avoidance strategies, the GRAT was dreamed up in a law firm and released into the wild to see if it could survive the courts. In 2000, the IRS challenged its use by the former wife of the brother of the Walmart founder, Sam Walton—and lost. "The tax court's decision just blew this loophole wide open," Lord said. "For twenty-two years, everyone has known you can do this. You've got a tax court decision that basically blesses it, and Congress hasn't done anything about it." In honor of its first patron, the tactic is often called a Walton GRAT.

The ethics around avoiding taxes are themselves a form of inheritance. "Families just grow up in it," McCaffery said. "The patriarch never paid much in taxes. And you're just in a world in which, four times a year, you're going to Nevada or wherever."

*   *   *

For half a century, Gordon Getty has lived in a grand yellow Italianate mansion in Pacific Heights, with sweeping views of the Golden Gate Bridge and Alcatraz. Over the years, he and Ann, a publisher and a decorator, expanded their living space, buying the house next door (to make room for his work at the piano) and then the house next door to that. They hosted charity events, opera stars, and fundraisers for politicians, including Kamala Harris and Gavin Newsom. (Newsom's father, William, one of Gordon's friends since high school, managed the family trust for years.)

Sonn became accustomed to the rhythms of life in the Getty orbit: the talk of political allies, the family's trips on their Boeing 727, known as "the Jetty." And yet, by 2018, after four years of crisscrossing the country to attend to the Gettys' finances, elements of the job were making her increasingly uncomfortable. For one thing, she said, her employers had refused to contribute to her health insurance or her payroll taxes, to avoid the appearance of operating in New York, where she lived. For another, helping to manage a family's most sensitive financial deliberations could be an emotional process; these are "blood-sucking" jobs, as one finance professional put it. Sarah Getty told me, "My anxiety mind will take over sometimes and be, like, Should I spend less? Should I spend more? Am I being selfish right now? I didn't need that massage chair." (She added, "I didn't get a massage chair, don't worry. But I thought about it.") For Sarah, it complicated matters that Sonn "was also representing Kendalle, who I don't always get along with."

There were disputes about the dispensation of funds. Sarah supported animal advocacy groups, such as the World Wildlife Fund, but Sonn advised her instead to donate to the Amazon Basin, to protect the landscape and its Indigenous people from environmental harm. "I care about those things as well, don't get me wrong," Sarah told me. "It's just the fact that she picked it, and I felt manipulated." There was also friction over Sonn's compensation. She had started at a base salary of $180,000, along with her fees as an investment adviser, and though her salary eventually more than doubled, she discovered that some other suppliers of advisory services to Getty trusts had collected at least $1 million a year. She complained to Kendalle and Sarah, who agreed to pay her a hefty bonus when the trust fund opened, a percentage that she calculated would come to about $4 million.

Another debate was far more sensitive: Sonn suspected that members of the Getty family might be violating California tax laws. By getting on the plane four times a year to vote elsewhere, and keeping the back office in Reno, they had justified putting off the payment of an estimated $116 million in California taxes on the sisters' trust, according to Sonn. Employing a similar approach with at least two other family funds, they had, by Sonn's estimate, deferred a combined $300 million in payments. In truth, she said, they often worked on the Pleiades Trust while in California; in 2016, for instance, she had visited Gordon's house in Pacific Heights to help interview a battery of prospective financial advisers. "All of the candidates flew into San Francisco," she said.

At first, she thought that some members of the family might agree with her. In a 2018 email, Nicolette Getty, the third sister, described the expense and the logistics of the quarterly ritual as "distasteful." She wrote, "The trusts should become California trusts and pay the California tax that we rightfully owe." But advisers in Gordon's family office apparently disagreed, and by the following spring Nicolette was expressing a similar view. "We can live in California for now if we want to, without penalty, as long as we move out of state for a year before we are ready to access the trust principal," she wrote in an email to her siblings and others. She elaborated on the idea in a message days later, arguing that "those of us living in [California] at the time of dad's death would then make plans to move out of state for 1-2 years." (In theory, relocating could allow an heir to escape tens of millions of dollars in California's "throwback" tax, which vanishes if you move away for long enough.)

But moving away for "1-2 years" to avoid California taxes struck Sonn as a dubious charade. By the onset of the pandemic in 2020, Kendalle and Sarah had resettled in California, and though Sonn had prospered by facilitating their juggling of geography, she now concluded that the tax strategy was becoming untenable. At one point, she texted Kendalle that "emails, texts and phone conversations go back and forth all the time inside CA, and all of those are traceable to CA, pandemic or not. We've interviewed Trust consultants at your Dad's house. I don't think we're being in integrity re: the spirit of the law." She added, "I'm compelled to tell you the truth here, even though it's an ugly shitshow and not of either of our makings."

Kendalle replied with one word: "Zoinks."

Eventually, Sonn wore out her welcome. In January 2021, Sarah fired her from ASG Investments, but she offered to work out a severance package, signing off, "I love you." Sonn asked for a payout of about $2.5 million plus a year's salary. "That seems fair," Sarah replied. But days later Sarah sent a blistering criticism, in which she said that an employment lawyer was "appalled" by Sonn's proposed terms. "I now don't trust you in any regard," she wrote. By the end of the year, Kendalle had fired Sonn, too. She had agreed to give her $2.5 million, in installments, but she stopped after the first payment; she said the family office had discouraged her from sending more.

The following spring, Kendalle and KPG Investments filed suit in Nevada state court, alleging that Sonn had breached her fiduciary duties and deceived her client into agreeing to the bonus. In May, Sonn filed suit in the Eastern District of New York against her former clients and employers, as well as others involved. According to the *Los Angeles Times*, the Gettys' battle with their former financial adviser could "serve as a roadmap for California tax investigators, should they choose to follow the route."

The legal survival of a multimillion-dollar tax dodge can hinge on minutiae. Auditors have been known to examine not only what state you claimed to call home but also where you swiped your gym card, the locations of your social media posts, and where you keep your most treasured belongings—an examination known in the industry as the "Teddy-bear test." To gauge what investigators might think of the approach laid out in Sonn's suit, I interviewed five tax lawyers. They said the final tax bill would likely rest on subtle facts—for instance, how much trust business was done in California, or whether the beneficiaries moved away from the state with plans to return.

Darien Shanske, a law professor at UC Davis, characterized the Gettys' approach as "aggressive, obnoxious tax planning," saying, "They are at the limit, or perhaps beyond the limit." But the family's larger strategy, he told me, might be simply to take their chances with

California's version of the IRS, the Franchise Tax Board. The FTB, like many agencies, has a finite capacity for complex cases, especially when faced with a well-resourced litigant. "They're probably guessing that, in the unlikely event that the FTB challenges them, it may well lose, thanks to their preparatory work—or that, faced with this work and the legal uncertainties, it'll just decide to settle." Robert Leberman, the trust administrator, told me that the "major portion" of work was kept "outside the State of California," and that the family intends to "fulfill any and all tax obligations." In Shanske's view, this is a slender pledge; fulfilling narrowly conceived legal obligations, while avoiding taxes in a state so closely associated with the Getty family, undermines their claim to social responsibility. "There's a price schedule that we set amongst ourselves as a polity," he said. "And they decided they want to pay less."

*   *   *

Spend enough time around wealth managers and their clients and you can start to see the whole story of American power and suffering as a function of the simple arithmetic of compounding—of money making money, of lobbyists layering on new exemptions each decade, of the cultural amnesia that makes ideas about wealth come to seem normal, honorable, inevitable. In private moments, even Old Paul Getty marveled at his drive to accumulate. "I don't know why I continue to be active in business," he wrote in his diary in 1952, four decades after he first tried to retire. "Force of habit, I suppose."

What motivates those who already have so much to strategize so hard to have a little more? Greed is not always about money for money's sake. For some, it's power. ("The prize of the general is not a bigger tent but command," Oliver Wendell Holmes said.) For others, cheating on your taxes is a nihilistic triumph. ("That makes me smart.") For more than a few, it's about fear. Luke Weil, an heir to a gambling industry fortune, once told a documentarian that the prospect of losing his inheritance haunted him like the threat of "losing a parent or a sibling."

The deepest motive may be even more primal, an innate appetite for status. "If you measure the blood levels of the chimp on top of the hierarchy, they tend to have high serotonin and testosterone levels, which are mood-enhancing," Brooke Harrington, the sociologist, said. Putting that in human terms, she continued, "If you don't preserve the wealth enough so that the intermarriage and education and status-maintenance activities continue, then you're also letting the institution crumble." Perpetuity, after all, is priceless. "The fortune is the monument you build to yourself," she said. (For those who are truly mortality-avoidant, there is the option of a "personal-revival trust," a product geared to clients who plan to be cryogenically frozen and want to be assured of coming back in comfort.)

In their current condition, taxes on American wealth are, effectively, on the honor system, with opt-outs for the flagrantly defiant. Could it be different? In recent years, the highest-profile ideas have been wealth taxes, such as Senator Warren's proposal for a 2 percent annual levy on fortunes greater than $50 million, and an extra one percent above a billion. Critics say that the idea fails to distinguish trustafarians from entrepreneurs, and that people will cheat—though we don't usually abandon speed limits just because speeders will speed.

Other ideas have received less attention. In 2021, Democrats proposed to narrow the angel of death loophole, expand the estate tax, impose a billionaires' income tax, and eliminate some of the most popular trusts, including the GRAT. But lobbyists mobilized, reviving some of the same arguments that once gutted the estate tax; by Christmas, the GRAT and other exemptions had been saved. "Closing the loopholes is not rocket science," Bob Lord, the Arizona lawyer, said. "All you need is a couple of bought-off senators."

Still, the perversities of the tax code have become so glaring that even some of their most devoted protectors suspect that change is coming. Marvin Blum, the Texas lawyer, lamented in his seminar that Congress had "shined a spotlight on many of the best tools in our toolbox that we use to avoid estate tax." He warned, "Now that the general public is aware, there is a growing outcry to shut down these benefits. This is a wake-up call that, sooner or later, the tax landscape will likely drastically change."

Many of the ideas for reform converge around the need to prevent the re-feudalization of American wealth—the Spartan scenario, which early Americans fought so hard to escape. For the moment, restoring real taxes on what we leave behind could be more politically viable than levying a wealth tax. Instead of colliding with American myths about the pursuit of success, such taxes could tap into Americans' ambivalence about inherited riches. Some proponents suggest a federal rule against perpetuities, which would put a universal ban on dynasty trusts. Others suggest stronger financial incentives for whistle-blowers. "Governments have limited budgets, the stuff is complicated, and the advisers know what's going on," McCaffery said. "They know where the bodies are buried."

In one of my conversations with Sonn, I asked why more people from her rarefied wing of financial services don't speak out. "Anybody who is within the industry, and has been there a long time, has accepted certain tenets," she said. "Climate change is an 'externality.' Social injustice, and the various social crises that we're experiencing right now, would be considered 'externalities.' And they're actually mandated by corporate law to say, 'You cannot think about the externalities. You have to think about the profit first.'"

Sonn told me she didn't know anyone else in finance who had publicly criticized a client or the underlying assumptions of the business. "There's an unspoken omertà," she said. People "become engaged in the wrongdoing themselves. So they're able to enforce a certain kind of culture of silence around bad behavior." Sonn had started out in wealth management determined to help people find "tax-efficient" ways of clearing their conscience but had come to see an ethical flaw in that ambition. "The financial services industry lives between the letter of the law and the spirit of the law," she said. "That's what tax efficiency is."

Sarah Getty insisted that the sisters had acted in accordance with their family's values. "Everything we were trying to do was lawful," she said. "I'm not against paying taxes at all, because I think they're very important, especially if they go in the right things. I would want the right government to be in control, though, because, if the wrong government is in control, then they go to all the stuff I don't support. I'm very against military and guns and weapons, and very pro-planet." Like many others I spoke to while reporting on Sonn's dispute with the Gettys, Sarah described a feeling of captivity to industries and laws that enriched her but tried her conscience. Nicolette told me, "This Nevada trust arrangement was made before I became a trustee or was included in the trust or Getty matters at all." She went on, "I'll admit that for a time I did consider the option of moving out of California in order to avoid the tax, because it is quite substantial." But, she said, she abandoned the idea, and expects to pay about $30 million in taxes on her share of the trust. "I'm one who thinks the tax burden needs to be higher on the wealthy such as myself and my family," she said. Her sister Kendalle, who declined to comment for this article, is fond of retweeting posts by Bernie Sanders: "Billionaires get richer & pay less in taxes while millions are unemployed, kids go hungry, veterans sleep on the street. We must stand up to the billionaire class and create an economy for all, not just a few."

Sarah has experienced the dispute as a personal betrayal. "I've learned that you can't even trust the people you hire," she told me. Sonn, too, seemed bruised by the experience. In her suit, she accused her former patrons of threatening to ruin her professional reputation if she went ahead with the case. If the case eventually settles, it isn't clear what she might win or lose. In some places, whistle-blowers who allege tax fraud can receive financial rewards from the state, but there is no such provision in California. And there isn't much of a market for a disgruntled wealth manager.

"My career in finance is over," Sonn said. I asked what her parents made of that. She gave a wan laugh and said, "I fulfilled a lot of their intergenerational ambitions." She had reached the heights of wealth management, optimized her position, and sued in pursuit of millions. Viewed from a certain angle, it was a capitalist fairy tale. When the Pleiades Trust opens, each of the sisters can expect to receive at least $300 million, minus whatever taxes their office does not succeed in avoiding. Sonn, whether or not she obtains the rest of her payout, will have made millions of dollars from her association with the Gettys. One wealth manager told me that it would have been unusual for Sonn to spend eight years as "a slave to these prima-donna girls, without the expectation that there's something at the end of the rainbow."

Sonn said she had come to believe that, unless wealthy Americans made some sacrifices to undo the stagnation of social mobility, stories like hers would become impossible: "My parents came here imagining that they could build a better life, and I am a product of that. And I think that some of what we're experiencing is that window has been closing for the last ten or twenty years."

But, despite the dispute, Sonn blamed her former clients less than their enablers in finance and politics. Loopholes, like dynasties, do not survive without good help. Why didn't reform work? I asked. She thought for a moment and said, "The system will always do whatever it can to preserve itself."

In January 2023, six days after this article appeared, Kendalle Getty posted a photo of herself in a makeshift guillotine with the caption, "You only think you know the truth about me." Her lawyers, citing Sonn's comments in The New Yorker *to accuse her of breach of contract, asked a Nevada judge to seal documents in the case. The judge denied the request. In August 2024, Sonn and the Gettys reached a confidential settlement. Sonn, who still lives in New York, now works at the Solidaire Network, which connects wealthy donors to social movements.*

Gordon Getty celebrated his ninetieth birthday in 2024, with hundreds of well-wishers, including Nancy Pelosi and Governor Gavin Newsom, as well as his three daughters. In Washington, Senator Ron Wyden, an Oregon Democrat, and Senator Angus King, an Independent from Maine, have introduced the GRATS Act. The bill—officially named the "Getting Rid of Abusive Trust Schemes Act"—aims to amend the rules on trusts to reduce their tax benefits.

THE PERILS

How to Lose It

Land of Make-Believe

*Zach Horwitz was a mystifying presence
on the big screen, until the FBI showed up*

— 2024 —

Anyone who visited Zach and Mallory Horwitz in 2019 would have said that they had made it in Hollywood. They lived in a $6 million home on Bolton Road, within walking distance of Beverly Hills; there was a screening room, a thousand-bottle wine cellar, and a cabana laced with flowering vines by the pool. The Horwitzes had hired a celebrity decorator and installed a baby grand piano and framed photographs of Brigitte Bardot and Jack Nicholson. On social media, Zach posted pictures of himself courtside at Lakers games; Mallory shared images of their toddler playing in the California sun. For Mallory's thirtieth birthday, Zach paid the R&B artist Miguel to perform for friends at the Nice Guy, a voguish restaurant in West Hollywood.

The couple, college sweethearts from Indiana University, had arrived in California seven years earlier, in search of a new life. They had started the cross-country drive with their dog, Lucy, on New Year's Eve. In L.A., Mallory trained to be a hair stylist, like her mother and grandmother back home in Santa Claus, Indiana. Zach, who had secretly wanted to act ever since he saw his first Broadway play as a child, landed a few tiny parts: he played Demon 3 in one film, an unnamed basketball player in another. He was not quite movie-star handsome, but he had gleaming

195

teeth, an aquiline nose, imposing biceps, and turquoise eyes. For a stage name, he chose Zach Avery.

Although Zach was not an overnight success, bigger roles came soon enough. In 2017, he flew to Serbia for a film directed by Ralph Fiennes, then he was off to Virginia to shoot a movie with the Hollywood veteran Bruce Dern, in which he played opposite Olivia Munn. Before long, he starred in a thriller featuring Brian Cox, who played the patriarch Logan Roy on *Succession*. In an interview after the production, Zach praised Cox for "taking me under his wing," and marveled, with self-flattering deference, "When you're sitting across the table from him, doing scenes, you almost have to pinch yourself and say, 'How is this real?'"

Like many young stars, Zach dabbled in tech investments and started companies to produce and distribute films; he named his enterprises 1inMM, after his favorite saying, "When odds are one in a million, be that one." Eventually, he encouraged Mallory to stop working at the salon. They had $40 million in the bank, he told her. Why go to work? All the while, Zach kept in touch with the friends who'd been with him during his rise. He took them to parties by private plane and always paid their way; he even made some of them rich, by dealing them into his businesses. In 2018, during a dinner in Montreal with three old friends from Indiana, one of them proposed a toast to Zach: "You've changed my life, my wife's life, my children's lives."

But even in Hollywood, where professional envy is as ubiquitous as dental veneers, people around Zach were unusually puzzled by the divide between his success and his talent. "He is the worst actor I've ever worked with," a former colleague told me. Sharing a scene with Zach, he said, was like interacting with a banana. The director Michele Civetta, who worked with Zach, told me that he was forced to invent ways to help him unlock emotion; otherwise, it was like "dealing with a dead horse." Audiences reached a similar conclusion. After Zach appeared with Cox in *Last Moment of Clarity*, one reviewer wrote that he delivered "such a dull, unappealing performance that the movie has a void at the center." A viewer of another of his films declared, "Zach Avery's acting was like a cancer to this movie. Every time he was on screen it died a little more. Good god, how did he make it past the auditions?"

Still, many people who encountered Zach thought that he seemed like just another lucky beneficiary of the capricious entertainment business. Gina Dickerson, a real estate agent who met with him and Mallory, said, "In L.A. more than anywhere else, nobody really ever knows where the money is coming from." Her colleague Tracy Tutor told me, "In Hollywood, the more you fake it, the more people actually buy it. You have the right car? You're wearing the right suit? You know the right people? No one does the diligence."

If anything, Zach struck people as too blandly genial to be anything other than what he appeared. Civetta, the director, noticed that he seemed determined to project wholesome simplicity—"milk and apple pie, his wife, his kids." Tutor, the real estate agent, who often appears with her clients on a reality show called *Million Dollar Listing Los Angeles*, considered casting Zach but concluded that he was too undistinguished to put on TV: "I said to the show, 'This is the most boring, vanilla person.'"

*   *   *

As a teenager on the outskirts of Fort Wayne, where subdivisions give way to farmland, Zach Horwitz was an athlete, not a theater kid. The Carroll High School yearbook featured a picture of him shirtless in the gym, under the headline "Best Bodies." He was popular, but prone to telling fanciful stories that seemed engineered to draw attention. According to a classmate named Steve Clark, Horwitz once told peers that he had met the baseball star Derek Jeter at a mall in Florida, and that Jeter had invited him to dinner. The story seemed ludicrous, but Horwitz was beyond reproach. "He was handsome, and he was a football player, which is to say he was high school royalty," Clark said.

Horwitz's parents, Susan and Howard, had divorced when he was young. For a time, he lived with his mother and sister in Tampa.

During a visit to New York City when he was in grade school, he thrilled to a performance of *Annie Get Your Gun*. He asked his mother about the actors, and she explained that they were professionals, paid to entertain the crowd. Back home, he took to memorizing lines from movies like *Forrest Gump* and *Jerry Maguire*, and he talked of quitting school to become an actor, but his mother insisted that he get an education. By his sophomore year of high school, they had moved to Indiana; his mother had married Robert Kozlowski, a prosperous manufacturing executive. The family lived comfortably, with a vacation house on a lake.

In 2005, Horwitz started college in Bloomington, majoring in psychology. One day at the gym, he met Jake Wunderlin, who, like him, was a brawny former athlete from Fort Wayne. Unlike Horwitz, though, Wunderlin did not come from money. He was a scholarship kid—a tall, reserved honors student in finance who worked at the campus food court to help pay expenses. They grew close, and Wunderlin joined him on visits to his mother and stepfather, who had a big house near Zionsville, the richest town in Indiana. Horwitz gained a reputation for spending freely on friends, covering late-night drinks and pizza. "He was the one that would pay for everything," Wunderlin told me. "He loved it. He never was mad about it, like, 'Are you going to pitch in?'" Joe deAlteris, a business student who had been friends with Wunderlin since kindergarten, grew close with Horwitz, too. "I knew him as the guy who had a ton of family money," he told me. "It felt like every semester he came back with a new car."

Horwitz also had a knack for identifying a need in another person, a point of emotional access. DeAlteris was outgoing, a wide receiver on the Indiana team and a member of the Beta Theta Pi fraternity, but in 2009 his stepfather died, and he was overwhelmed with grief. It was not a subject that he discussed easily with the college gym crowd, but Horwitz lost his own stepfather around the same time, and the two bonded. At social occasions, Horwitz liked to pose questions that generated moments of self-revelation. He once asked a circle of friends,

"How much money is enough? How much would it take in your life to do whatever you want?"

Mallory met Zach at a tailgate party in 2008, just before her twentieth birthday, and was taken with his attentive manner. "Everyone loved him," she recalled. "If there was a homeless person on the street, he'd say, 'Let's give some money.' I felt like I had an extremely deep, rare connection with this person." After graduating, she followed Zach to Chicago. She walked him to classes at the Chicago School of Professional Psychology; when he told her that he was dropping out after less than a year, she strove to be supportive. He harbored fantasies of getting into the Chicago improv scene, but kept them to himself. Instead, he talked enthusiastically about a job as a salesman, providing accounting software to small businesses.

Wunderlin was working in the Indianapolis office of the wealth-management division at J.P. Morgan, and Horwitz called periodically to compare notes. Among friends, he let it be known that he had inherited money—as much as $10 million, some said—and Wunderlin got used to hearing him talk about the "crazy returns" that his mother's financial team had achieved. In fact, the family's money was contested. Horwitz's stepbrother Steven had filed suit against several relatives, alleging that they had shortchanged him on his inheritance. He accused Horwitz's mother, Susan, of fraud and manipulation, suggesting that she may have forged his father's signature on a will while he was sick, in order to secure most of an estate that totaled more than $11 million. Lawyers for Susan called the allegations "false and distorted" and fought the case; in 2011, they reached a confidential settlement.

As the case was nearing resolution, Horwitz called Wunderlin and told him about an enticing opportunity: he had attended a small-business convention, where he'd pitched a chain of fast casual healthy restaurants—in effect, juice bars with supplements. He said that he'd caught the attention of venture capitalists backed by Howard Schultz, the founder and CEO of Starbucks, who had a sideline as an investor in food start-ups. (Not long before, a VC firm that Schultz cofounded had put almost $30 million into Pinkberry frozen yogurt.) Schultz himself had expressed interest, Horwitz told him. "He said, 'I have a meeting with Howard,'" Wunderlin recalled.

Days later, Horwitz reported back that the meeting had gone well; if he could get a restaurant built, Schultz would consider an investment. Horwitz invited his friend to join the venture, saying, "I need to build a team." Wunderlin wasn't about to leave J.P. Morgan for a juice bar, but then Horwitz put him in contact with Schultz directly. In March 2011, Wunderlin got a long email from Schultz's account, reflecting on the lessons of building Starbucks and declaring, "I have faith in you. Your team has faith in you." It ended on a note of inspiration: "Be the person that you have always dreamed of becoming, Jake, and all the rest will fall into place." Elated, Wunderlin showed the email to his parents, quit his job, and moved to Chicago.

The restaurant, called FÜL, opened that summer. Mallory, who got her own galvanizing email from Schultz, had signed on, and Horwitz recruited other friends. In the next six weeks, he shared exciting news: undercover test shoppers had visited and approved the restaurant; Schultz was preparing a $30 million offer. Better yet, they had received a rival offer from a private-equity firm in Florida.

Though the business consisted of a single storefront, Horwitz gave out grandiose titles, naming himself the CEO and Wunderlin the CFO, with a starting salary of $250,000. He leased an office capacious enough for each of them to have a suite. While Mallory ran the restaurant and Wunderlin plotted its growth, Horwitz spent most days in his office, with the door closed. One afternoon, he invited Wunderlin to join him at the bank, but had him wait in the lobby while he signed documents to prepare for a deal.

Then, all of a sudden, it was gone. The private-equity offer had collapsed, Horwitz said, for complex reasons involving his inheritance, his private investments, and the Securities and Exchange Commission. Worse, he added, when FÜL looked unavailable, Schultz had moved on to another health food chain. Wunderlin was devastated. Without new investments, the restaurant would be finished by the end of the year. "We were left to fend for ourselves," he said. He began looking for other work.

The only good news, Horwitz said, was that Schultz had offered him a job at Maveron, his venture capital firm. Mallory later recalled that he showed her a contract for a position at the firm's "Entrepreneur Outreach Program," based in Los Angeles. It would be perfect, he told her: he would visit campuses and small-business conventions, cultivating young strivers. He did not mention that the move would also allow him to pursue his dream of being a star.

*   *   *

Acting is a discouraging business, but Hollywood aspirants have sustained themselves for decades with tales of predecessors who outhustled the competition. Dick Van Dyke danced to stardom in *Bye Bye Birdie* despite having never before taken a class. Eddie Redmayne got cast in *Les Misérables* by claiming that he was a seasoned equestrian, even though he hadn't been on a horse since childhood. Making it through an audition often requires bluffing not just the casting director but also yourself. It's a mentality that Ryan Gosling once called "self-mythologizing"—the ability to face a "hundred other people that are better-looking and more talented and somehow think that you should get the job."

When Horwitz got to Los Angeles, he set about bluffing two audiences: his old friends at home and his potential new friends in Hollywood. Soon after arriving, he wrote on Twitter, "I normally wouldn't name drop BUT I asked H. Schultz this AM what his goal is for me in my role, he simply says, 'Just be good. Don't stink.'" Before long, though, he started telling Mallory that he was bored with his job and talking about shifting his attention to acting. "I'm, like, 'OK, if this is going to make you happy, do what you want to do—as a hobby,'" she recalled. He tried acting classes and auditions. Then, when he struggled to get parts, he changed tack. Ever since Warren Beatty produced *Bonnie and Clyde*, it has been common for accomplished actors to develop movies and then star in them. Horwitz wondered, Why can't I produce, too? He befriended two brothers, Julio and Diego Hallivis, who were looking to establish themselves in the film industry. Diego, who wore his hair in a tall black pompadour, was a fledgling director. Julio, wiry and intense, ran the business side. Horwitz recruited them for 1inMM Productions to make low-budget independent films—essentially B movies in which he might star. He leased office space in Culver City and three black Mercedes coupes for them to drive to meetings. When Horwitz wasn't around, Julio spoke scathingly about him. An associate recalled that he often said, "He's such a terrible actor. But he's the money guy. He has family money, and he knows rich people."

Horwitz had arrived in L.A. at a time of unusual opportunity. Five years before, Netflix had started streaming films and television shows, and, as Amazon worked to keep up, the two companies competed for talent and content. By 2019, Netflix would be spending more than $12 billion a year on programming. Disney launched Disney+, and WarnerMedia created HBO Max. All told, there were more than 250 online video services in America, feeding a seemingly inexhaustible demand. Money was coursing through the industry; *The New York Times* reported: "Florists, caterers, set decorators, chauffeurs, hair stylists, headhunters—it's gravy train time."

In March 2013, Horwitz announced a partnership to buy the rights to cheap movies and distribute them to the Latin American divisions of Netflix, HBO, and other platforms. His new partner, Gustavo Montaudon, was well suited to the endeavor: he had spent decades at Twentieth Century Fox, distributing content across Latin America. The deal was covered in the trade press, helping to secure a transformation of Horwitz's image. The struggling actor with a failed juice bar was identified in *Variety* as "the entrepreneur behind fitness-driven lifestyle brand FÜL." (Some of his marketing materials went further, describing FÜL as a "multi-million dollar, multi-pronged fitness brand" with "seven locations" and "apparel sold in Target, Dick's Sporting Goods and Sports Authority.")

One of the first people Horwitz approached with his venture was Jake Wunderlin. By the spring of 2014, Wunderlin was in Chicago, working as a trader. He had just received a bonus of $35,000, and he was engaged to be married. He and Horwitz remained friends, but they rarely talked business anymore, until Horwitz started dropping hints that Schultz was backing his work in the movie business. "Zach said, 'I can let you in on a deal,'" Wunderlin told me. It was small by his usual standards, Horwitz said, but if Wunderlin could put up $37,000, he could make $9,000 in ninety days. The contract showed that Horwitz was selling Sony the rights to a Mexican rom-com called *Deseo*, described in the official summary as "A succession of erotic encounters weaved into a daisy chain of delightful sensuality."

Wunderlin had recovered from the failure of the juice bar, but he was still wary: "I said, 'I can't lose this money. This is everything that I've ever saved.'" Horwitz persuaded him by pledging his own assets in case anything went wrong. The deal went through as promised; Wunderlin got his money, which he put toward a down payment on a house. He was hooked.

That fall, he flew to Los Angeles to be a groomsman at Zach and Mallory's wedding at the Four Seasons. Wunderlin was awed by his friend's new life: "He was doing three-hundred-thousand-dollar deals."

Back in Chicago, Wunderlin sat on a roof deck one night with some of their other college friends, including deAlteris, who was working in private equity. He asked if they wanted to pool their money on a larger film deal. "None of us had the gift of inheritance or anything like that," he told me. "All of us were focused on what's next in banking or private wealth or sales and trading. We were all trying to figure out how to be successful." They agreed to buy into a series of deals, and got lucrative returns, often 20 percent or higher. Soon, they started taking out loans to fund more of Horwitz's investments, and thought of quitting their jobs to do it full-time. DeAlteris said, "We're getting paid on time. Real cash. Without fail."

Before long, they were encouraging their parents to put money in. DeAlteris's mother, a widow and a retired physician's assistant, invested $40,000. Wunderlin's parents put up half their retirement savings. Within two years, the college friends had profited on twenty-seven of Horwitz's movie deals. To handle the business, four of them formed a company—called JJMT Capital, for the initials of their first names—and started bringing in money from outsiders, including wealthy investors on Chicago's North Shore. "People were banging down our door—'I hear you guys have this great opportunity. Do you have any room for me?'" deAlteris said.

When Horwitz visited Chicago, he resumed his old conspicuous generosity. At a pizza parlor, he tipped the server $2,000. "She came back out in tears," Wunderlin recalled. At nightclubs, Horwitz might pick up a $40,000 check and leave another $30,000 for a tip. As the party swirled around him, he would lean back in silence, with a blissfully satisfied look.

His friends felt a tinge of satisfaction, too; they were proud of the money that they made for their parents and friends. None of them knew much about the entertainment business, but they thought they knew due diligence. "I would pepper him with questions, and he would come back with answers to everything," deAlteris said. They showed the contracts to industry experts, and Horwitz arranged for a member of their team to speak by phone with his main contact at HBO. Horwitz was always available to answer questions, but he told investors never to contact the streaming platforms directly, because he had signed non-disclosure agreements. "I've got basically three relationships—HBO, Netflix, and Sony," he'd say. "If you guys go around me, you're going to blow up my business."

In fact, there was no business. Horwitz was not buying or selling movie rights. He had got his hands on a few distribution contracts, then copy-and-pasted them in Microsoft Word to make hundreds of fakes, forging signatures of executives that he found on LinkedIn. As new investors bought in, he paid off earlier investors with the proceeds—

a Ponzi scheme. (Montaudon, his partner, has not been charged with any wrongdoing.) He sent out fake bank statements and ginned up bogus emails and text messages from HBO and Netflix, often using apps to send fake messages to himself at predetermined times. He arranged for a female accomplice, who has never been identified, to impersonate the contact at HBO. This kind of deception requires relentless discipline; Bernie Madoff insisted that every screw he might see on his yacht have its head turned in the same direction. Horwitz, too, had a fastidious streak. He held to a rigid schedule, growing upset if he couldn't fit in a workout before noon, and he calmed himself by insuring that everything around him was in the proper place. He never went more than two weeks between haircuts.

His fraud rested on perceptions of Hollywood as a money factory—an idea that reached back to the 1930s, when Louis Mayer, the cofounder of M-G-M, was the highest-paid executive in the country. (Nineteen of the next twenty-five highest-paid execs also ran Hollywood studios.) The reality is that hits are unpredictable and the business is clannish and opaque—"a closed world," as one longtime industry executive put it to me, "with its own language, own rules, own economics and caste system." The finances are obscured by "Hollywood accounting," invented by studios to shield revenues from inspection by stars, writers, and others who want a cut. (The screenwriter for *Men in Black* has said that the film earned more than half a billion dollars, but that the studio refuses to declare it profitable.) And yet, for all that volatility, movies have a charismatic appeal for the distant investor—the proverbial dentist from Omaha, lured by the unspoken prospect that he will somehow end up clinking glasses with Tom Hanks. "People try to buy their way in," the executive said, "and what happens is they lose a lot of money and still get kicked to the curb."

It's tempting to wonder why Horwitz's friends in Chicago thought they had found a vast source of revenue that people in Hollywood had somehow overlooked. But they didn't think they had beaten the insiders; they thought their friend had become an insider. DeAlteris said, "It's an old boys' club, and it seemed like we just so happened to be old boys with somebody who knew some of the old boys."

As their partnership flourished, their personal lives became more entwined; they attended one another's weddings and took joint vacations. In 2016, Horwitz flew Wunderlin by chartered jet to Miami for a mutual friend's bachelor party that stretched for a week. Late one night, the two set off from shore on paddleboards, pausing in the water to reflect on their good fortune. Wunderlin recalls that Horwitz said, "I have more money than I know what to do with. It's like Monopoly money."

*   *   *

By funneling cash into his production company, Horwitz had provided himself with a string of minor roles, including that of a murderous psychopath in a short film made in homage to the Joker, and that of a victim of a home invasion in a movie called *Trespassers*. But after five years in Hollywood he seemed to be confined to B movies—until he devised a way to get closer to real stardom.

In June 2017, Horwitz cofounded a company called Rogue Black, with Andrew Levitas, a filmmaker and a sculptor who had directed Amy Adams, Jennifer Hudson, and other prominent actors. (Levitas, who is not alleged to have been aware of Horwitz's scheme, declined to comment.) In the next four years, according to court documents, Horwitz poured about $20 million into Rogue Black, and Levitas arranged investments in eight movies, including *The White Crow*, directed by Ralph Fiennes, and *Last Moment of Clarity*, with Brian Cox. Horwitz received parts in four of them.

Some were so small that he was barely visible on screen, but still he could claim proximity to famous actors. In 2018, he hired a publicist, Nedda Soltani, who had represented cast members of *Breaking Bad* and the *Real Housewives* franchise. He gave her pictures of himself on the red carpet at the Golden Globes. (He had never attended the awards ceremony, but a photo outside an after-party made it appear that he had. Soltani told me, "No one talks about that, but you could get a hotel room and wear your tux and just sort of be in the mix.") When she asked for a biography, he conjured a story of humble Midwestern roots: an injury had kept him out of the NFL, so he supported himself as a door-to-door salesman before making his way to Hollywood. (In truth, Horwitz had played intramural football in college.) Soltani's boyfriend was from Indiana, so Horwitz felt instantly relatable. "There was something about his eyes. He smelled good, his haircut was nice, he had a nice watch. He made you believe," she said. "We built this little bio on him, and that became my pitch: Johnny Football turns to acting, rags to riches."

The outlets that Soltani persuaded to feature her client were mostly obscure online venues—the kind, she said, that people solicit articles in "just to post them on their Instagram stories and say, 'Look at me.'" But investors researching Horwitz could now find unquestioning recitations of his story. In an interview on AfterBuzz TV, a YouTube channel focused on "Hollywood's rising talent," the host mentioned his "burgeoning career in football, which was derailed," and asked about his association with Fiennes. Horwitz warmly recalled showing up for filming in Belgrade. "Walk on set, he's in the back of this auditorium, and he says, 'Zach!'" He described Fiennes's avuncular instructions: "I loved what you did there. Bring exactly the same thing, but, if you turn just a little bit to the right, the light is going to hit you in a way that's going to look amazing." (Fiennes's publicist said that she was unable to reach her client for comment.)

Hollywood has long had an ambivalent relationship with facts. The screenwriter William Goldman once described overhearing a producer tout so many bogus figures while working the phone that he finally had to cover the mouthpiece and ask, "Which lie did I tell?" In time, Horwitz had deceived so many friends and investors that he had to discourage them from talking to one another; he was always "building moats," as one put it. He told an associate that he had sold FÜL for

$11 million but warned him not to mention it to Mallory, claiming that she had a small-town discomfort with people knowing their business.

Yet Horwitz never stopped stoking belief. Late one night at a club, he showed an investor named Craig Cole a string of text messages telling him that Ted Sarandos, the CEO of Netflix, was seeking long-term rights to the full library of films that he distributed. When the fake Sarandos asked what would secure the deal, Horwitz replied, "The zeros." Moments later, a text came back with an offer in the hundreds of millions. Horwitz slumped to the floor, in a pantomime of triumph and gratitude. In *Bad Actor*, a documentary about the case, Cole recalled that Horwitz started crying: "He says, 'Craig, we made it! We did it!'" Cole wept, too; when he got home that night, he told his girlfriend that they were set for life.

Like other accomplished swindlers, Horwitz excelled by knowing his audience. In Chicago, he was a wealthy heir who flew private jets to movie shoots. In L.A., he was a plucky football talent selling door-to-door. (A surprising number of people he dealt with in California mentioned how good he smelled.) His difficulty showing emotion, a detriment on screen, turned out to be useful for enticing investors. Edgar Allan Poe, in an essay on swindling, noted the power of "nonchalance"— the kind of take-it-or-leave-it indifference that conveys credibility—and Horwitz often succeeded by convincing investors that he didn't much care whether they bought in. "Remember Zach does not need any money from us," one wrote to another in 2017.

That June, Horwitz met investors at the Four Seasons in Beverly Hills. Over dinner, he sat beside Jim Russell, a Las Vegas steel executive, and, according to court documents, said that he had made some $20 million the previous year. Russell was concerned when Horwitz insisted that his business records were too confidential to share, and later sent an email to one of his partners describing the evasion as a "Red Flag!!" But the partner dismissed the concern, writing, "This is the goose that lays the golden egg." Russell relented, and his group put in another $5 million.

By 2019, Horwitz even seemed to be improving his acting. In May, he showed up in Norfolk, Virginia, to shoot a movie called *The Gateway*. It was understood that his financial support guaranteed him a place on screen. "This is truly not uncommon," Michele Civetta, the director, told me. "I've heard countless stories from friends who've made films. It's, like, 'Oh, yeah, if you want half a million dollars, this wealthy industrialist's daughter has to have a secondary role.'"

Horwitz was assigned the role of a volatile ex-con named Mike, but in rehearsals he got timid and self-conscious; his voice went high and his mannerisms grew labored. So Civetta contacted a nearby jail and arranged for Horwitz to spend the night, talking to inmates and being searched and fingerprinted. When he returned, he showed a new ability to "change tonalities," Civetta said. "He could go places relatively quickly in terms of diabolical rage." When the movie came out, *Variety* observed, "Probably the best turn is by Avery," who "makes potentially cardboard villain Mike into a frighteningly credible sociopath."

*   *   *

As the end of 2019 approached, Horwitz had raised $358 million in the past year. He was running what scholars of confidence games call an "affinity fraud," built around trust and personal connections. He found wealthy investors—in Napa Valley, Orange County, Las Vegas, and Chicago—who then spread the word on the tennis court and the charity circuit. But every network has limits, and the arithmetic of a Ponzi scheme is unforgiving. When you run out of new investors, the mechanism begins to collapse. After Thanksgiving, Horwitz fell behind on his payments for the first time.

To fend off concerns, Horwitz blamed the delay on the big media platforms and promised a speedy resolution. On January 4, though, Wunderlin and deAlteris arrived at his house on Bolton Road to figure out what was happening. For three days, Horwitz walked them through documents; he had thousands of pages of fake contracts and emails and bank statements, which he presented calmly. "Cool as a cucumber," deAlteris recalled. The possibility of fraud never occurred to him, deAlteris said: "I thought it was wild disorganization that he had so much money coming into his bank account." The friends went back to Chicago feeling relieved.

But Horwitz fell further behind, and he gave more excuses. Covid-19 was disrupting business; HBO was reorganizing its operation; Netflix was auditing its distribution deals. He needed time with his family, he said—Mallory had recently given birth to their second child. All the while, he kept up his patter. In October, he texted an investor, "just heard from HBO," and then passed along a fake email from executives asking for a "week grace period." He commiserated: "always something w them."

Near the end of 2020, Horwitz bought one last bit of time by saying that money was piling up at Freeway Entertainment, an account-management firm, and would soon be distributed. But the delays were becoming untenable for his friends in Chicago. People who had given them money to invest were threatening to sue. One was Marty Kaplan, a financier who, along with partners and family members, had $10 million at risk. According to Kaplan's lawyer, deAlteris had reassured him by citing his friendship with Horwitz, adding, "I wouldn't be able to pay rent if something went wrong."

In all, Horwitz owed the Chicago group $165 million. He had got his lawyer at the prominent firm K&L Gates to send a letter warning them that the details of the deals were "strictly confidential," but on February 23 Wunderlin and deAlteris decided to call Freeway to check the account balance. Wunderlin made the call from his home in Chicago; he patched in deAlteris, at his kitchen table across town. Horwitz had given them a copy of his contract with Freeway, as well as statements showing a growing balance. DeAlteris flipped through the paperwork to find the account number, then read it aloud. The representative paused and asked to hear the name again. The firm had no record of a Zach Horwitz, he said. DeAlteris grew impatient: "I'm looking at the fucking bank statement! You clearly misheard me."

By the time they hung up, they could see an impending catastrophe. "All the dominoes fell after that one," deAlteris said. Wunderlin, who had been pacing during the call, dropped to his knees. He had been the first of the friends to put money into Horwitz's scheme, followed by his family and then by outsiders who contributed a harrowing sum. When I asked him about it more than two years later, he fell silent and struggled not to cry. "I still can't really talk about it without doing this," he said.

That afternoon, their lawyer contacted the FBI to report a suspected fraud. Other investors were reaching similar conclusions. On March 15, FBI agents came to deAlteris's house to record a call with Horwitz. Wunderlin was there, too. On the phone, Horwitz ran through his usual reassurances, until Wunderlin cut in: "Here's the problem with that. That's not fucking true. We spoke to Freeway. Where in the fuck is our money?"

There was a long pause—long enough that they had to ask Horwitz if he was still on the line. Finally, he said, "I think the lawyers should do the talking." Wunderlin couldn't restrain himself: "You're not going to tell me where any of the money is? What did you do with it?" He talked about his mother's savings, his father's savings, but Horwitz stayed silent. Wunderlin sensed that he might have realized he was being recorded. "It was like talking to the wall," he said.

In L.A., Horwitz's friends noticed that he seemed paranoid, worrying that he was being monitored through their phones. When they asked what was going on, he evaded the question, saying that he didn't want to expose them to trouble.

According to court documents, Horwitz had been using Adderall and Xanax and drinking heavily, sometimes staying up most of the night. Mallory was worried about his behavior, but she believed that he had just been having trouble recouping money that HBO and Netflix owed him. They had begun to talk about a simpler life—maybe somewhere quieter, like Nashville or Austin. By spring, they had put their house on the market and found a buyer. The offer was set to be officially accepted on April 6.

That morning, before dawn, Mallory was asleep beside Zach and their three-year-old when she awoke to banging on the front door. From down the hall, she could hear their baby crying, and she ran to soothe him. Looking through the window, she saw FBI agents, guns drawn, and heard them shouting Zach's name. Mallory rushed downstairs with the baby in her arms and opened the door. Agents streamed in. Zach, now on the stairs, asked if he could put on a shirt. The agents refused, and walked him out onto Bolton Road. John Verrastro, the agent in charge, was startled by Horwitz's behavior. He had come to expect defendants in white-collar cases to express something during their arrests—bewilderment, outrage, despair—but Horwitz showed none of that. "He didn't seem surprised," Verrastro said.

Mallory quickly filed for divorce. According to her filings, their joint accounts had been frozen by the authorities; the only money in her name was a checking account with a balance of $100.75. Horwitz was charged with thirteen counts of fraud, in the service of what prosecutors called an "intricate illusion"—the largest Ponzi scheme in Hollywood history. He had raised more than $690 million by deceiving hundreds of investors, beginning with his closest friends. A woeful actor on screen turned out to have been an astonishingly convincing performer in life.

The extent of the lie was almost too great for Mallory to grasp. Her husband never had any deals with HBO or Netflix. He had never even met Howard Schultz. When Zach left for late-night meetings, there were no meetings. The only thing real was his slender imprint on the screen. In her filings, she wrote, "I loved him. I idolized him. Zach is a masterful manipulator and liar and brainwashed and gaslit me into believing he was this perfect man, something he made everyone around him feel. Only a sociopath can live the sort of deceptive life Zach lived for nearly ten years." Mallory's father bought her and the children one-way tickets to Indiana. On May 1, 2021, she flew home.

*   *   *

Horwitz got out on bail: a million dollars, posted by his mother. For a week or two, the case made headlines worldwide, but he stayed out of sight, telling his kids that he was working as a dog-walker. Among people who knew him, the reaction that I encountered most often was disbelief that he was bright enough to manage such a scheme. "I don't know how the fuck he was capable of it," one of his closest friends told me. Another associate said, "If you had asked me if this man even had Photoshop downloaded to his computer, I would've told you, 'Absolutely not.'" More than a few surmised that his Latin American distribution network must have been a front for a drug cartel.

The government didn't agree. The SEC named him as the sole defendant, noting that he alone had controlled the bank accounts at 1inMM. When I told Verrastro, the FBI agent, that many people were perplexed nobody else was charged, he said he couldn't go into detail about that decision. But he hastened to add, "The one thing that's clear in this case is there was no one above him. He is the main guy."

As with many frauds, the prosecution triggered a series of lawsuits, as investors fought over the remaining assets and accused one another, as well as various banks and law firms, of failing to spot the crime. Alexander Loftus, a lawyer representing some of the investors, filed suits against Horwitz's friends in Chicago. "When you're acting like a broker, it's your job to see if this is good or not before you sell it," he told me. Ultimately, Loftus said, the friends in Chicago agreed to give up more than $9 million—though they maintain that they acted in good faith. "My family members who trusted me, they're not savvy," deAlteris said. "I thought that I was being fairly objective with how I approached it. My family members weren't. One chip became two chips, which became all their chips." Their lawyer, Brian Michael, told me, "It's inconceivable that they would've questioned a fraud that was rooted in a friendship long before Zach went to Hollywood, that they allowed their own families to participate in."

In the end, there was surprisingly little money to recoup. A receiver, appointed by the court to hunt for assets, reported that an "unknown" sum might be "hidden." But lawyers involved in the case told me that Horwitz expended most of the money keeping the scheme going. The rest he used to pay for jets and yachts and the pursuit of stardom: prosecutors listed $605,000 to Mercedes-Benz and Audi, $174,000 to party planners, $54,600 for a "luxury watch subscription" service. Six months after his arrest, confronted by extensive evidence of his deceptions, Horwitz pleaded guilty.

On the afternoon of February 14, 2022, I attended the sentencing in a federal courtroom in L.A. Horwitz arrived early, in a tailored blue suit and brown wingtips. His mother and other relatives filled the rows behind the defense table. Prosecutors declared, in a written argument to the judge, "It is difficult to conceive a white-collar crime more egregious." They noted that Horwitz had begun his scheme by "betraying the trust of his own friends, people who lowered their guard because they could not possibly imagine that someone they had known for years would unflinchingly swindle them and their families out of their life savings."

Victims had been invited to submit descriptions of the impact on their lives. One investor, identified as a sixty-four-year-old who lost $1.4 million, described coming out of retirement to pay for food and shelter: "I cry every day and have stopped seeing friends or family because of the shame of this financial loss and have a now severe distrust of other human beings. If it was not for my spiritual beliefs, I would have committed suicide." Another wrote, "I am the mother of a 46-year-old special needs daughter. . . . I will never be able to earn what has been taken from me and my daughter but the emotional damage . . . is even greater."

Some victims chose to speak in person. Robert Henny, a lanky screenwriter with two young children, stepped to the microphone. "I don't live an extravagant lifestyle," he said. "My career could hit bumps and we'd be O.K. Even after my wife's cancer diagnosis, we were O.K. For fifteen years, we lived frugally." They had lost $1.8 million in the scheme. "For the first time, we are not O.K. I don't know if we ever will be," he said.

When it was Horwitz's turn to speak, he stood before the judge, his shoulders hunched and hands clasped. "I became the exact opposite person from who I wanted to be," he said. He wept and paused to collect himself. "I am destroyed and haunted every day and night by the harm that I have caused others." He asked the judge for a lenient sentence, one that would allow him to "return to my young boys when they are still boys."

The judge, Mark C. Scarsi, was unmoved. He applied the maximum sentence that prosecutors had requested: twenty years in prison. (Elizabeth Holmes, the founder of the disgraced biotech start-up Theranos, was sentenced to eleven years; Sam Bankman-Fried, the billionaire founder of FTX, is serving twenty-five.) As the sentence was announced, Horwitz stared into the distance and then up at the ceiling.

After the courtroom emptied out, Henny stopped at the bathroom. As he was preparing to leave, the door opened and Horwitz walked in. "We look at each other," Henny recalled. "And he goes, 'Hey, I just want to tell you, I'm so sorry.'" Henny, who is six feet four, towered over him. "You took everything from us," he said.

One of Horwitz's relatives poked his head in the door and said, "Hey, are we all good here?"

Horwitz reassured him, "Yeah, we're OK," and the door closed again.

Henny could have asked him why he did it, or how he lived with himself. But, as a writer, he was interested in only one thing: "How did you think you were going to get out of this? What was your endgame?"

Horwitz paused, and then said, "I didn't have one."

Until the end, Horwitz seemed to have believed that one of his identities was going to save him—actor, producer, investor. Something had to work. Fake it till you make it.

*   *   *

One morning in November 2023, I took a cab out to the Federal Correctional Institute at Terminal Island. It sits on a peninsula at the far end of an industrial strip south of Los Angeles, jutting into the waters of the harbor. The facility is surrounded by barbed wire and gun towers, but tauntingly close to the city. Walking inside, I could hear seagulls and the distant rumble of cranes on the docks.

I had exchanged letters and emails with Horwitz since his sentencing, in which he agreed to keep the "lines of communication open" but wouldn't say "anything specific." He seemed more interested in projecting a narrative of rehabilitation. He described a shift in his mind-set and said, "I am healthier for it every single day." He imagined teaching a class to fellow-inmates, called "Emotional Intelligence Through Acting," that would give them a "safe space to express vulnerability."

I had stopped by the prison hoping to get Horwitz to speak more frankly about his crimes. In the visiting room, he wore a khaki shirt tucked into khaki pants, his hair cropped. He was relaxed and unfailingly polite. But, for all his talk of expressing vulnerability, he was still unwilling to answer questions on the record. In an email later, he told me that publicity doesn't help, because "all the wounds keep getting ripped open and additional salt being poured on top."

I was wary of whatever he might tell me, in any case. He had always been conscious of his ability to persuade. At family Thanksgivings, when relatives went around the table saying what made them grateful, he treated it as a "performance," he wrote later, prepping an answer and "artificially manufacturing it in order to get the sought after result."

In prison, Horwitz had access to a computer for fifteen minutes at a time. He used it to start a blog, which he called Be That 1, a new variation on his favorite slogan about beating the odds. He offered occasional glimpses of his thinking during the scam—how he'd been "obsessed with belief in a superior life that existed just beyond my grasp"; how he had "put on the smile" despite "living an absolute hell," with the knowledge that his life was "all bullsh*t"; how he had portrayed "utmost confidence to everyone" to mask "deep, unresolved internal insecurities." He recalled the feeling of living a "fabricated life that I had forced myself to believe was reality." To sustain the delusion, he developed self-protective habits—"avoiding phone calls . . . avoid opening mail . . . avoid checking e-mails"—even though "on some level it was simply denial of what was inevitably coming."

He also indulged in the language of self-help. Prison, he wrote, was a "journey" of "mending the wounds" and finding "genuine emotion." People he had tricked were infuriated by the blog; it seemed glib or, perhaps, strategic—a way of assembling material for a relaunch of his life after prison. "I think he wants to be the next version of that guy from *Wolf of Wall Street*," Mallory told me. "He loved that movie and watched it over and over again."

Even from prison, Horwitz couldn't seem to control his instinct for imposture and assimilation. Reading his blog, the producers of the documentary *Bad Actor* came upon lines that sounded out of place; they turned out to be copied from *Never Finished*, a self-help book by David Goggins, a former Navy SEAL. Goggins wrote that "humility is the antidote to self-pity. It keeps you rooted in reality and your emotions in check." Horwitz had published that passage in his own voice, changing only "you" and "your" to "me" and "my."

*   *   *

In Horwitz's fantasies, you hear echoes of the long tradition of American artifice: of Napoleon Hill, who wrote in *Think and Grow Rich* that "whatever the mind of men can conceive and believe, it can achieve," and of the clergyman Norman Vincent Peale, who declared, "As you act and persevere in acting, so you tend to become"—a principle impressed on a young real estate scion named Donald Trump when his family attended Peale's sermons. At times, this tendency still seems strong enough to overwhelm the systems that we've developed to punish it. Even after Elizabeth Holmes was convicted, she voiced a belief that lies are just a stop on the way to truth. Asked what she thought would've happened if she had not courted so much attention, she told an interviewer, "We would've seen through our vision."

In my conversations with people who knew Horwitz, many wondered why he risked so much. If it was all for money and fame, why not get out before it became so destructive? I concluded that he was seeking something harder to attain. He spent years performing the parts of a life he desired—the chosen protégé, the coveted talent, the loyal friend. He needed applause, from the server at a pizza restaurant and from his friends toasting him at dinner.

In the end, Horwitz got fame only where most people would want it least: from the true crime audience. After his arrest, a commenter on Reddit wrote, "This is 100% going to be a movie." Another agreed: "I'd watch the shit out of this." Before long, Horwitz's scheme was the focus of podcasts with names like *Scamfluencers*, *Crime and Wine*, and *Oh My Fraud*. His story was re-created for episodes of *The Con* on ABC, and *American Greed* on CNBC.

But most of the people who had worked with him were eager to forget him. When I wrote to a Hollywood veteran, asking about the experience, the response was "Your e-mail is something that I have dreaded in the back of my head for a long time." The traces of Horwitz's Hollywood life have been scattered or effaced. The house on Bolton Road was sold and the contents auctioned off. A poster with the slogan that inspired the name of his scheme went for forty-five dollars. And, despite all that Horwitz risked to make it on the big screen, his acting is hard to find. In *The White Crow*, his appearance was edited down to half a second. When *The Gateway* came out in 2021, he was nowhere on the posters, and Olivia Munn never mentioned him on the press tour. When Brian Cox published a memoir, the movie he made with Zach Avery did not even make the index.

Looking back through his hours of effortful acting, there is one scene that stands out. It's in *Trespassers*, the home invasion movie, when his character admits to his wife that he has cheated on her. On set, the director, frustrated with his attempts to get Horwitz to perform, finally told him to ignore the script and let himself go: "Just strip it away. Throw away the line. Just tell her." After a pause, Horwitz gave himself over to a few seconds of unconcealed feeling. "I fucked up," he said. "I'm a piece of shit!" He sounded present and broken and strangely relieved. For a moment, you could almost forget that Horwitz was acting.

———————————

Zach Horwitz is scheduled to be released from prison on March 10, 2038.

Patriot Games

*The billionaire Guo Wengui was linked to Chinese intelligence,
the FBI, and Donald Trump. What was he after?*

— 2022 —

The Sherry-Netherland, a slender neo-Renaissance tower at 781 Fifth Avenue, is known as one of New York's "white glove" co-ops, for the linen gloves that the elevator attendants wear. It has panoramic views of Central Park, décor inherited from a Vanderbilt mansion, and amenities befitting a luxury hotel; room service comes from the Harry Cipriani restaurant downstairs. Through the years, the Sherry has accommodated the occasional celebrity—Diana Ross, Francis Ford Coppola, David Bowie—but, like other buildings of its kind, it tends to prefer quieter money.

On a winter day in 2015, the Sherry's co-op board received an unusual application. A Chinese businessman calling himself Miles Guo wanted the most expensive unit in the building—a penthouse that occupies the entire eighteenth floor, with six bedrooms, nine bathrooms, and three terraces. There was no need to secure a mortgage; he could send $68 million in cash. Although Guo didn't know anyone at the Sherry who could vouch for him, his lawyers, at prominent firms in Washington and New York, delivered confidential documents that identified him as a married father of two, who owned a Beijing real estate enterprise with assets of nearly $4 billion. He was No. 74 on a list of China's richest people, but he avoided public attention, and even basic photographs were scarce. A reference letter from UBS, the Swiss bank, characterized him as a "modest gentleman with a warm heart." A personal recommendation from Tony Blair, Britain's former prime minister, said, "Miles is honest, forthright and has impeccable taste."

The co-op board, moving with unusual alacrity, convened to approve the application. Guo arrived soon afterward, accompanied by a coterie of attendants and, later, by a white Pomeranian named Snow. Around the building, the new tenant was hard to miss. He was a handsome, ebullient man in his late forties, with an array of trim-cut Brioni suits and a broad smile.

From his adopted home on the Upper East Side, Guo spent lavishly and gained access to new worlds. He paid $43 million for a silver superyacht, *Lady May*, which had space to entertain fifty people and a living room that revolved on a cushion of compressed air. In London, he socialized at Mark's Club, a members-only establishment, and traveled around town in a white Rolls-Royce. On one visit, he implored an acquaintance, whom he'd met only hours before, to borrow the car for as long as he needed.

Donald Trump became the Republican presidential front-runner that summer, and Guo's instincts proved well suited to the emerging era; he had already joined Mar-a-Lago, Trump's club in Palm Beach, and he wasn't shy about praising his own business acumen ("I'm a genius at making money!"). He boasted of expensive tastes: handmade Louis Vuitton shoes, a rare variety of tea said to be worth a million dollars a kilo. Even before he was introduced to Steve Bannon, Bannon had heard enough about Guo to pronounce him "the Donald Trump of Beijing." (Years later, when federal agents went looking for Bannon in connection with an allegedly fraudulent scheme to raise money for a wall on the Mexican border, they found him aboard Guo's yacht in Long Island Sound.)

At the Sherry, though, Guo rapidly developed a reputation for peculiar habits. He seemed obsessed with the risk of intruders; he tried to block the fire exit in his penthouse, and residents complained that he stationed bodyguards in the lobby. In March 2015, a spate of reports in the Chinese press offered an explanation for his anxiety: Guo—whom the reports referred to by his Mandarin name, Guo Wengui—was at the center of a burgeoning scandal involving corruption and espionage.

For nearly a decade, he had maintained a secret partnership with one of China's most powerful spymasters, an intelligence officer named Ma Jian, who had recently been arrested by his own government. Caixin, a Chinese investigative news organization, reported that Ma and Guo had used surveillance, blackmail, and political influence to amass fortunes and evade scrutiny.

Guo denied any wrongdoing; he told a Hong Kong newspaper that he and Ma were just friends, who had met through work and bonded over a shared appreciation for architecture. But, two years later, he changed his story dramatically. He acknowledged that he had been a longtime "affiliate" of China's all-pervasive Ministry of State Security. The agency, he said, had tasked him with "handling things for them" and connecting with "sensitive figures" abroad, traveling on eleven different passports and employing the code name Wu Nan.

Even more startling, he subsequently declared himself an enemy of the Chinese Communist Party—a position almost unheard-of among China's elite. He applied for political asylum in the United States, and founded a media network, which broadcast incendiary criticisms of the CCP and enthusiastic support for Trump. His businesses reportedly paid hundreds of thousands of dollars to Trump advisers, including Bannon, Rudy Giuliani, and the attorney L. Lin Wood, who joined efforts to overturn the 2020 election. As Guo's neighbors at the Sherry-Netherland watched in confusion, he established himself as an election denier, a vaccine skeptic, and a right-wing provocateur, with a degree of political influence that is especially rare among foreign citizens on American soil.

Through the decades, Washington has attracted no shortage of wealthy figures who learned to surf the rivalries in American politics. But how, exactly, a Chinese intelligence collaborator was reborn as a darling of Trump Republicans is a measure of the shifting folkways of conservative politics, and the extraordinary power that accrues to people with the wealth and savvy to command the technologies of influence. Depending on whom you believe, Guo has been either an asset of the FBI or a target of its suspicions, or perhaps both at the same time. Under one alias or another—including Miles Kwok, Guo Haoyun, and Ho Wan Kwok—he has been sued numerous times for defamation, libel, and inflicting emotional distress, and has sued many others on similar grounds. The Chinese government says that he is under investigation in at least nineteen cases, for allegations that include bribery, money laundering, and rape—all of which he denies, attributing them to a propaganda campaign. (Guo and his attorneys declined requests to comment for this article.)

Some observers argue that Guo's disruptive behavior makes sense only if he is still linked to the Chinese state. In a federal court filing from 2019, a private intelligence firm in a business dispute with him claimed that he "was, and is, a dissident-hunter, propagandist, and agent in the service of the People's Republic of China." Guo denied the accusation and won the case, but the court left open the question of his actual identity. "The evidence at trial does not permit the Court to decide whether Guo is, in fact, a dissident or a double agent," Judge Lewis J. Liman wrote. "Others will have to determine who the true Guo is."

*   *   *

The farming village of Xicaoying, in the flatlands of Shandong Province, takes gritty pride in its history. A monument marks the spot nearby where Emperor Qin, who unified China more than two thousand years ago, is said to have ordered an embankment built at such speed that workers who died from the toil were entombed in their own earthworks. Guo grew up there in the 1970s, in an impoverished family with eight children. He started out without much more than the gift of gab— a "tireless tongue," as it is known in Chinese. He had little interest in school. When Chinese reporters later probed his background, a teacher recalled, "he led a group that mostly fought, gambled, and chased girls."

At thirteen, Guo dropped out, and for a time he found work selling clothes and electronics. But in 1989, before he could build much of a career, he was put in jail. He has offered a high-minded explanation for his imprisonment: inspired by the pro-democracy protests in Tiananmen Square, he sold his motorcycle and sent thirty-six hundred yuan—about a thousand dollars—to the student activists. When police came to arrest him, his younger brother objected and was fatally shot. Guo served twenty-two months, and, according to a brisk narrative in his court filings, underwent a storybook transformation: "After his release from prison, Mr. Guo became a successful real estate developer and investor."

But a copy of the verdict in Guo's case makes no mention of political activism; it lists his crime as fraud, for bilking buyers in a local oil scheme. Moreover, he was detained a week before the crackdown on protests in Beijing. (Guo suggested that prosecutors falsified the charges.)

In any case, jail did change Guo's life, providing him with contacts that shaped his early career. After his release, a fellow-inmate led him to an entry-level job with a wealthy entrepreneur in Hong Kong, a woman named Xia Ping. Guo's new position offered heady opportunities. In 1993, when he was in his twenties, he was running a company called Big Boss Furniture. Soon, he joined a project to build the first skyscraper hotel in Zhengzhou, the capital of Henan Province.

Henan is a rough place, where a legacy of poverty feeds an image of endemic crime, as well as a cruel caricature across China. (A Beijing newspaper once lamented that the locals are "generally regarded as cheaters, thieves, troublemakers, and bumpkins.") But Guo thrived there. The business scene ran on a quasi-legal symbiosis between entrepreneurs and Party officials. Builders needed land and protection from regulators; apparatchiks wanted kickbacks, and they wanted to be linked with the kinds of projects—hotels, railways, coal mines—that inspire promotions. Over time, Guo built enough trust with patrons in high office that he was allowed to handle their most delicate business deal-ings. In China, such attendants are known as "white gloves," because they help politicians make money while keeping their hands clean.

Life as a white glove is lucrative but risky. "We were like the fish that clean the teeth of crocodiles," a former white glove named Desmond Shum recalled in *Red Roulette*, a memoir that he published after fleeing China. According to his account, in the 2000s Shum, an entrepreneur in Beijing, became a white glove for the wife of China's premier, Wen Jiabao. To succeed, he had to master what he called the "infinite fungi-bility of Chinese laws." He and his wife, Whitney Duan, learned how to find political sponsors and how to win deals by supplying bureaucrats with gifts; they learned when to flatter an official's knowledge of poetry and when to buy him a thousand-dollar bowl of soup, made from cov-eted fish maw. The business relied on appeasing officials' vanity. One of Shum's employees accompanied "so many people to so many bathhouses that his skin started peeling off."

Perhaps the most important principle of survival, Shum wrote, was that Party officials "used corruption investigations to purge their polit-ical foes," so they were fanatical about hiding business deals from one another. A prominent Beijing venue dedicated two staff members to staggering the arrivals and departures of politicians at dinnertime, so that no one could see whom anyone else was eating with. The couple knew they had joined a "life-and-death" game, but they accepted the risk. "We'd come from nothing," Shum wrote. "So why not go for it all?" They were divorced in 2015; two years later, Duan disappeared, presumably detained by the government. Shum has said that his family has not heard from her since, except for two phone calls pleading with him not to publish the book.

*   *   *

Having launched his rise in the provinces, Guo turned his focus to Beijing, where the prospects, and the stakes, were far higher. In the

capital, he developed a reputation for transactional generosity. A regulator whom Guo was courting for an approval is said to have walked
out of his apartment to find a new sports car waiting for him. In the
glove compartment was a gift card, loaded with the equivalent of several
hundred thousand dollars. (Guo has emphatically denied paying bribes.)

Word got around that Guo could be as ruthless as he was generous.
He seemed to have access to compromising information—the power
to "grab someone by the handle," as the Chinese expression goes. In
2006, while Guo was trying to secure a building permit for a patch of
land beside the site of the upcoming Summer Olympic Games, he was
rebuffed by Liu Zhihua, a powerful vice mayor of Beijing. In retaliation,
Guo obtained a tape of Liu having sex with a mistress and delivered it
to the government. The vice mayor was soon accused of corruption and
of leading a "decadent lifestyle," and given a suspended death sentence.
Guo got his building permit.

Guo later revealed that he had obtained the tape from government
agencies. Caixin reported that it came from Ma Jian, the spymaster, a
man with heavy-lidded eyes, a rosebud mouth, and sturdy jowls. In three
decades at the security services, he had risen to the top of the counterintelligence department—the shadowy specialty of seeking out moles,
double agents, and conspirators. He not only led the hunt for snooping
foreigners; he also collected files on his comrades in the Communist
Party, on the theory that thwarting potential blackmail requires cata-
loguing the weaknesses of one's own side—who has a young lover, say,
or a drug habit that an enemy could exploit. As a former diplomat put
it, Ma was the man with a "safe full of papers."

The Chinese security services have long cultivated relationships
with "commercial cadres"—businesspeople who share information, and
sometimes profits, in return for protection. The ethos, as one leader put
it, is to "use business to cultivate intelligence, so that intelligence and
business thrive together."

At times, the linkages have extended to criminal enterprises. In 1993,
one of China's top law enforcement officials, Tao Siju, praised "patriotic"

elements of the Hong Kong Mafia, a brutal network of drug runners and blackmailers who were known to attack their rivals with meat cleavers. For decades, the security services have built relationships with scrappy young rogues whose ingenuity and underworld contacts might prove useful. A scholar who is familiar with China's security apparatus told me, "They find people in their early stage. They can change their name; they can change their story. They need to be picked up from nowhere."

By the time Guo befriended the spymaster, he had already shown a knack for borrowing the government's power: in Beijing, he paid a transportation official for license plates bearing the letter "A," which typically signal connections with high officials. (For years, cars with these plates were effectively exempt from traffic laws, because cops rarely dared to pull them over.) Now he evidently began to benefit from his association with the security services. When a man named Qu Long tried to report Guo for strong-arm tactics, he was himself arrested by a team that included an officer from Ma's ministry and sent to prison.

These kinds of gambits fed a fearsome reputation among Guo's business rivals, who nicknamed him the "god of war." Even some of his employees were frightened of him. Chen Zhiyao, a Taiwanese businessman, was once summoned to a company office to discuss a dispute over money. Before going, Chen told his wife to call him every thirty minutes; if he didn't answer, she was to contact his friends—he gave her a list of ten—and raise the alarm. At the office, according to allegations that Chen later published in Taiwan, he was detained, beaten, and threatened with a gun. He sued in a Beijing court, but lost the case.

At the building site that Guo had wrested from the grip of the vice mayor, he developed the Pangu Plaza, a complex containing the Pangu 7 Star Hotel (Guo assigned the rating himself) and a row of luxury high-rises arranged in the shape of a dragon. The tallest of the buildings, with a crown designed to resemble an Olympic flame, became a new landmark on the Beijing skyline. But journalists looking into Guo's background quickly ran aground; the *Beijing News*, a local paper, said that its editors received a letter from Ma's ministry directing them to

drop a story for reasons of "national security." Even at the grand opening of the high-rises, where Guo presided, photographers did not take
his picture.

Guo's relatively low profile made him useful to the spy agency. Operating as a cutout—a civilian who can circulate without attracting official attention—he took several trips to meet with the Dalai Lama, the
Tibetan spiritual leader, whom Beijing regards as a dangerous separatist.
Guo said that he conveyed messages back and forth, and that the government offered him awards for his services, which he modestly declined.
But, before long, he began to draw international notice. Randal Phillips,
who was then the CIA station chief in Beijing, noted that the head of
the Chinese military's clandestine service arranged meetings at Guo's
hotel—a sign that intelligence officers considered it safe territory.

Eventually, Guo began talking to American officials directly, though
he revealed little of himself. A former government official told me, "The
first time the U.S. embassy ran across Guo Wengui, that wasn't the name
he was using—it was Miles Kwok. He introduced himself and talked to
the embassy, and the embassy filed several cables. The narrative he gave
was that he was a princeling"—a son of the powerful elite. "He made
up this whole biography. The embassy did a little bit of digging, and it
all fell apart." Still, it seemed possible that he had valuable information.
Diplomats dined with Guo at his hotel periodically, and he spoke with
unusual candor about which Chinese leaders were womanizing and
embezzling. He claimed to have witnessed some of them cavorting on
his own private jet. "He'd dish," the former diplomat said.

In Washington, some of those who heard Guo's tales suspected that
they were exaggerations, or disinformation meant to tarnish rivals and
confuse Americans about Beijing politics. But people who encountered
Guo were struck by his unmistakable access to power. Not long after
the 2008 Olympics, Orville Schell, a journalist and author who leads
the Center on U.S.-China Relations at the Asia Society, was invited to
join Guo in his private dining room at the Pangu Plaza. Guo gave him
an effusive welcome, Schell told me: "Miles takes to you like a long-lost

friend." After dinner, Guo took him down to a basement garage, to show off a collection of luxury cars: "Lamborghinis, Porsches, Maseratis—the whole nine yards." The display was about more than cars; in Beijing, no one acquires such ostentatious wealth without high-ranking protection.

The two stayed in touch, and Schell noticed that Guo seemed able to draw anyone to his dinner table: Henry Kissinger, George Shultz, politicians from Hong Kong and Macau. He once returned from a visit to North Korea with a pompadour in the style of Kim Jong-il. "He waxed quite elegiac about Kim, and what a close buddy he'd become," Schell said.

At one point, Schell, who had written critically of China's record on human rights, encountered resistance to his visa application, and Guo volunteered to help. "He said, 'I'm going to fix this for you. But you've got to talk to some people.'" Guo took Schell to a series of meetings with two officials of indeterminate portfolio. "Every session was at some fancy tearoom," Schell said. "They never wanted to tell me directly who they were in the government. But we would get together to talk for hours about U.S.-China policy." Schell concluded that they were intelligence officers. "I learned more from them about the inner thinking in Party organs than in all my decades of experience in China. I'm certain they were trying to flip me. They tried to give me presents and take me on trips, but I thought, Well, I know these guys are spooks, and the room is obviously wired." As Schell got to know Guo, it became increasingly clear how closely he was entwined with Ma. "We would be eating dinner, and he'd be on the phone every ten minutes with this guy," Schell said. "This was how he got everything done: Ma Jian."

*   *   *

The competition among China's elite usually takes place behind a kind of virtual curtain. Officials do their best to obscure their infighting, and local Chinese journalists know that reporting on such behavior is forbidden—unless, that is, it becomes too public to be ignored. A decade ago, a charismatic party boss named Bo Xilai was purged after his wife murdered one of their white gloves with a dose of cyanide. The deceased was an Englishman, Neil Heywood, and, once the British embassy publicly acknowledged suspicions about his death, censors had no choice but to allow the topic into the news.

In Guo's case, he might still be in China if it weren't for a secretive power play that spilled into public view. In late 2014, while trying to win control of a financial firm, he accused a rival, Li You, of corruption. But Li did not go without a fight. When police came to a Beijing hotel one night to arrest him, his bodyguards stalled while he escaped—reportedly still in his pajamas. Li was eventually caught, but the conflict with Guo had become too visible to censor. A Chinese reporter had even witnessed the fracas in the hotel, and details of Guo's ties to the spymaster started to appear in the overseas Chinese media.

Leaders of the Communist Party were alarmed. If the spymaster with a "safe full of papers" went rogue, he could do unimaginable damage. On January 16, 2015, the Party announced that Ma was under investigation. A former intelligence official told me that Guo was nearly arrested, too, but he received a warning just in time: "When the security guys came to Ma's office, trying to detain him, his senior aide was on the phone to Guo, saying, 'Get the fuck out now.'"

While the government started to seize his assets and arrest his relatives and employees, Guo flew to Hong Kong, and then to London, where he had powerful connections—including the former prime minister Tony Blair, whom he had been courting for years. Shortly after Blair and his wife, Cherie, departed Downing Street, Guo bought five thousand copies of Cherie's autobiography, saying that it would inspire his employees. He also donated to Blair's charities. An affinity grew. By 2013, Blair was working for a sovereign wealth fund in Abu Dhabi. According to Caixin, he agreed to introduce Guo to members of the Royal Family, and Guo raised $3 billion from the royals. (A spokesman said Blair "has never had a commercial contract with Mr. Kwok" and denied that Blair agreed to "make the introduction as is claimed.")

After Guo landed in New York, he submitted his application for the penthouse at the Sherry-Netherland. He might never go back to China. He needed to master a new terrain, and so he started with a game he knew: intelligence. Around the world, the FBI maintains thousands of formal and informal sources, ranging from high-flying financiers to shoe shiners who monitor foot traffic on a street corner. Some have civic motives, in the way of a grandmother on a porch who quietly notes the make and model of a drug dealer's car. But in most cases the relationships are transactional. The source wants money or protection from prosecution; the handler, as one former agent told me, is "trying to juice as much utility out of that person" as possible.

In New York, Guo spoke to the FBI about Chinese leaders' financial and private lives, according to two sources familiar with the arrangement. "He knew who had girlfriends, who had boyfriends," a former Bureau official recalled. More important, Guo knew which Party families profited from which companies: "Just going to Miles and asking him these questions will save you three or four months of analytical work." In one instance, the official said, Guo provided information about Xi Jinping's daughter while she was attending college in the U.S.

The CIA was less impressed; analysts concluded that Guo could not be trusted to keep secrets. But the FBI remained in contact. "If you ask ten different FBI and CIA people about Miles, you're going to get seven different answers," the former Bureau official said. "It's not always perfect. But no source is." The official added, "He knows that he needs us to protect him. So he'll constantly give just enough." Guo looked for other forms of protection, too, trying to hire people with connections to the local power structure. In New York, he invited Jeh Johnson, who ran the Department of Homeland Security under President Obama, to his apartment at the Sherry-Netherland. Johnson had left the government and was working as a lawyer at a white-shoe firm, and Guo wanted to hire him. During their meeting, Johnson responded politely, telling Guo, "I feel like you're somebody I want to help." After doing more research into Guo, however, Johnson declined to take him on.

*   *   *

In China, Guo had honed an instinct for aligning himself with politicians. After splashing ashore in the U.S., he sussed out potential new allies in Washington. Though both the Republican and Democratic parties were growing tougher toward China, only Republicans had made aggression toward China a key measure of conservative credibility. In January 2017, shortly after Trump's inauguration, Guo activated his Twitter account and started giving incendiary interviews in the overseas Chinese media, accusing some of China's leaders of corruption. He started livestreaming from the penthouse and the deck of *Lady May*, offering other salacious, often unproved, allegations. His social media accounts attracted hundreds of thousands of followers, mostly Chinese expatriates—many of whom avidly supported Trump because of Trump's criticisms of China. Guo declared it the beginning of a "whistle-blower movement," and extolled his own courage: "Guo Wengui is from the grass roots, born as a farmer, and not afraid of death."

In China, Guo's disclosures came as a bombshell. The Party asked Interpol, the global police organization, to issue a "red notice" seeking Guo's extradition. A video confession from his former patron, the spymaster Ma Jian, was uploaded to YouTube. Looking bedraggled and reading carefully, Ma said that he had accepted some sixty million yuan in bribes from Guo and had intervened repeatedly to aid his businesses. (Guo denied bribing Ma.)

One day in May 2017, a team of four officers from China's security services—Guo's former allies—turned up at the Sherry-Netherland. The lobby is an ornate place, with hand-loomed French carpets, marble mosaics, and a ceiling painted with cherubs inspired by frescoes at the Vatican. The officers didn't linger; they headed for the penthouse, where Guo was expecting them.

Guo and the security officers spoke for hours, arrayed on the gold-colored furniture in his solarium. The visit was an audacious effort to get him back. He later released excerpts of a recording, in which they could be heard discussing a deal: return to China, and they would leave his family alone and unfreeze his assets. The officers, Guo said afterward, had brought his wife and their daughter from Beijing; permitting his family to leave was a gesture of goodwill. But Guo didn't trust them. "Unless I get Secretary Xi's approval, I won't go back," he said.

Having failed to entice Guo to return home, authorities in China tried to use another form of leverage. They approached Steve Wynn, who was then the finance chair of the Republican National Committee. Wynn, a hotelier, was burdened by restrictions on his casino operations in Macau. In June 2017, according to federal court filings, he spoke by phone with Sun Lijun, the vice minister of public security, who asked for help in getting Guo back to China. Wynn agreed to raise the issue with President Trump. At a dinner in Washington, Wynn conveyed the request and gave Trump's secretary a packet that included the Interpol notice, press reports, and copies of Guo's passport. Afterward, he heard from Elliott Broidy, a venture capitalist and the deputy finance chair of the Republican National Committee, who was in contact with Sun Lijun. Broidy texted that Sun was "extremely pleased and said that President Xi Jinping appreciates [the] assistance." Wynn wrote to another person, who was also involved in the communications, "I remain grateful for the privilege of being part of the Macau and PRC [People's Republic of China] business community."

Soon after the dinner with Wynn, Trump was in the Oval Office, receiving a briefing on China. According to two attendees, he called out to his secretary, "Bring me the letter that Steve Wynn brought from Xi." Trump told the group, "We should get this guy out of here. He's a rapist." But H. R. McMaster, the national security advisor, looked at the packet and concluded that it would be wrong to act on the request. "Trump never followed up on it," an attendee recalled. "He just moved on." Wynn tried once more: in a meeting with White House staff, according to a participant, he offered the use of his private jet to transport Guo to China. "It was a rendition that he was proposing," the participant said. "No one answered." (Broidy and Wynn maintain that they never acted as agents of the Chinese state. The Justice Department sued Wynn, to force him to register under the Foreign Agents Registration Act, but in 2022 the case was dismissed. His attorney said that Wynn believed he was acting as a "patriotic messenger," and that the offer of his jet was "a hundred percent tongue-in-cheek.")

The politics of Beijing had prepared Guo well for navigating Trump's Washington—another realm where money bought influence, business mixed with government, and truth merged with fiction. Guo used his wealth to make inroads in Trump's world. Bill Gertz, a China specialist at *The Washington Free Beacon*, posted stories on Guo and his claims, calling him a "leading Chinese dissident"—until Gertz left, in 2019, after failing to disclose that he took a hundred-thousand-dollar loan from one of Guo's associates. (Gertz did not respond to a request for comment.) Nevertheless, Gertz helped introduce Guo to influential conservatives, including the man who would become his most important collaborator: Steve Bannon.

Bannon had taken a special interest in corruption among the Chinese elite. Earlier in his career, he had been a naval officer aboard ships in the South China Sea, worked as a banker at Goldman Sachs, and run an online gaming company with offices in Hong Kong and Shanghai. He had come to believe that China's leverage over American businesses was a threat, and he was intent on making China a central target of his brand of extreme conservative politics. Bannon said of Guo's allegations, "This guy knows details. He's not just throwing shit out there."

Bannon had been in the Oval Office during the discussion about deporting Guo. Afterward, he told others that he had retrieved the packet that Wynn had brought and put it in his office, to make sure that Guo wasn't extradited.

After Bannon was pushed out of the White House in August 2017, he and Guo met at the Hay-Adams Hotel in Washington. "We spent six hours just talking," Bannon said. Like Guo, Bannon was in search of new allies. The Mercer family, the conservative funders who had backed his earlier ventures, were breaking with him. Bannon was preparing to relaunch his media career, and, as a White House colleague put it, he needed a "new sugar daddy."

*   *   *

On the afternoon of June 4, 2020, bobbing on a boat in New York Harbor, Guo and Bannon held a livestreamed press event to announce a joint initiative. The two were an unusual sight: the exuberant Chinese tycoon in a dark, double-breasted suit, alongside the glowering American with his rumpled silver hair and distinctive assemblage of collared shirts. The setting had been carefully arranged, with planes trailing banners overhead and Guo's yacht and the Statue of Liberty in the background. The date marked the anniversary of the crackdown at Tiananmen Square.

Peering into a camera, Guo announced the establishment of a shadow government, which he called the New Federal State of China. In Mandarin, he made an impassioned call to arms. "We can't keep dreaming anymore. We need to take action, action, action!" he shouted, slicing the air with his hand. Bannon, who does not speak Chinese, stood by awkwardly. In 2018, he had signed a yearlong deal with one of Guo's companies for "strategic consulting services," at a cost of a million dollars.

Guo built toward a climactic finish, chanting a slogan—"Take Down the CCP!"—in Chinese. After the ninth repetition, he switched to English, and Bannon joined in. Guo was in a celebratory mood. He kissed Bannon on the cheek and, gazing up at him, said, "Love you."

"Thank you," Bannon said. "Are we still on live?" To close out the ceremony, they presented a statement of principles, which Guo signed in his own blood. (Bannon skipped that part.)

For all their differences in style, the two shared an unsentimental view of human affairs, a conspiratorial mind-set, and a belief in the power of calculated alliances. They formed a joint venture called GTV Media Group, an alternative-news platform, which ran Bannon's *War*

Room podcast, dubbed in Mandarin, along with frequent livestreams from Guo and his fans. The broadcasts touted the Rule of Law Foundation, which Guo and Bannon had founded to reveal the Communist Party's corrupting effects at home and abroad. (Guo pledged a hundred million dollars; Bannon was chairman.) And they hyped Guo's business initiatives, including cryptocurrencies, called G-Coins and G-Dollars; a membership group called G-Clubs; and an apparel line called G-Fashion.

Bannon had instructed Guo that success in the media required simplified messages put on a loop—a principle that he has described as "wash, rinse, repeat." On the air, Guo spoke constantly of the Communist Party's crimes and the hypocrisy of its leaders. "Everything is fake," he said. Guo's network pulled in hundreds of millions of dollars, mostly from Chinese expats, who thrilled to the promise of challenging the Party. (When Bannon was arrested on the yacht, he left his position as chairman; he was pardoned by Trump of federal charges, and he pleaded not guilty to a similar case in state court.)

Guo's platforms became popular venues for Covid misinformation, antivaccine rhetoric, and the promotion of folk cures. His fashion line included a button-down shirt emblazoned with the word "Ivermectin," for almost twenty-two hundred dollars. As the boundary between his businesses and his politics faded, he made wildly unsubstantiated claims. He announced that his media venture would be a good investment if the Chinese currency collapsed, and promised investors, "I will not let you lose any money." He told fans that donating to his initiatives would give them an advantage on their immigration applications. "It's very simple," he said in a video in 2020. "If you say you support the whistle-blower movement and you've applied for political asylum, your application for asylum will one hundred percent get approved."

In the intelligence community, Guo's disclosures on China were met with skepticism. When he released what he described as an internal Party plan to increase the number of spies in America, some specialists deemed it a forgery. "It had some of the right things, but it's a very particular kind of art—how they number, where they put certain markings," the former government official said. But it was not until the fall of 2020 that the Chinese expats who formed the core of Guo's audience began to question his loyalties. Faced with growing criticism of his falsehoods and his dubious ventures, Guo denounced many of the most prominent Chinese dissidents in America as "fake pro-democracy activists," and said that they "should be beaten up as soon as we see them." He called on his followers to join what he called Operation Elimination of Fake Activists.

Teng Biao, a legal scholar at Hunter College, who fled China after being persecuted for advocating human rights, began seeing comments online from people seeking his home address. One wrote, "I wanna send him a bullet directly into his head!" In December, Teng was at his house in a quiet cul-de-sac near Princeton, New Jersey, teaching a class on Zoom, when his wife came into his office. She was nervous. Sixteen people were standing in front of their house with signs and bullhorns, shouting that Teng was a "CCP spy."

The protesters returned the next day in a convoy of vehicles, and the day after that, chanting, cursing, and shouting so loudly that Teng's children could hear them from inside the house. The protesters live-streamed the scene on GTV and YouTube, and argued with neighbors who came out to defend Teng.

Similar protests appeared outside more than a dozen dissidents' homes in Texas, Virginia, and California. In Vancouver and Los Angeles, people in the crowd harassed their targets till they emerged, then beat and kicked them. (In a statement made at the time, Guo said that he had "never condoned any type of violence toward any individuals.") For nearly two months, the protesters showed up at Teng's house every day, as if they were punching a clock—shouting from 10:30 in the morning to 4:30 in the afternoon, with a break for lunch. A memo from the New Federal State of China, which was subsequently cited in a lawsuit, showed that some had been recruited for fees of as much as $300 a day, with a reward of $10,000 for "excellent performance." Guo's animosity toward dissidents might have been surprising, but it wasn't new. In a leaked recording of a phone call from 2017, he had expressed contempt for them. "They never say anything good about China," he said. "They deserve to die," he added. "I can take these bastards down and help our leaders get revenge."

*   *   *

Some American observers speculated that Guo never entirely broke away from Chinese intelligence. One popular theory held that he maintained ties to factions in Beijing because he hoped to return to China and regain some of his stature. Chris Johnson, a former CIA analyst on China, told me that Guo's disclosures must be read not only for "the people that he chooses to name, but also the people he does not name."

If Guo did represent a faction of the Chinese government, the best bet was that it was composed of powerful families and security officials who had been harmed by Xi's many purges. "This is an intra-CCP fight," the attendee at the Oval Office meeting said. For all Guo's fulminating against the Party, "he's not anti-CCP. He just views himself as a counter to Xi." Teng, the dissident, shares that view. He suspected that Guo was seeking to "replace some CCP leaders with officials more inclined in his favor." The goal, he said, was to "replace well-fed tigers with hungry tigers."

But in the serpentine logic of intelligence, another theory suggested that Guo was actually representing a faction loyal to Xi, which was using him to attack its rivals. He hardly ever criticized Xi by name, and some of the strongest evidence against Guo's description of himself as a dissident had come from his own words. In the summer of 2017, shortly after the Chinese security officers visited him in New York, he released a public letter to Communist Party leaders. He suggested that he could use his "influence and resources" on their behalf, and asked them to "assign me a clear, targeted task, so that I can atone for my past mistakes, and demonstrate my patriotism and support for President Xi."

He claimed that his revelations in America were made "under pressure," and promised, "I will continue not to cross the red lines." Hoping to "safeguard our nation's interests and image," he offered to be a "propagandist," employing "my own style of propaganda."

In the years after that letter, Guo's efforts turned more squarely to promoting division and cynicism in U.S. politics. He claimed that the Communist Party had a plan to subvert the U.S., using leaked documents, bribery, and blackmail for what he called 3F: "foment weakness, foment chaos and foment the destruction of America." It was an approach that, Guo's critics noted, uncannily described his own patterns. The national security official, who was involved in Guo's case, described him as a chaos agent working on China's behalf: "You could make a circumstantial argument that this guy is here to fuck us up. Just tie us in knots."

The divisive power of Guo's network became clear as the 2020 presidential election approached. A study conducted by Graphika, an analytics firm, found thousands of social media accounts spreading his quotes, along with conspiratorial claims about dissidents, vaccines, Joe Biden, and QAnon. Chat groups for Guo's fans were stocked with templates of pro-Trump messages that users were encouraged to distribute as if they were spontaneous.

During the 2016 campaign, when Trump allies circulated anti-Clinton propaganda, they relied on Twitter and Facebook, but those platforms had since cracked down on election disinformation. Now Guo's network provided an alternative. Nothing demonstrated its impact more than its promotion of doctored reports about Hunter Biden's laptop. The first known public mention of a laptop abandoned by the president's son and recovered from a repair shop, came from a guest on the YouTube channel of Wang Dinggang, one of Guo's collaborators. Some of Guo's allies followed up by turning a kernel of truth into an array of fictions, creating and spreading fabricated images, according to Jack Maxey, a former co-host of Bannon's podcast. "It was a huge deflection from reality," Maxey recalled. "I said to Steve on Day

One, 'This is a bad idea.'" But, he added, "I can't tell Steve what to do. Apparently, Miles can."

In the final weeks of the race, Rudy Giuliani ignited a media campaign alleging that the computer's hard drive contained emails and pictures of Hunter Biden that compromised his father. Guo denied involvement in disseminating false information about the laptop, but messages which later leaked suggest that he coordinated his followers to edit images and to spread the story. Three days before the election, Bannon met with Guo's supporters and applauded their "editorial creativity over the pictures," according to a recording provided to *Mother Jones*. Bannon said that the laptop story stalled Biden's momentum and "drove up his negatives," which kept the race close enough that Trump could declare victory, whether or not he went on to win. "That's our strategy," Bannon told them. "So, when you wake up Wednesday morning, it's going to be a firestorm."

After Trump lost the 2020 election, Guo's network joined the effort to overturn the outcome. On November 14, hundreds of his supporters traveled to Washington for the Million MAGA March, erecting a stage and hiring advertising trucks to traverse the city. A company controlled by Guo spent more than $400,000 on the rally, according to *Mother Jones*, and also gave $100,000 to an organization headed by the attorney L. Lin Wood, who was suing to reverse Trump's loss in Georgia. On January 6, Guo's network carried livestreams of the siege of the Capitol, and promoted comments that hailed the attackers as "patriots."

*   *   *

In the strange economics of Trumpworld, his electoral loss in 2020 created a prime opportunity for his proxies in the media—the radio hosts and conspiracy theorists who profited from grievance. In the months after January 6, Guo's video network, GTV, and its related businesses operated from an office tower overlooking Columbus Circle. One day that September, he summoned a collection of former Trump aides to the office for a livestream on the subject of China. To Guo's left sat Peter Navarro, a former business school professor who had served as Trump's trade adviser and as his administration's most ardent China hawk. Navarro, who wore a windbreaker with "TeamTrump" stenciled on the chest, looked gaunt and glumly captive—a fierce critic of China working with a self-acknowledged former affiliate of the country's spy services. Bannon had on a black sport coat over a black shirt, with another shirt underneath. He was seated beside Jason Miller, the former spokesman and then-CEO of Gettr, one of several new social media networks vying to attract conservative users. It, too, had received funding from Guo.

They were all there to celebrate Navarro's installation as the "international ambassador" from the New Federal State of China. But Navarro wanted to talk about vaccines, too; he was a devoted proponent of hydroxychloroquine. "The illegitimate Biden regime is preventing the use of these therapeutics and killing people," he said. Guo agreed, and made a dark prediction, in his patchwork English: "In six months, ten months, you will see on the street talented drivers, driving their cars, immediately by accident, die because of Covid vaccine. That's murder."

The rhetoric was heated, but Guo seemed to sense that the scene wasn't much to look at. He encouraged his translators to ask questions, and one began to rave about Navarro's appearance: "I have a colleague who is a very beautiful lady, and she is the greatest fan of Mr. Navarro. So when you appear, every time she will just shout, 'Oh, here comes Peter Navarro!'" Navarro, shifting uncomfortably, gave a wan smile. Bannon seemed happy to maintain the spirit of admiration, though. "Miles is the George Washington of the new China," he said at one point. "We're talking about a new China and new Chinese—Chinese who finally have freedom after millennia of history." Toward the end, one of the translators asked when the U.S. government would recognize Guo's government-in-exile. Bannon answered, "Sometime after 2024—when Trump takes the White House back."

But even as Guo and his allies predicted victory, his operation was in turmoil. Two days earlier, the Securities and Exchange Commission had charged three companies associated with Guo—GTV Media Group, Saraca Media Group, and Voice of Guo Media—with illegal sales of stock and cryptocurrency. The companies neither admitted nor denied wrongdoing, but they agreed to pay more than $539 million, including restitution to thousands of investors in at least thirty-nine countries.

Guo's news site played down the charges, telling fans that the companies had reached a settlement "without penalty clauses." In reality, they had been ordered to pay $35 million in penalties, and the SEC said that it was continuing to investigate the matter. GTV shut down, and the case marked a turning point in Guo's movement. Some former aides and supporters rebelled, turning their social media and chat networks into venues for criticism and revelation. Guo lashed out, calling his erstwhile allies liars, rats, and "running dogs" of the Communist Party.

Ultimately, a different legal case dealt a heavier blow to Guo. The operators of a hedge fund, Pacific Alliance Asia Opportunity, had been suing him to repay a loan taken years ago to develop Pangu Plaza, in Beijing, but Guo had treated the case with contempt. "I think you guys are a bunch of thugs," he said in a deposition in October 2018. "I don't need to pay any attention to you." In 2021, a New York court ordered him to pay the fund $116 million in debt and interest; when he failed to do so, the court tacked on an additional $134 million in fines. The judge wrote that if "billionaire litigants" can "knowingly and intentionally violate Court orders, there is no rule of law."

Guo promptly filed for bankruptcy, claiming to have as much as half a billion dollars in debt and no more than $100,000 in assets. The yacht and the penthouse, he maintained, were actually not his at all, but properties of family members, shell companies, and other financial entities. His creditors called the bankruptcy "an obvious attempt to avoid both payment and possible incarceration."

As the case inched through the courts, the image that Guo had erected was wobbling. The signature high-rise in Pangu Plaza had been auctioned off for $734 million. Its most audacious design feature—the crown in the shape of the Olympic flame—was dismantled, rendering the building all but indistinguishable from others. In New York, Guo had put his penthouse at the Sherry-Netherland up for sale, and gradually reduced the price to $35 million, barely half of what he had paid. The co-op board that once welcomed Guo was now suing him for allegedly failing to pay maintenance fees, which amounted to some $82,000 a month.

As ever, Guo approached the challenges with exuberant aggression. He continued livestreaming from an estate in Greenwich, Connecticut, delivering his messages against the backdrop of a pool house and an expansive lawn. He harangued a lawyer who had been appointed as the bankruptcy trustee, denouncing him as "fully representing the CCP." And he dabbled in new ventures, including a hip-hop track titled "The Hero," which featured him in action movie garb, assuming a series of valiant poses: astride a white horse, wielding a lightsaber in ritual combat, commanding a squadron of backup dancers in front of luxury SUVs and a private jet. On the way to the chorus—"Take Down the CCP!"—Guo made a resolute proclamation: "To die on the battlefield is my honor."

Through it all, Guo insisted that he faced threats of assassination from China. But hunted men do not often release hip-hop tracks, and, as the former intelligence official observed, "If the MSS [Ministry of State Security] really wanted to kill his ass, they have the ability to do it."

*   *   *

In trying to untangle Guo's zigzagging identities and feuds and bluffs, I often thought of the late James Jesus Angleton, the longtime head of counterintelligence at the CIA. Angleton spent years hunting for Soviet moles in America, straining to see through ploys and misinformation to divine who was working to "confuse and split the West," as he put it. Angleton described his domain as a "wilderness of mirrors," a metaphor borrowed from T. S. Eliot's "Gerontion." The poem, written amid the ashes of the First World War, contains a warning: "History has many cunning passages, contrived corridors / And issues, deceives with whispering ambitions, / Guides us by vanities." By the time Angleton retired in 1974, his obsession had become so consuming that some people wondered if he himself was the mole.

What of Guo was real and what was fake? Was he pulled to and fro by the tensions between the U.S. and China, or was he exerting forces of his own? Was he heightening the chaos in American politics, or simply reflecting our own anxieties and frailties back to us?

At bottom, Guo might have been simply an adaptable, inveterate grifter. An American who worked at Pangu Plaza in its early years recalled that, two floors below the garage of luxury cars, there was an unfinished basement, a dark, wet place where wood planks formed a gangway over mud. One part was dedicated to storing high-end Japanese porcelain plates and gold-colored flatware. "You could see lights in the distance," he said. "It was some of the migrant workers, who lived down there. They'd built these little huts out of scaffolding pipes." The migrant laborers in the basement camp were building the fantasy that Guo was promoting up on the surface.

Guo never stopped selling aspiration; he just moved venues to the United States. In 2020, he proposed that passports from his government-in-exile be made available at a cost of $50,000 per family. *The Wall Street Journal* reported that the FBI was examining Guo and the funding of his media work with Bannon. (At the time, both Guo and Bannon said that the Bureau had not contacted them.) It was possible that his efforts to cultivate various government connections could afford him some protection. Guo's dealings with the FBI could make him "messy" to prosecute, according to a former Justice Department official. He could adopt the strategy that prosecutors call "graymail"—threatening to disclose national security secrets in the process of defending himself. The official said, "Even if you win it, he might be revealing a lot more than anyone ever wants revealed."

Teng Biao, the dissident, saw a lesson for critics of Chinese authoritarianism who made the Faustian choice to support Trump and, later,

Guo. "They think the end justifies the means," Teng said. He made a moral argument against cooperating with dubious allies, asking, "Must the enemy of the enemy be a friend? Hitler and ISIS were also anti-communists."

Bannon, Guo's most prominent defender, heard all the criticisms—"Other guys are saying, 'Hey, all he's doing is feeding you bullshit.'"—but Bannon didn't care. He said, "I think in *outcomes*. Whether he's working for a faction or not, who knows?" Bannon suggested, reviving an old cliché, that China was an impenetrable mystery: "It's like the very end of the movie *Chinatown*," when Jack Nicholson's character is told to accept what he cannot understand. More important, from Bannon's perspective, was that Guo had altered American politics by forcing Republican contenders to adopt a more bellicose stance: "He's done more than anybody to wake this country up to the threats of the CCP as a transnational criminal organization and an existential threat to America. Whether he's working for a faction or he's hedging his bets, the stuff he's done and what he's galvanized is just relentless."

On March 15, 2023, the FBI arrested Guo at his penthouse in the Sherry-Netherland. Prosecutors accused Guo and a codefendant, Kin Ming Je, of conducting a fraud worth more than a billion dollars, by soliciting investments in bogus ventures involving cryptocurrency, online membership programs, and digital media. Guo had employed a particular American formula: use the technologies of influence to attract followers, then use their cash to buy political access, status, and luxury—which, in turn, furnished an image that attracted more followers. Even in an era of excess, his range of indulgences stood out, including a fifty-thousand-square-foot mansion in Mahwah, New Jersey, a twelve-thousand-square-foot mansion in Greenwich, a $3.5 million Ferrari, a $4.4 million Bugatti, a $62,000 television, two $36,000 mattresses, and a $53,000 "fireplace log cradle holder." Guo's lawyer framed his extravagance as a form of political activism: "Mr. Guo is simply *trying to show people that they could live the same life afforded to China's elites." Prosecutors named Bannon as an unindicted co-conspirator but did not charge him with a crime. In an unrelated case, Bannon served four months in jail for contempt of Congress and was released in October 2024.*

After a seven-week trial, a jury convicted Guo on nine of twelve counts, including racketeering conspiracy and securities fraud. His co-defendant, Je, a financier, became a fugitive, believed to be hiding in the United Arab Emirates. While Guo awaited sentencing, his penthouse was for sale at a reduced price of $19.5 million.

The Big House

Life after white-collar crime

— 2021 —

In the 1990s, Jeffrey D. Grant had a law firm in Westchester County, a seat on the local school board, and an ownership stake in a bistro called, if you'll forgive the irony, the Good Life. He was in his early forties, garrulous and rotund, and he gloried in his capacity to consume. Each year, he took his wife and daughters on half a dozen "shopping vacations," though they sometimes neglected to open the bags between trips.

Grant had developed an early appreciation for personal displays of wealth and power. Born in 1956, the son of a marketing executive, he grew up on Long Island, graduated from SUNY Brockport, and worked his way through New York Law School as a shoe salesman. By then, his parents had divorced, and his father had moved in with Lynda Dick, a wealthy widow whose properties included one of the most storied mansions in Greenwich, Connecticut, a hilltop estate known as Dunnellen Hall. (It later became famous as the home of Leona Helmsley, the hotel magnate convicted of tax evasion in 1989, after a trial in which a housekeeper testified that Helmsley had told her, "We don't pay taxes. Only the little people pay taxes.")

Grant cultivated an ability to muscle his way into one opportunity after another. In law school, he approached the box office of a concert venue in Boston and, pretending to be the son of a music promoter, threatened revenge if he and three friends were not admitted free of charge. The brazen charade worked so well that the headliner, the rock 'n' roll pioneer Gary U.S. Bonds, hosted the group backstage and, at the concert, sang "Happy Birthday" to one of Grant's friends. As a lawyer, Grant specialized in real estate and corporate work and regarded himself as an "assassin." In business and out of it, his philosophy was "Win, win, win."

As he reached his mid-forties, however, Grant found himself unraveling. He had become addicted to painkillers—first Demerol, prescribed for a torn Achilles tendon, and then OxyContin. He was increasingly erratic and grandiose, betting wildly on dot-com stocks. In 2000, as his debts mounted, he started filching money from clients' escrow accounts. The following year, after the terrorist attacks of September 11, Grant applied for a disaster relief loan from the Small Business Administration, claiming to have lost the use of an office near Ground Zero. That was a fiction. He received $247,000, which he used to cover personal and office expenses.

In July 2002, under investigation for breaching his clients' accounts, he surrendered his law license and was later disbarred. That summer, as he sat in a Ralph Lauren wicker chair in his greenhouse in Rye, he attempted suicide, swallowing forty tablets of Demerol. He survived, and entered drug and alcohol rehab. He and his wife moved to Greenwich, seeking a fresh start, but the marriage was too badly frayed to survive.

Grant's undoing was not yet complete: officers of the Internal Revenue Service discovered the false claim on his loan application, and in 2004 a warrant was issued for his arrest. He pleaded guilty to wire fraud and money laundering, and a judge sentenced him to eighteen months in prison, chastising him for exploiting a national tragedy. On Easter Sunday 2006, two friends drove Grant three hours west from Greenwich to Allenwood Low, a federal prison in the mountainous Amish country of central Pennsylvania. Grant quickly learned the rules: never take someone's seat in the TV room or ask a stranger what landed him in prison. And he mastered the black-market economy that runs on "macks," or foil packages of smoked mackerel, which sell for about a dollar in the commissary. He marked time mostly by walking—circling an outdoor track three or four hours a day, listening to NPR on headphones. "In the morning, all the airplanes from the East Coast would fly over going west, and at night they would come the other way," he told me. "I would remember myself as a businessman."

Grant was released to a halfway house in June 2007 after fourteen months in prison. He had walked thirty-five hundred miles around the track and shed sixty-five pounds. He returned to Greenwich with no idea of what to do next.

*   *   *

Many people who have served time for white-collar felonies look to get back into business. Barely six months after the home wares mogul Martha Stewart emerged from prison—she had been convicted of lying to investigators about a stock trade—she was hosting two new television shows. Grant, who no longer had a law license, tried applying himself to good works instead. He volunteered at rehab facilities that had helped him get sober. He joined the board of Family ReEntry, a nonprofit in Bridgeport, which aids formerly imprisoned people and their families, and he later served as its executive director. Hoping to improve his inner life, he studied for a divinity degree at Union Theological Seminary in Manhattan. In 2009, he married Lynn Springer, a Greenwich event planner he had met in recovery. In 2012, they founded the Progressive Prison Project, a ministry focused on white-collar and other nonviolent offenders.

As word of his experience spread, Grant started hearing from neighbors who were heading to prison or had recently returned and were seeking advice or companionship. At the time, a sense of alarm was animating conversations among businessmen along the Metro-North corridor: Preet Bharara, the U.S. attorney for the Southern District of

New York, had imposed a crackdown on insider trading, leading to more than eighty guilty pleas and convictions. Some of these cases were later invalidated by an appeals court, but Operation Perfect Hedge, as it was known, had punctured the realm of traders, analysts, and portfolio managers. "My phone would ring in the middle of the night," Grant said. One financier, under indictment, called while hiding in his office with the lights out. "He said, 'I'm afraid that people will recognize me on the street,'" Grant recalled. A reporter from *Absolute Return*, a trade publication for the hedge fund industry, asked Grant, "How do Wall Street skills usually translate in prison?" His reply: "These skills are not only in large degree useless, they are probably counterproductive." As he told me, "Business rewards a certain type of attitude and assertiveness— all things that will get you killed in prison."

Grant, in his pastoral role for anxious brokers, fallen hedgies, and other wobbling pillars of late capitalism, came to expect fresh inquiries from desperate people each morning when he opened his email. "Everyone going through this is freaking out, so they're up all night, googling," he said. In the hope of nourishing his unlikely flock, Grant developed an ambitious reading list, which included *Letters and Papers from Prison*, by Dietrich Bonhoeffer, and *The Gulag Archipelago*, by Aleksandr Solzhenitsyn. If some callers found that Bonhoeffer's words of resistance to the victims of National Socialism did not seem immediately applicable, Grant also offered practical tips. Before reporting to prison, he advised them, mail yourself the phone numbers of family members and friends on the visitors' list, because "you'll be too discombobulated to remember them once you're inside." And remind your wife never to touch paper money on the morning of a visit; almost every bill bears traces of drug residue, which will set off the scanners.

In 2016, Grant established what he called the White Collar Support Group, an online meeting inspired by twelve-step programs for drug and alcohol addiction. He described the program as a step toward "ethics rehab" and, on his website, explained that it was for people who wanted to "take responsibility for our actions and the wreckage we caused." In blunter terms, he told me that it was for "guys detoxing from power and influence."

The first session attracted four attendees, including a hedge fund manager and a man who had pilfered from his child's youth soccer club. But soon the program grew. In the next five years, more than three hundred people cycled through, either on their way to prison or just out and trying to reestablish a semblance of their old order. Some of Grant's flock were familiar from front-page scandals, born of Ponzi schemes, insider trading, and other forms of expensive corruption; others were virtually unknown to the public. In the summer of 2021, I asked him if I could sit in on a meeting of the White Collar Support Group. He agreed, but alerted his members in advance, in case anyone wanted to preserve his privacy.

At seven o'clock one evening in July, I signed on to Zoom and found myself with twenty-eight people, mostly male and white, each identified by a name and a location. Meetings are free, though Grant suggests a donation of five dollars to his ministry. He draws a distinction between his work and the industry of white-collar "prison coaches" who offer bespoke services for a price. Among them, Wall Street Prison Consultants promises to "ensure you serve the shortest sentence possible in the most favorable institution." It sells consulting packages at the levels of Bronze, Silver, and Gold, the finest of which includes "Polygraph Manipulation Techniques," "Prison Survival Orientation Coaching," and an "Early Release Package" that helps clients apply for a drug treatment program to reduce the length of a sentence.

Grant, who now lives in Woodbury, Connecticut, appeared on camera wearing a pale blue oxford shirt and sitting before a stone fireplace. As he called the meeting to order, we recited Reinhold Niebuhr's Serenity Prayer, and then Grant reminded everyone of the rules: with few exceptions, anyone who talked for more than three minutes would hear a snippet of music—on this occasion, the Parliament funk classic "Mothership Connection (Star Child)" —signaling him to wrap it up. Surrendering control, Grant likes to tell his charges, may not come naturally.

*   *   *

Before the meeting, Grant had warned me not to expect universal contrition. "Almost everyone who contacts us has been successful, controlling, and perhaps narcissistic," he said. "The elements that made them successful are also the elements that contributed to their demise." Throughout their pre-indictment careers, aggression and rule-bending were considered strengths. In American culture, white-collar crime is often portrayed less as evidence of unfettered greed than as a misguided sibling of success. After the stock market crashed in 1929, Congress faced public pressure to curb the backroom manipulation that had helped devastate millions of shareholders. But Richard Whitney, the president of the New York Stock Exchange, a graduate of Groton and Harvard, told senators in Washington, "You gentlemen are making a great mistake. The exchange is a perfect institution." In 1938, Whitney was caught embezzling from the New York Yacht Club, his father-in-law, and a number of others. He went to Sing Sing dressed in a double-breasted suit.

Not long after Whitney's fall, the sociologist Edwin Sutherland devised the term "white-collar crime" to describe wrongdoing committed "by a person of respectability and high social status in the course of his occupation." Since then, each cycle of boom and bust has delivered new iterations of rapacious self-dealing, often indelibly linked to time or place, like schools of painting—the naked fraud of the Savings & Loans, the whimsical math at Arthur Andersen. In 2001, following the accounting scandals at Enron and other companies, a publication called *CFO Magazine* quietly abandoned its annual Excellence Awards, because winners from each of the previous three years had gone to prison.

Since the turn of the millennium, the prosecution of white-collar crime has plummeted—but this should not imply a surge in moralism among our leading capitalists. Rather, it reflected a change in the capacity to prosecute. After the attacks of September 11, the FBI began to shift resources toward counterterrorism. Meanwhile, Republican lawmakers cut the budget of the Internal Revenue Service so sharply that it had the same number of special agents in 2017 as it had half a century earlier, even though the national population had grown by two-thirds.

The atmosphere of impunity has become more conspicuous since the Great Recession of 2007–09, when, infamously, scarcely any top executives went to prison—despite the loss of more than $19 trillion in household wealth. At the time, leaders at the Department of Justice claimed that they could not prove fraudulent intent by Wall Street titans, who were many layers removed from the daily handling of toxic securities. Jed Rakoff, a judge in the Southern District of New York, believes that this was a catastrophic misreading of the law. Executives, he argues, could have been prosecuted under the principle that they were "willfully blind" to patterns of abuse that enriched them. "Dozens of people defrauded millions of people out of probably billions of dollars," Rakoff told me. The imperatives had less to do with compensating victims than with deterring crimes not yet conceived. "There are studies that are more than a hundred years old that show that the best way to deter any crime is to catch the perpetrators quickly," he said.

In the years since, the failure to hold top executives accountable has become intertwined with historic levels of income inequality, a phenomenon that Jennifer Taub, a professor at Western New England University School of Law, calls "criminogenic." In her 2020 book, *Big Dirty Money*, she wrote, "In our society, extreme wealth often confers tremendous power. So just as power tends to corrupt, so does excessive wealth." But nothing expressed America's ambivalence toward white-collar crime more eloquently than the election of Donald Trump, whose life and career as a business fabulist merited no fewer than 125 mentions in *Big Dirty Money*. During his first term as president, federal prosecutions of white-collar crime reached an all-time low. In 2020, Trump delivered pardons and clemency to a slew of affluent felons, including Michael Milken, the junk bond trader who had pleaded guilty to securities violations three decades earlier. Taub noted that the official White House announcement about the pardoned businessmen used the word "successful" to describe them four times.

*   *   *

Measurements of success, or something like it, haunt the conversations in the White Collar Support Group. In the Zoom meeting, one of the first people to speak up was Andy Tezna, a thirty-six-year-old former executive at NASA who had been sentenced the previous week for fraud. Applying for Covid relief in the name of fictitious businesses, Tezna had collected more than $350,000, including loans issued under the Paycheck Protection Program. He used the money to finance a Disney Vacation Club timeshare, a swimming pool ($48,962), and, to ease the social isolation of the pandemic, a French bulldog ($6,450).

"I got eighteen months," Tezna told the group, glumly. "Definitely not the number I had in mind." He was sitting beside a window covered by venetian blinds; he wore white earbuds and several days' growth of beard. He was waiting for word on when to report to prison. In court, Tezna and his lawyer had presented him as an American success story gone wrong. His family had come from Colombia when he was thirteen and lived in an unfinished basement, while he helped his mother clean houses. Later, he earned a degree from George Mason University and landed a job at NASA, which paid him $181,000 a year. In the job, he attended a space launch with members of Trump's cabinet and Elon Musk. "I just thought, My life is great," he told the group.

To the judge, Tezna had framed his malfeasance narrowly, arguing, "I was bad at managing my finances." The Justice Department thought it was worse than that. "These are not one-off mistakes," a prosecutor told the court. "This was greed."

A voice on the call piped up: "Hey, Andy? It's Bill Baroni."

It took me a moment to place the name. Then I remembered Bridge-gate. In 2013, after the New Jersey governor Chris Christie appointed Baroni as the deputy executive director of the Port Authority, he was accused of helping to arrange a traffic jam on the George Washington Bridge in order to punish the mayor of Fort Lee, who had refused to endorse Christie for reelection. Baroni was convicted of fraud and served three months in prison. But he denied the charges, and eventually the Supreme Court overturned his conviction. Justice Elena Kagan wrote that, even though the evidence showed "deception, corruption, abuse of power," the Bridgegate episode did not meet the legal threshold of fraud. Baroni's victory in the Supreme Court gave him unique status in the group. "I got the exact same sentence you did—eighteen months," he told Tezna. "I know what's in your head today."

For the next ninety minutes, the mood veered between grave and celebratory. Members swapped tidbits about mutual friends ("He got moved out of the private prison in Mississippi") and applauded new ventures ("I signed a lease last week"). Grant has developed a soothing vocabulary—about strength regained and community embraced—which collided occasionally with members' laments. "As a single guy, I can tell you dating sucks," a man in Delaware said, "because the reactions from women run the gamut from 'Oh, my God, you're the worst form of life on earth' to 'Oh, that's cool! Women like bad boys.'" A former hedge fund manager in Chicago was still smarting over the publicity around his indictment. "Reporters were calling my parents and my brother," he said. "I don't even know how they got their phone numbers." Members of the group arrive in disparate circumstances: some have managed to keep significant assets, while others are tapped out after restitution and legal expenses. According to Grant, the biggest distinction is between those who have been to prison and those who have not. Those who haven't served time, he told me, are "sort of outside the club."

More than a few members attributed their crimes to consumerist inadequacy. Craig Stanland, who defrauded the networking company Cisco of equipment worth more than $800,000, told the group, "It was just pure shame from the beginning—not being able to tell my wife that I couldn't afford that lifestyle, all the way through getting arrested. And then the scarlet letter." But Bill Livolsi, speaking from the Tulsa suburbs, who went to prison for his role in a Ponzi scheme that passed itself off as a hedge fund, had come to see his new circumstances as an unburdening. "I finally got a job after a year of being out. It makes a whopping fifteen dollars an hour, but I've never been happier with a job," he said. "My focus isn't on what flight I'm taking or where I'm going on this particular vacation. It's on how my family's doing and how I'm doing."

Grant is solicitous. He asks new members to introduce themselves and, when needed, draws them out. Richard Bronson, a former Lehman Brothers stockbroker with cropped gray hair and a beard, said, "I used to work on Wall Street. I did very well." In fact, Bronson became a partner at Stratton Oakmont, the firm made infamous by Martin Scorsese's *The Wolf of Wall Street*. He moved to Florida and converted a trading house called Biltmore Securities into a firm with five hundred employees. In Miami, he joined the boards of the ballet and the museum of contemporary art, opened a nightclub and started a magazine, and held court at an oceanside villa. But prosecutors said that all this was built on deceit; they accused him of running a boiler room that fed investors a stream of bogus stocks, causing losses estimated at $96 million. Bronson disputed this figure, and insisted that he had repaid his clients. Nevertheless, he pleaded guilty to securities and wire fraud in 2002, and served twenty-two months in prison.

Bronson told the group, "This is really the first time I've ever been around people who have similar comeuppances." He has been trying to revive his business career, launching 70 Million Jobs, a post-prison employment service, and an app called Commissary Club ("the exclusive social network for people with criminal histories"). "I've been out of prison for sixteen years, and I committed my crimes more than twenty-five years ago, and yet I wake up every morning with this gaping hole in my heart, out of regret for the things that I did." He choked up momentarily and paused to collect himself. "I don't suspect that I'll get over this feeling," he said, "and that saddens me."

Others tried to buck him up. "I think we're going to have to have a meeting about self-care soon," Grant said.

*   *   *

Behind each new revelation of white-collar crime lurks an uncomfortable question about some of America's most lucrative businesses: Are they attracting rogues or grooming them? Eugene Soltes, a professor at Harvard Business School, told me that regulations were partly to blame. "There is more white-collar crime today because there are more things that are criminal today than fifty years ago," he said. Bribing a foreign official, for instance, was legal until the Foreign Corrupt Practices Act of 1977, and insider trading was rarely prosecuted until the 1980s. Today, those are among the most common offenses. But, Soltes went on, "I suspect that you might be asking the more intuitive version of this question. Given the same laws, same number of people, et cetera, is the *proclivity* for someone to engage in white-collar crime higher than it was fifty years ago?"

To answer that question, Soltes had interviewed scores of people convicted or accused of white-collar crime. In a book titled *Why They Do It*, he concluded that he saw no evidence of a basic change in the willingness to break laws. What had changed, though, was what he called the "psychological distance" between perpetrators and their victims: "Business is done with individuals at greater length now, which reduces the feeling that managers are harming others." In experiments, people agree, in theory, to sacrifice the life of someone they can't see far more readily than that of someone who stands before them. In Soltes's interviews with people who had committed price-fixing or fraud, he found that many of them had never personally encountered their victims. In effect, an increasingly remote world was an increasingly lawless world.

In recent years, the sense that moral constraints are weakening has been voiced not just by critics of Wall Street but also by practitioners. John C. Bogle, an iconic investor who founded the Vanguard Group and spent more than six decades in finance, wrote in 2012, "When I came into this field, the standard seemed to be 'there are some things that one simply doesn't do.' Today, the standard is 'if everyone else is doing it, I can do it too.'" Soon afterward, the law firm Labaton Sucharow conducted a survey of finance professionals, in which a quarter of them said that they would "engage in insider trading to make $10 million if they could get away with it." Around the same time, Greg Smith, an executive director at Goldman Sachs, announced his resignation, decrying a "decline in the firm's moral fiber." Writing in *The New York Times*, he observed, "Over the last 12 months I have seen five different managing directors refer to their own clients as 'muppets.' . . . You don't have to be a rocket scientist to figure out that the junior analyst sitting quietly in the corner of the room hearing about 'muppets,' 'ripping eyeballs out' and 'getting paid' doesn't exactly turn into a model citizen."

Researchers have gained a deeper understanding of the way that dubious behavior moves through a community of colleagues or neighbors. In the mid-2000s, the federal government brought criminal and civil cases for backdating stock options—manipulating records so that executives could take home a larger return than their options truly merited. Studies found that the practice had started in Silicon Valley and then infected the broader business world; the vectors of transmission could be traced to specific individuals who served as directors or auditors of multiple companies. An unethical habit spreads through subtle cues that psychologists call "affective evaluations." If people are rising on one measurement (wealth or status) even as they are falling on another (ethics or lawfulness), the verdict about which matters more will hinge on the culture all around them—on which values are most "exalted by members of their insular business communities," Soltes wrote. In other words, as he told me, "If you spend time with people who pick locks, you will probably learn to pick locks."

In 2013, prosecutors announced an indictment of S.A.C. Capital Advisors—named for its founder, Steven A. Cohen—calling it a "veritable magnet for market cheaters." Cohen, like a considerable number of his peers, lived in Greenwich. In the previous decade, as the hedge fund industry surged in scale and profits, the rise of the internet had allowed funds to leave Wall Street, and many moved to southern Connecticut to take advantage of favorable tax rates and easy commutes. By 2005, hedge funds had taken over two-thirds of Greenwich's commercial real estate.

After the charges against Cohen were announced, David Rafferty, a columnist for *Greenwich Time*, a local paper, published a piece with the headline "Greenwich, Gateway to White-Collar Crime." He wrote, "A few years ago you might have been proud to tell your friends you lived in 'The Hedge Fund Capital of the World.' Now? Not so much."

Rafferty, in his column, described a "growing sense of unease in certain circles as one hedgie after another seems to be facing the music." Cohen, however, faced the music for a limited interlude. Under an agreement brokered with prosecutors, his firm pleaded guilty to insider trading and was sentenced to pay $1.8 billion in penalties. After a two-year suspension, Cohen returned to the hedge fund business, and made enough money to buy the New York Mets. The price was $2.4 billion, the largest sum ever paid for a North American sports franchise.

Luigi Zingales, a finance professor at the University of Chicago, told me that he wishes his profession spoke more candidly about accountability and impunity. Most of the time, he said, business schools find "every possible way to avoid the moral questions." He added, "I don't know of any alum that has been kicked out of the alumni association for immoral behavior. There are trustees of business schools today who have been convicted of bribery and insider trading, and I don't think people notice or care." He went on, "People are getting more and more comfortable in the gray area."

*   *   *

One of the longest-running members of the White Collar Support Group is a lean and taciturn man in his forties named Tom Hardin—or, as he is known with some notoriety in Wall Street circles, Tipper X. Not long after graduating from business school at Wharton, Hardin went to work for a hedge fund in Greenwich. He had much to learn. Almost instantly, he began hearing that some competitors, such as the billionaire Raj Rajaratnam, were suspected of relying on illegal tips from company insiders. (Rajaratnam was later convicted and sentenced to eleven years.) In 2007, after Hardin became a partner at Lanexa Global Management, a hedge fund in New York, he got his own inside tip, a heads-up on an upcoming acquisition, and he traded on the information and beat the market. He repeated similar stunts three times. "I'm, like, I would never get caught if I buy a small amount of stock," he told me. "This is like dropping a penny in the Grand Canyon." He went on, "You can say, 'I'm highly ethical and would never do this.' But once you're in the environment, and you feel like everybody else is doing it, and you feel you're not hurting anybody? It's very easy to convince yourself."

One morning in 2008, Hardin was walking out of the dry cleaner's when two FBI agents approached him. They sat him down in a Wendy's nearby and told him that they knew about his illegal trades. He had a choice: go to jail or wear a wire. He chose the latter, and became one of the most productive informants in the history of securities fraud. The FBI gave him a tiny recorder disguised as a cell phone battery, which he slipped into his shirt pocket, to gather evidence in more than twenty criminal cases brought under Operation Perfect Hedge. For a year and a half, his identity was disguised in court documents as Tipper X, fueling a mystery around what *The New York Times* called "the secret witness at the center of the biggest insider-trading case in a generation."

In December 2009, Hardin pleaded guilty, and his identity was revealed in court filings. He had avoided prison but become a felon, which made features of a normal life all but impossible, from opening a brokerage account to coaching his daughters' soccer team. He was unsure how he could earn a living. "I would ask my attorney, 'Are there any past clients you can connect me with who've got to the other side of this and are back on their feet?' He was, like, 'Sorry, not really.'"

He heard of Grant's group through a friend. "I had no idea something like this existed," Hardin said. "Jeff was the first one who said, 'Hey, here's a group of people just in our situation. Come every Monday.'" In 2016, the FBI called him again—this time, to invite him to brief a class of freshman federal agents. Hardin's lecture at the FBI led to more speeches—first for free, and eventually for a living. He was back on

Wall Street, as a teller of cautionary tales. It was not quite motivational speaking; his niche, as he put it, dryly, was "overcoming self-inflicted career decimation."

In his dealings with his peers, Hardin has learned to distinguish who is genuinely remorseful from who is not. "I'll hear from white-collar felons who tell me, 'I made a mistake,'" he told me. "I'll say, 'A mistake is something we do without intention. A bad decision was made intentionally.' If you're classifying your bad decisions as mistakes, you're not accepting responsibility."

*   *   *

In the era of rising discontent over injustice, some Americans accused of white-collar crimes have sought to identify with the movement to curb incarceration and prosecutorial misconduct. So far, the spirit of redemption has not extended to the members of the White Collar Support Group, whose crimes relate to some of the very abuses of power that inspire demands for greater accountability. For the moment, they are caught between competing furies, so they rely, more than ever, on one another. "A white-collar advocate still doesn't have a seat at the table of the larger criminal justice conversation," Grant told me. "We exist because there's no place else for us to go."

The group members' predicament rests on an unavoidable hypocrisy: after conducting themselves with little concern for the public, they find themselves appealing to the public for mercy. Bill Baroni, the former Port Authority executive, told me, "I can't go back. All I can do now is to take the experiences that I've had and try and help people." His regrets extend beyond his scandal. He had been a New Jersey state senator, and, he said, "I voted to increase mandatory minimum sentencing. I never would have done that had I had the experience of being in prison."

Baroni helped establish a nonprofit called the Prison Visitation Fund, which, if it can raise money, promises to pay travel expenses for family members who can't afford to travel. His partner, and first funder, in the endeavor is the former lawyer, Gordon Caplan, one of fifty-seven defendants in the college admissions scandal. (He was the one known for saying, "I'm not worried about the moral issue here.") After pleading guilty, he had been sent to a federal prison camp in Loretto, Pennsylvania.

Caplan was one of America's most prominent lawyers, but he never paid much attention to complaints about the criminal justice system until he was in the maw of it. "What I saw is other people going through a system that's built for failure, built for recidivism," he told me. Caplan used to assume that inmates had access to job training and reading materials. He was wrong. "The only courses that were offered were how to become a certified physical trainer and automotive repair." Inmates could create their own classes, and Caplan taught a short course on basic business literacy. "I had fifteen to twenty guys every class," he said. "'Do I set up an LLC versus a corporation?' 'Should I borrow money or should I get people to invest in equity?'" After getting out, Caplan was alarmed by the barriers that prevent even nonviolent felons from returning to normal life. "I have assets and I have family and I've got all that. But how does a guy who came out for dealing marijuana even start a painting business?"

Hearing Caplan, Grant, and others talk about their sudden awareness of America's penal system put me in mind of the work of Bryan Stevenson, a leading civil rights lawyer and the founder of the Equal Justice Initiative, which advocates for criminal justice reform. He beseeches people to "get proximate"—to step outside the confines of their experience. Stevenson often quotes his grandmother, the daughter of enslaved people, who went on to raise nine children. "You can't understand most of the important things from a distance, Bryan," she told him. "You have to get close."

But getting close is not the same as staying close. After serving twenty-eight days in prison, Caplan returned to Greenwich, where he lived in a $7 million Colonial, down a gentle hill from the old Helmsley estate. For all his recent concern about the failings of criminal justice, I suspected that the country might have more to learn from him about his own failings. What, I asked, possessed him to pay someone to falsify his kid's college admissions test results? He was not eager to answer. "Achievement, I think, is like a drug," he said, after a pause. "Once you achieve one thing, you need to achieve the next thing. And, when you're surrounded by people that are doing that, it becomes self-reinforcing. When you also have insecurities, which a lot of highly motivated people do, you're more apt to do what is necessary to achieve. And it's easy to step off the line." Caplan had convinced himself that paying to change his daughter's test results was scarcely more objectionable than other forms of influence and leverage that get kids into school. "I saw what I believed to be a very corrupt system, and I've got to play along or I'll be disadvantaged."

Greed, of course, is older than the Ten Commandments. But Caplan's experience illuminated the degree to which greed has been celebrated in America by the past two generations, engineered for lucrative new applications that, in efficiency and effect, are as different from their predecessors as an AR-15 rifle is from a musket. If you have the means, you can hone every edge, from your life expectancy to the amount of taxes you pay and your child's performance on the ACTs. It's not hard to insure that the winners keep winning, as long as you don't get caught.

*   *   *

The most candid moments in the White Collar Support Group tended to be when people acknowledged the havoc they had caused their spouses and children. Seth Williams, a former district attorney of Philadelphia, pleaded guilty in 2017 to accepting gifts in exchange for favors, and served nearly three years in federal prison. Afterward, he struggled to find an apartment that would accept a felon. His first job was stocking shelves overnight at a big-box store; eventually, after an online course, he became a wedding officiant for hire. He was not surprised that former colleagues avoided him, but watching the effects on his family left him in despair. "It affects all of us in how our children are treated at their schools, on the playground," he said. "Some of our spouses, people want nothing to do with them."

Not long ago, Grant regained his law license in the State of New York, based largely on his work as a minister and as an expert on prison. Nineteen years after being disbarred, he rented an office on West 43rd Street in Manhattan and started practicing again, as a private general counsel and a specialist in "white-collar crisis management." At seminary, he had studied migrant communities, and he came to see an analogy to people convicted of white-collar crimes. "We have one foot in the old country, one foot in the new," he told me. If they hoped to thrive again, they would have to depend on one another. "Greek Americans funded each other and opened diners. They lift each other up." He went on, "The problem we have in the white-collar community is that people who have been prosecuted for white-collar crimes want to become so successful again that they are no longer associated with it. I've approached some of the household names, and to a one they've rejected it." I asked him if he was referring to people like Michael Milken and Martha Stewart. Grant demurred. "My mission is to help people relieve their shame, not to shame someone into doing something."

Grant will tell you that shame does not help in recovery. But America's record in recent years suggests that shamelessness might be a larger problem. If the country has begun to appreciate the structural reasons that many of its least advantaged people break the law, it has yet to reckon with the question of why many of its most advantaged do, too. Members of Grant's group usually come to accept that they got themselves into trouble, but more than a few hope to follow Milken and Stewart back to the club they used to belong to—winners of the American game.

As the Zoom meeting wound down, Grant asked Andy Tezna, the former NASA executive on his way to prison, if there was anything else he wanted to say. "I had a lapse of judgment," he began, then caught himself and confessed impatience with the language of confession. "I'm so tired of using that word, but, whatever it was that led me to make my mistake, it's not going to define me for the rest of my life." He thanked the members of the group for helping him get ready to embark on his "government-mandated retreat." He'd see them afterward, he said, "once I'm out, a little wiser, a little older, with a few more gray hairs."

In 2022, Gordon Caplan regained permission to practice law. He became the CEO of a strategic advisory firm. Raj Rajaratnam, after serving seven and a half years for insider trading, established a family office based in New York City, where, as a headline put it, he was "hunting for his next big trade."

The Supreme Court has continued to limit the scope of prosecution for white-collar crimes. The latest decision, in 2024, cleared the way for officials to receive gratuities for past acts, as long as there was no quid pro quo. Ruling along partisan lines, the justices overturned the conviction of a former Indiana mayor who had solicited and accepted a $13,000 tip from a garbage truck company after it was awarded city contracts.

On the day of Trump's second inauguration, he imposed a hiring freeze on federal civilian workers to last ninety days; the Internal Revenue Service, however, was singled out for special treatment—the only agency where the hiring freeze was imposed indefinitely.

Acknowledgments

O ne of the earliest discoveries in the reporting of this book came, by chance, from a stranger, sitting next to me on a flight nearly a decade ago. He worked in Silicon Valley, and when I asked what kinds of stories were overlooked there, he started to talk—less about technology than about changing conceptions of wealth, government, and the future. We stayed in touch. He remains anonymous; I remain grateful.

Because these essays took life, in their original shape, in *The New Yorker*, they benefited, immeasurably, from the institution that has been my professional home for seventeen years. For help on these pieces, I'm particularly grateful to David Remnick, Dorothy Wickenden, Deirdre Foley-Mendelssohn, Daniel Zalewski, Michael Luo, and, especially, Nick Trautwein, who edited most of these essays and lent them his expertise and taste. Even more than usual, the subject matter called upon the talents of the fact-checking department, led by Fergus McIntosh and Teresa Mathew. The fact-checkers' determination to find the truth, when that pursuit is increasingly difficult, is the essence of good journalism. Lucie Koenig conducted further valuable fact-checking for the book.

I owe a great debt to reporters and scholars who have explored subjects in these pages, beginning with my Washington colleagues Jane Mayer and Susan Glasser, who have returned repeatedly to matters of money, influence, and politics. I have also learned an immense amount from the work of Jesse Eisinger, Justin Elliott, Jeff Ernsthausen, Mike Forsythe, Dan Friedman, Brooke Harrington, Joshua Kaplan, Paul Kiel, and Bob Lord.

My friend and agent, Jennifer Joel, at CAA, has a rare combination of judgment, grit, and good humor. I'm also fortunate to work with CAA colleagues Michael Glantz, Will Watkins, and Sindhu Vegesena. At Scribner and Simon & Schuster, I am privileged to have the editorial wisdom and enthusiasm of Nan Graham, Colin Harrison, Jonathan Karp, and Marysue Rucci. Major thanks to the other members of their publishing team, including Ana Chan, Annie Craig, Mark Galarrita, Kyle Kabel, Mark LaFlaur, Jaya Miceli, Karen Pearlman, Emily Polson, Nicholas Poser, Paul Samuelson, Stu Smith, and Brianna Yamashita.

My greatest debt, always, is to those who tolerate this writing life, with its many absences and distractions, including Susan and Peter Osnos, Katherine and Colin Sanford, and a great many Bermans. My astonishing children, Oliver and Rose, have learned to read and write with gusto in the time it took me to finish this project. Above all, my gratitude is to Sarabeth. Without your creativity, integrity, and encouragement, there would never be much of anything on the page.

Index

About the Author

Evan Osnos has been a staff writer at *The New Yorker* since 2008. His most recent book, *Wildland: The Making of America's Fury*, was a *New York Times* bestseller. He is also the author of *Age of Ambition: Chasing Fortune, Truth, and Faith in the New China*, which won the National Book Award. Previously, he was a foreign correspondent for the *Chicago Tribune*, where he shared two Pulitzer Prizes. He lives with his wife and children near Washington, D.C.